1995 SUPER HOROSCOPE

YOUR CANDID, DAILY, INDIVIDUAL, COMPREHENSIVE 15-MONTH FORECAST

LEO

JULY 21 – AUGUST 21

ARROW

CONTENTS

THE PUBLISHERS REGRET THAT THEY CANNOT ANSWER INDIVIDUAL LETTERS
REQUESTING PERSONAL HOROSCOPE INFORMATION.

FIRST PUBLISHED IN GREAT BRITAIN BY ARROW BOOKS,
20 VAUXHALL BRIDGE ROAD, LONDON SW1V 2SA, 1994
© GROSSET & DUNLAP, INC., 1974, 1978, 1979, 1980, 1981, 1982
© CHARTER COMMUNICATIONS, INC., 1983, 1984, 1985
COPYRIGHT © 1986, 1987, 1988, 1989, 1990, 1991, 1992, 1993, 1994
THE BERKLEY PUBLISHING GROUP
THIS EDITION PUBLISHED BY AGREEMENT WITH THE BERKLEY PUBLISHING
GROUP

PRINTED IN GREAT BRITAIN BY
THE GUERNSEY PRESS CO. LTD
GUERNSEY, C.I.
ISBN 0 09 930601 8

NOTE TO THE CUSP-BORN

First find the year of your birth, and then find the sign under which you were born according to your day of birth. Thus, you can determine if you are a true Leo (or Cancer or Virgo), according to the variations of the dates of the Zodiac. (See also page 7.)

Are you *really* a Leo? If your birthday falls during the fourth week of July, at the beginning of Leo, will you still retain the traits of Cancer, the sign of the Zodiac before Leo? And what if you were born late in August—are you more Virgo than Leo? Many people born at the edge, or cusp, of a sign have difficulty determining exactly what sign they are. If you are one of these people, here's how you can figure it out, once and for all.

Consult the following table. It will tell you the precise days on which the Sun entered and left your sign for the year of your birth. If you were born at the beginning or end of Leo, yours is a lifetime reflecting a process of subtle transformation. Your life on Earth will symbolize a significant change in consciousness, for you are either about to enter a whole new way of living or are leaving one behind.

If you are a Leo, born during the fourth week of July, you may want to read the horoscope book for Cancer as well as Leo. Cancer holds the keys to many of your secret uncertainties and deep-rooted problems, and your secret needs and wishes. You are the spirit of independence and creativity, or want to be. Yet through Cancer you reveal your deep, but often hidden, need to have strong ties. You may be trying to leave dependencies behind, yet you find yourself drawn again and again to the past or to family responsibilities.

You reflect the birth of a new sign, a ripe, whole person, fully able to tap and realize all your potentials for love and creativity.

If you were born after the third week of August, you may want to read the horoscope book for Virgo as well, for through Virgo you learn to put all your talents as a lover or creator to work. Your love for life is infectious, and your zest and sunny disposition are an inspiration to everyone around you. You are capable of seriousness, discipline and great diligence.

iii

You are a lover—ardent, passionate and determined that love will not elude you. Though you may try to avoid it, you will find yourself in work, health or duty situations that demand less emotion and more mind. You are not afraid of taking a gamble and are reluctant to give up your love of enjoyment for work or studies. You can blend professionalism and propriety in perfect amounts. You are the natural mixture of creativity and discipline, able to feel and to analyze. You symbolize the warmth and fullness of a late summer day, a natural ripeness and maturity that is mellow and comfortable to be near.

DATES SUN ENTERS LEO
(LEAVES CANCER)

July 23 every year from 1900 to 2000, except for the following:

July 22:

1928	1953	1968	1981	1992
32	56	69	84	93
36	57	72	85	94
40	60	73	86	96
44	61	76	88	97
48	64	77	89	98
52	65	80	90	

DATES SUN LEAVES LEO
(ENTERS VIRGO)

August 23 every year from 1900 to 2000, except for the following:

August 22:			August 24:	
1960	1980	1992	1903	1919
64	84	93	07	23
68	88	96	11	27
72	89	97	15	
76				

HISTORY AND USES
OF ASTROLOGY

Does astrology have a place in the fast-moving, ultra-scientific world we live in today? Can it be justified in a sophisticated society whose outriders are already preparing to step off the moon into the deep space of the planets themselves? Or is it just a hangover of ancient superstition, a psychological dummy for neurotics and dreamers of every historical age?

These are the kind of questions that any inquiring person can be expected to ask when they approach a subject like astrology which goes beyond, but never excludes, the materialistic side of life.

The simple, single answer is that astrology works. It works for tens of millions of people in the western world alone. In the United States there are 10 million followers and in Europe, an estimated 25 million. America has more than 4000 practicing astrologers, Europe nearly three times as many. Even down-under Australia has its hundreds of thousands of adherents. The importance of such vast numbers of people from diverse backgrounds and cultures is recognized by the world's biggest newspapers and magazines who probably devote more of their space to this subject in a year than to any other. In the eastern countries, astrology has enormous followings, again, because it has been proved to work. In countries like India, brides and grooms for centuries have been chosen on the basis of astrological compatibility. The low divorce rate there, despite today's heavy westernizing influence, is attributed largely to this practice.

In the western world, astrology today is more vital than ever before; more practicable because it needs a sophisticated society like ours to understand and develop its contribution to the full; more valid because science itself is confirming the precepts of astrological knowledge with every new exciting step. The ordinary person who daily applies astrology intelligently does not have to wonder whether it is true nor believe in it blindly. He can see it working for himself. And, if he can use it—and this book is designed to help the reader to do just that—he can make living a far richer experience, and become a more developed personality and a better person.

Astrology is the science of relationships. It is not just a study of planetary influences on man and his environment. It is the study of man himself.

We are at the center of our personal universe, of all our rela-

1

tionships. And our happiness or sadness depends on how we act, how we relate to the people and things that surround us. The emotions that we generate have a distinct affect—for better or worse—on the world around us. Our friends and our enemies will confirm this. Just look in the mirror the next time you are angry. In other words, each of us is a kind of sun or planet or star and our influence on our personal universe, whether loving, helpful or destructive, varies with our changing moods, expressed through our individual character.

And to an extent that includes the entire galaxy, this is true of the planetary bodies. Their radiations affect each other, including the earth and all the things on it. And in comparatively recent years, giant constellations called "quasars" have been discovered. These exist far beyond the night stars that we can observe, and science says these quasars are emitting radiating influences more powerful and different than ever recorded on earth. Their effect on man from an astrological point of view is under deep study. Compared with these inter-stellar forces, our personal "radiations" are negligible on the planetary scale. But ours are just as potent in the way they affect our moods, and our ability to control them. To this extent they determine much of the happiness and satisfaction in our lives. For instance, if we were bound and gagged and had to hold some strong emotion within us without being able to move, we would soon start to feel very uncomfortable. We are obviously pretty powerful radiators inside, in our own way. But usually, we are able to throw off our emotion in some sort of action—we have a good cry, walk it off, or tell someone our troubles—before it can build up too far and make us physically ill. Astrology helps us to understand the universal forces working on us, and through this understanding, we can become more properly adjusted to our surroundings and find ourselves coping where others may flounder.

Closely related to our emotions is the "other side" of our personal universe, our physical welfare. Our body, of course, is largely influenced by things around us over which we have very little control. The phone rings, we hear it. The train runs late. We snag our stocking or cut our face shaving. Our body is under a constant bombardment of events that influence our lives to varying degrees.

The question that arises from all this is, what makes each of us act so that we have to involve other people and keep the ball of activity and evolution rolling? This is the question that both science and astrology are involved with. The scientists have attacked it from different angles: anthropology, the study of human evolution as body, mind and response to environment; anatomy, the study of bodily structure; psychology, the science of the human mind; and so on. These studies have produced very impressive classifications and valuable information, but because the approach to the problem is fragmented, so is the result. They remain "branches" of science. Science generally studies effects. It keeps turning up wonderful answers but no lasting solutions. Astrology, on the other hand approaches the question from the broader viewpoint. Astrology began its inquiry with the totality of human experience and saw it as an effect. It then looked to find the cause, or at least the prime movers, and during thousands of years of observation of man and his *universal* environment, came up with the extraordinary principle of planetary influence—or astrology, which, from the Greek, means the science of the stars.

Modern science, as we shall see, has confirmed much of astrology's foundations—most of it unintentionally, some of it reluctantly, but still, indisputably.

It is not difficult to imagine that there must be a connection between outer space and the earth. Even today, scientists are not too sure how our earth was created, but it is generally agreed that it is only a tiny part of the universe. And as a part of the universe, people on earth see and feel the influence of heavenly bodies in almost every aspect of our existence. There is no doubt that the sun has the greatest influence on life on this planet. Without it there would be no life, for without it there would be no warmth, no division into day and night, no cycles of time or season at all. This is clear and easy to see. The influence of the moon, on the other hand, is more subtle, though no less definite.

There are many ways in which the influence of the moon manifests itself here on earth, both on human and animal life. It is a well-known fact, for instance, that the large movements of water on our planet—that is the ebb and flow of the tides—are caused by the moon's gravitational pull. Since this is so, it follows that these water movements do not occur only in the oceans, but that all bodies of water are affected, even down to the tiniest puddle.

The human body, too, which consists of about 70 percent water, falls within the scope of this lunar influence. For example the menstrual cycle of most women corresponds to the lunar month; the period of pregnancy in humans is 273 days, or equal to nine lunar months. Similarly, many illnesses reach a crisis at the change of the moon, and statistics in many countries have shown that the crime rate is highest at the time of the full moon. Even human sexual desire has been associated with the phases of the moon. But, it is in the movement of the tides that we get the clearest demonstration of planetary influence, and the irresistible correspondence between the so-called metaphysical and the physical.

Tide tables are prepared years in advance by calculating the future positions of the moon. Science has known for a long time that the moon is the main cause of tidal action. But only in the last few years has it begun to realize the possible extent of this influence on mankind. To begin with, the ocean tides do not rise and fall as we might imagine from our personal observations of them. The moon as it orbits around the earth, sets up a circular wave of attraction which pulls the oceans of the world after it, broadly in an east to west direction. This influence is like a phantom wave crest, a loop of power stretching from pole to pole which passes over and around the earth like an invisible shadow. It travels with equal effect across the land masses and, as scientists were recently amazed to observe, caused oysters placed in the dark in the middle of the United States where there is no sea, to open their shells to receive the non-existent tide. If the land-locked oysters react to this invisible signal, what effect does it have on us who not so long ago in evolutionary time, came out of the sea and still have its salt in our blood and sweat?

Less well known is the fact that the moon is also the primary force behind the circulation of blood in human beings and animals, and the movement of sap in trees and plants. Agriculturists have established that the moon has a distinct influence on crops, which explains why for centuries people have planted according to moon cycles. The habits of many animals, too, are directed by the movement of the moon. Migratory birds, for instance, depart only at or near the time of the full moon. Just as certain fish, eels in particular, move only in accordance with certain phases of the moon.

Know Thyself—Why?

In today's fast-changing world, everyone still longs to know what the future holds. It is the one thing that everyone has in common: rich and poor, famous and infamous, all are deeply concerned about tomorrow.

But the key to the future, as every historian knows, lies in the past. This is as true of individual people as it is of nations. You cannot understand your future without first understanding your past, which is simply another way of saying that you must first of all know yourself.

The motto "know thyself" seems obvious enough nowadays, but it was originally put forward as the foundation of wisdom by the ancient Greek philosophers. It was then adopted by the "mystery religions" of the ancient Middle East, Greece and Rome, and is still used in all genuine schools of mind training or mystical discipline, both in those of the East, based on yoga, and those of the West. So it is universally accepted now, and has been through the ages.

But how do you go about discovering what sort of person you are? The first step is usually classification into some sort of system of types. Astrology did this long before the birth of Christ. Psychology has also done it. So has modern medicine, in its way.

One system classifies men according to the source of the impulses they respond to most readily: the muscles, leading to direct bodily action; the digestive organs, resulting in emotion, or the brain and nerves. Another such system says that character is determined by the endocrine glands, and gives us labels like "pituitary," "thyroid" and "hyperthyroid" types. These different systems are neither contradictory nor mutually exclusive. In fact, they are very often different ways of saying the same thing.

Very popular and useful classifications were devised by Dr. C. G. Jung, the eminent disciple of Freud. Jung observed among the different faculties of the mind, four which have a predominant influence on character. These four faculties exist in all of us without exception, but not in perfect balance. So when we say, for instance, that a man is a "thinking type," it means that in any situation he tries to be rational. It follows that emotion, which some say is the opposite of thinking, will be his weakest function. This type can be sensible and reasonable, or calculating and unsympathetic. The emotional type, on the other hand, can often be recognized by exaggerated language—everything is either marvelous or terrible—and in extreme cases they even invent dramas and quarrels out of nothing just to make life more interesting.

The other two faculties are intuition and physical sensation. The sensation type does not only care for food and drink, nice clothes and furniture; he is also interested in all forms of physical experience. Many scientists are sensation types as are athletes and naturelovers. Like sensation, intuition is a form of perception and we all possess it. But it works through that part of the mind which is not under conscious control—consequently it sees meanings and connections which are not obvious to thought or emotion. Inventors and original thinkers are always intuitive, but so, too, are superstitious people who see meanings where none exist.

Thus, sensation tells us what is going on in the world, feeling (that is, emotion) tells us how important it is to ourselves, thinking enables us to interpret it and work out what we should do about it, and intuition tells us what it means to ourselves and others. All four faculties are essential, and all are present in every one of us. But some people are guided chiefly by one, others by another.

Besides these four types, Jung observed a division into extrovert and introvert, which cuts across them. By and large, the introvert is one who finds truth inside himself rather than outside. He is not, therefore, ideally suited to a religion or a political party which tells him what to believe. Original thinkers are almost necessarily introverts. The extrovert, on the other hand, finds truth coming to him from outside. He believes in experts and authorities, and wants to think that nature and the laws of nature really exists, that they are what they appear to be and not just generalities made by men.

A disadvantage of all these systems of classification, is that one cannot tell very easily where to place oneself. Some people are reluctant to admit that they act to please their emotions. So they deceive themselves for years by trying to belong to whichever type they think is the "best." Of course, there is no best; each has its faults and each has its good points.

The advantage of the signs of the Zodiac is that they simplify classification. Not only that, but your date of birth is personal—it is unarguably yours. What better way to know yourself than by going back as far as possible to the very moment of your birth? And this is precisely what your horoscope is all about.

What Is a Horoscope?

If you had been able to take a picture of the heavens at the moment of your birth, that photograph would be your horoscope. Lacking such a snapshot, it is still possible to recreate the picture—and this is at the basis of the astrologer's art. In other words, your horoscope is a representation of the skies with the planets in the exact positions they occupied at the time you were born.

This information, of course, is not enough for the astrologer. He has to have a background of significance to put the photograph on. You will get the idea if you imagine two balls—one inside the other. The inner one is transparent. In the center of both is the astrologer, able to look up, down and around in all directions. The outer sphere is the Zodiac which is divided into twelve approximately equal segments, like the segments of an orange. The inner ball is our photograph. It is transparent except for the images of the planets. Looking out from the center, the astrologer sees the planets in various segments of the Zodiac. These twelve segments are known as the signs or houses.

The position of the planets when each of us is born is always different. So the photograph is always different. But the Zodiac and its signs are fixed.

Now, where in all this are you, the subject of the horoscope?

Your character is largely determined by the sign the sun is in. So that is where the astrologer looks first in your horoscope.

There are twelve signs in the Zodiac and the sun spends approximately one month in each. As the sun's motion is almost perfectly regular, the astrologers have been able to fix the dates governing each sign. There are not many people who do not know which sign of the Zodiac they were born under or who have not been amazed at some time or other at the accuracy of the description of their own character. Here are the twelve signs, the ancient zodiacal symbol, and their dates for the year 1995.*

ARIES	Ram	March 20–April 20
TAURUS	Bull	April 20–May 21
GEMINI	Twins	May 21–June 21
CANCER	Crab	June 21–July 23
LEO	Lion	July 23–August 23
VIRGO	Virgin	August 23–September 23
LIBRA	Scales	September 23–October 23
SCORPIO	Scorpion	October 23–November 22
SAGITTARIUS	Archer	November 22–December 22
CAPRICORN	Sea-Goat	December 22–January 20
AQUARIUS	Water-Bearer	January 20–February 18
PISCES	Fish	February 18–March 20

The time of birth—apart from the date—is important in advanced astrology because the planets travel at such great speed that the patterns they form change from minute to minute. For this reason, each person's horoscope is his and his alone. Further on we will see that the practicing astrologer has ways of determining and reading these minute time changes which dictate the finer character differences in us all.

However, it is still possible to draw significant conclusions and make meaningful predictions based simply on the sign of the Zodiac a person is born under. In a horoscope, the signs do not necessarily correspond with the divisions of the houses. It could be that a house begins halfway across a sign. It is the interpretation of such combinations of different influences that distinguishes the professional astrologer from the student and the follower.

However, to gain a workable understanding of astrology, it is not necessary to go into great detail. In fact, the beginner is likely to find himself confused if he attempts to absorb too much too quickly. It should be remembered that this is a science and to become proficient at it, and especially to grasp the tremendous scope of possibilities in man and his affairs and direct them into a worthwhile reading, takes a great deal of study and experience.

*These dates are fluid and change with the motion of the Earth from year to year.

If you do intend to pursue it seriously you will have to learn to figure the exact moment of birth against the degrees of longitude and latitude of the planets at that precise time. This involves adapting local time to Greenwich Mean Time (G.M.T.), reference to tables of houses to establish the Ascendant, as well as making calculations from Ephemeris—the tables of the planets' positions.

After reading this introduction, try drawing up a rough horoscope to get the "feel" of reading some elementary characteristics and natal influences.

Draw a circle with twelve equal segments. Write in counterclockwise the names of the signs—Aries, Taurus, Gemini etc.—one for each segment. Look up an ephemeris for the year of the person's birth and note down the sign each planet was in on the birthday. Do not worry about the number of degrees (although if a planet is on the edge of a sign its position obviously should be considered). Write the name of the planet in the segment/sign on your chart. Write the number 1 in the sign where the sun is. This is the first house. Number the rest of the houses, counterclockwise till you finish at 12. Now you can investigate the probable basic expectation of experience of the person concerned. This is done first of all by seeing what planet or planets is/are in what sign and house. (See also page 72.)

The 12 houses control these functions:

1st.	Individuality, body appearance, general outlook on life	(Personality house)
2nd.	Finance, business	(Money house)
3rd.	Relatives, education, correspondence	(Relatives house)
4th.	Family, neighbors	(Home house)
5th.	Pleasure, children, attempts, entertainment	(Pleasure house)
6th.	Health, employees	(Health house)
7th.	Marriage, partnerships	(Marriage house)
8th.	Death, secret deals, difficulties	(Death house)
9th.	Travel, intellectual affairs	(Travel house)
10th.	Ambition, social standing	(Business and Honor house)
11th.	Friendship, social life, luck	(Friends house)
12th.	Troubles, illness, loss	(Trouble house)

The characteristics of the planets modify the influence of the Sun according to their natures and strengths.

Sun: Source of life. Basic temperament according to sun sign. The will.
Moon: Superficial nature. Moods. Changeable. Adaptive. Mother.
Mercury: Communication. Intellect. Reasoning power. Curiosity. Short travels.
Venus: Love. Delight. Art. Beautiful possessions.
Mars: Energy. Initiative. War. Anger. Destruction. Impulse.
Jupiter: Good. Generous. Expansive. Opportunities. Protection.
Saturn: Jupiter's opposite. Contraction. Servant. Delay. Hardwork. Cold. Privation. Research. Lasting rewards after long struggle.
Uranus: Fashion. Electricity. Revolution. Sudden changes. Modern science.
Neptune: Sensationalism. Mass emotion. Devastation. Delusion.
Pluto: Creates and destroys. Lust for power. Strong obsessions.

Superimpose the characteristics of the planets on the functions of the house in which they appear. Express the result through the character of the birth (sun) sign, and you will get the basic idea of how astrology works.

Of course, many other considerations have been taken into account in producing the carefully worked out predictions in this book: The aspects of the planets to each other; their strength according to position and sign; whether they are in a house of exaltation or decline; whether they are natural enemies or not; whether a planet occupies his own sign; the position of a planet in relation to its own house or sign; whether the planet is male, female or neuter; whether the sign is a fire, earth, water or air sign. These are only a few of the colors on the astrologer's pallet which he must mix with the inspiration of the artist and the accuracy of the mathematician.

The Problem of Love

Love, of course, is never a problem. The problem lies in recognizing the difference between infatuation, emotion, sex and, sometimes, the downright deceit of the other person. Mankind, with its record of broken marriages, despair and disillusionment, is obviously not very good at making these distinctions.

Can astrology help?

Yes. In the same way that advance knowledge can usually help in any human situation. And there is probably no situation as human, as poignant, as pathetic and universal, as the failure of man's love.

Love, of course, is not just between man and woman. It involves love of children, parents, home and so on. But the big problems usually involve the choice of partner.

Astrology has established degrees of compatibility that exist between people born under the various signs of the Zodiac. Because people are individuals, there are numerous variations and modifications and the astrologer, when approached on mate and marriage matters makes allowances for them. But the fact remains that some groups of people are suited for each other and some are not and astrology has expressed this in terms of characteristics which all can study and use as a personal guide.

No matter how much enjoyment and pleasure we find in the different aspects of each other's character, if it is not an overall compatibility, the chances of our finding fulfillment or enduring happiness in each other are pretty hopeless. And astrology can help us to find someone compatible.

History of Astrology

The origins of astrology have been lost far back in history, but we do know that reference is made to it as far back as the first written records of the human race. It is not hard to see why. Even in primitive times, people must have looked for an explanation for the various happenings in their lives. They must have wanted to know why people were different from one to another. And in their search they turned to the regular movements of the sun, moon and stars to see if they could provide an answer.

It is interesting to note that as soon as man learned to use his tools in any type of design, or his mind in any kind of calculation, he turned his attention to the heavens. Ancient cave dwellings reveal dim crescents and circles representative of the sun and moon, rulers of day and night. Mesopotamia and the civilization of Chaldea, in itself the foundation of those of Babylonia and Assyria, show a complete picture of astronomical observation and well-developed astrological interpretation.

Humanity has a natural instinct for order. The study of anthropology reveals that primitive people—even as far back as prehistoric times—were striving to achieve a certain order in their lives. They tried to organize the apparent chaos of the universe. They had the desire to attach meaning to things. This demand for order has persisted throughout the history of man. So that observing the regularity of the heavenly bodies made it logical that primitive peoples should turn heavenwards in their search for an understanding of the world in which they found themselves so random and alone.

And they did find a significance in the movements of the stars. Shepherds tending their flocks, for instance, observed that when the cluster of stars now known as the constellation Aries was in sight, it was the time of fertility and they associated it with the Ram. And they noticed that the growth of plants and plant life corresponded with different phases of the moon, so that certain times were favorable for the planting of crops, and other times were not. In this way, there grew up a tradition of seasons and causes connected with the passage of the sun through the twelve signs of the Zodiac.

Astrology was valued so highly that the king was kept informed of the daily and monthly changes in the heavenly bodies, and the results of astrological studies regarding events of the future. Head astrologers were clearly men of great rank and position, and the office was said to be a hereditary one.

Omens were taken, not only from eclipses and conjunctions of the moon or sun with one of the planets, but also from storms and earthquakes. In the eastern civilizations, particularly, the reverence inspired by astrology appears to have remained unbroken since the very earliest days. In ancient China, astrology, astronomy and religion went hand in hand. The astrologer, who was also an astronomer, was part of the official government service and had his own corner in the Imperial Palace. The duties of the Imperial astrologer, whose office was one of the most important in the land, were clearly defined, as this extract from early records shows:

"This exalted gentleman must concern himself with the stars in the heavens, keeping a record of the changes and movements of the Planets, the Sun and the Moon, in order to examine the movements of the terrestial world with the object of prognosticating good and bad fortune. He divides the territories of the nine regions of the empire in accordance with their dependence on particular celestial bodies. All the fiefs and principalities are connected with the stars and from this their prosperity or misfortune should be ascertained. He makes prognostications according to the twelve years of the Jupiter cycle of good and evil of the terrestial world. From the colors of the five kinds of clouds, he determines the coming of floods or droughts, abundance or famine. From the twelve winds, he draws conclusions about the state of harmony of heaven and earth, and takes note of good and bad signs that result from their accord or disaccord. In general, he concerns himself with five kinds of phenomena so as to warn the Emperor to come to the aid of the government and to allow for variations in the ceremonies according to their circumstances."

The Chinese were also keen observers of the fixed stars, giving them such unusual names as Ghost Vehicle, Sun of Imperial Concubine, Imperial Prince, Pivot of Heaven, Twinkling Brilliance or Weaving Girl. But, great astrologers though they may have been, the Chinese lacked one aspect of mathematics that the Greeks applied to astrology—deductive geometry. Deductive geometry was the basis of much classical astrology in and after the time of the Greeks, and this explains the different methods of prognostication used in the East and West.

Down through the ages the astrologer's art has depended, not so much on the uncovering of new facts, though this is important, as on the interpretation of the facts already known. This is the essence of his skill. Obviously one cannot always tell how people will react (and this underlines the very important difference between astrology and predestination which will be discussed later on) but one can be prepared, be forewarned, to know what to expect.

But why should the signs of the zodiac have any effect at all on the formation of human character? It is easy to see why people thought they did, and even now we constantly use astrological expressions in our everyday speech. The thoughts of "lucky star," "ill-fated," "star-crossed," "mooning around," are interwoven into the very structure of our language.

In the same way that the earth has been created by influences from outside, there remains an indisputable togetherness in the working of the universe. The world, after all, is a coherent structure, for if it were not, it would be quite without order and we would never know what to expect. A dog could turn into an apple, or an elephant sprout wings and fly at any moment without so much as a by your leave. But nature, as we know, functions according to laws, not whims, and the laws of nature are certainly not subject to capricious exceptions.

This means that no part of the universe is ever arbitrarily cut off from any other part. Everything is therefore to some extent linked with everything else. The moon draws an imperceptible tide on every puddle; tiny and trivial events can be effected by outside forces (such as the fall of a feather by the faintest puff of wind). And so it is fair to think that the local events at any moment reflect to a very small extent the evolution of the world as a whole.

From this principle follows the possibility of divination, and also knowledge of events at a distance, provided one's mind were always as perfectly undisturbed, as ideally smooth, as a mirror or unruffled lake. Provided, in other words, that one did not confuse the picture with hopes, guesses, and expectations. When people try to foretell the future by cards or crystal ball gazing they find it much easier to confuse the picture with expectations than to reflect it clearly.

But the present does contain a good deal of the future to which it leads—not all, but a good deal. The diver halfway between bridge and water is going to make a splash; the train whizzing towards the station will pass through it unless interfered with; the burglar breaking a pane of glass has exposed himself to the possibility of a prison sentence. Yet this is not a doctrine of determinism, as was emphasized earlier. Clearly, there are forces already at work in the present, and any one of them could alter the situation in some way. Equally, a change of decision could alter the whole situation as well. So the future depends, not on an irresistible force, but on a small act of free will.

An individual's age, physique, and position on the earth's surface are remote consequences of his birth. Birth counts as the original cause for all that happens subsequently. The horoscope, in this case, means "this person represents the further evolution of the state of the universe pictured in this chart." Such a chart can apply equally to man or woman, dog, ship or even limited company.

If the evolution of an idea, or of a person, is to be understood as a totality, it must continue to evolve from its own beginnings, which is to say, in the terms in which it began. The brown-eyed person will be faithful to brown eyes all his life; the traitor is being faithful to some complex of ideas which has long been evolving in him; and the person born at sunset will always express, as he evolves, the psychological implications or analogies of the moment when the sun sinks out of sight.

This is the doctrine that an idea must continue to evolve in terms of its origin. It is a completely non-materialist doctrine, though it never fails to apply to material objects. And it implies, too, that the individual will continue to evolve in terms of his moment of origin, and therefore possibly of the sign of the Zodiac rising on the eastern horizon at his birth. It also implies that the signs of the Zodiac themselves will evolve in the collective mind of the human race in the same terms that they were first devised and not in the terms in which modern astrologers consciously think they ought to work.

For the human race, like every other kind of animal, has a collective mind, as Professor Jung discovered in his investigation of dreams. If no such collective mind existed, no infant could ever learn anything, for communication would be impossible. Furthermore, it is absurd to suggest that the conscious mind could be older than the "unconscious," for an infant's nervous system functions correctly before it has discovered the difference between "myself" and "something else" or discovered what eyes and hands are for. Indeed, the involuntary muscles function correctly even before birth, and will never be under conscious control. They are part of what we call the "unconscious" which is not really "unconscious" at all. To the contrary, it is totally aware of itself and everything else; it is merely that part of the mind that cannot be controlled by conscious effort.

And human experience, though it varies in detail with every individual, is basically the same for each one of us, consisting of sky and earth, day and night, waking and sleeping, man and woman, birth and death. So there is bound to be in the mind of the human race a very large number of inescapable ideas, which are called our natural archetypes.

There are also, however, artificial or cultural archetypes which are not universal or applicable to everyone, but are nevertheless inescapable within the limits of a given culture. Examples of these are the cross in Christianity, and the notion of "escape from the wheel of rebirth" in India. There was a time when these ideas did not exist. And there was a time, too, when the scheme of the Zodiac did not exist. One would not expect the Zodiac to have any influence on remote and primitive peoples, for example, who have never heard of it. If the Zodiac is only an archetype, their horoscopes probably would not work and it would not matter which sign they were born under.

But where the Zodiac is known, and the idea of it has become worked into the collective mind, then there it could well appear to have an influence, even if it has no physical existence. For ideas do not have a physical existence, anyway. No physical basis has yet been discovered for the telepathy that controls an anthill; young swallows migrate before, not after, their parents; and the weaverbird builds its intricate nest without being taught. Materialists suppose, but cannot prove, that "instinct" (as it is called, for no one knows how it works) is controlled by nucleic acid in the chromosomes. This is not a genuine explanation, though, for it only pushes the mystery one stage further back.

Does this mean, then, that the human race, in whose civilization the idea of the twelve signs of the Zodiac has long been embedded, is divided into only twelve types? Can we honestly believe that it is really as simple as that? If so, there must be pretty wide ranges of variation within each type. And if, to explain the variation, we call in heredity and environment, experiences in early childhood, the thyroid and other glands, and also the four functions of the mind mentioned at the beginning of this introduction, and extroversion and introversion, then one begins to wonder if the original classification was worth making at all. No sensible person believes that his favorite system explains everything. But even so, he will not find it much use at all if it does not even save him the trouble of bothering with the others.

Under the Jungian system, everyone has not only a dominant or principal function, but also a secondary or subsidiary one, so that the four can be arranged in order of potency. In the intuitive type, sensation is always the most inefficient function, but the second most inefficient function can be either thinking (which tends to make original thinkers such as Jung himself) or else feeling (which tends to make artistic people). Therefore, allowing for introversion and extroversion, there are at least four kinds of intuitive types, and sixteen types in all. Furthermore, one can see how the sixteen types merge into each other, so that there are no unrealistic or unconvincingly rigid divisions.

In the same way, if we were to put every person under only one sign of the Zodiac, the system becomes too rigid and unlike life. Besides, it was never intended to be used like that. It may be convenient to have only twelve types, but we know that in practice there is every possible gradation between aggressiveness and timidity, or between conscientiousness and laziness. How, then, do we account for this?

The Tyrant and the Saint

Just as the thinking type of man is also influenced to some extent by sensation and intuition, but not very much by emotion, so a person born under Leo can be influenced to some extent by one or two (but not more) of the other signs. For instance, famous persons born under the sign of Gemini include Henry VIII, whom nothing and no-one could have induced to abdicate, and Edward VIII, who did just that. Obviously, then, the sign Gemini does not fully explain the complete character of either of them.

Again, under the opposite sign, Sagittarius, were both Stalin, who was totally consumed with the notion of power, and Charles V, who freely gave up an empire because he preferred to go into a monastery. And we find under Scorpio, many uncompromising characters such as Luther, de Gaulle, Indira Gandhi and Montgomery, but also Petain, a successful commander whose name later became synonymous with collaboration.

A single sign is therefore obviously inadequate to explain the differences between people; it can only explain resemblances, such as the combativeness of the Scorpio group, or the far-reaching devotion of Charles V and Stalin to their respective ideals—the Christian heaven and the Communist utopia.

But very few people are born under one sign only. As well as the month of birth, as was mentioned earlier, the day matters, and, even more, the hour, which ought, if possible, to be noted to the nearest minute. Without this, it is impossible to have an actual horoscope, for the word horoscope means literally, "a consideration of the hour."

The month of birth tells you only which sign of the Zodiac was occupied by the sun. The day and hour tell you what sign was occupied by the moon. And the minute tells you which sign was rising on the eastern horizon. This is called the Ascendant, and it is supposed to be the most important thing in the whole horoscope.

If you were born at midnight, the sun is then in an important position, although invisible. But at one o'clock in the morning the sun is not important, so the moment of birth will not matter much. The important thing then will be the Ascendant, and possibly one or two of the planets. At a given day and hour, say, dawn on January 1st, or 9:00 p.m. on the longest day, the Ascendant will always be the same at any given place. But the moon and planets alter from day to day, at different speeds and have to be looked up in an astronomical table.

The sun is said to signify one's heart, that is to say, one's deepest desires and inmost nature. This is quite different from the moon, which, as we have seen, signifies one's superficial way of behaving. When the ancient Romans referred to the Emperor Augustus as a Capricornian, they meant that he had the moon in Capricorn; they did not pay much attention to the sun, although he was born at sunrise. Or, to take another example, a modern astrologer would call Disraeli a Scorpion because he had Scorpio rising, but most people would call him Sagittarian because he had the sun there. The Romans would have called him Leo because his moon was in Leo.

The sun, as has already been pointed out, is important if one is born near sunrise, sunset, noon or midnight, but is otherwise not reckoned as the principal influence. So if one does not seem to fit one's birth month, it is always worthwhile reading the other signs, for one may have been born at a time when any of them were rising or occupied by the moon. It also seems to be the case that the influence of the sun develops as life goes on, so that the month of birth is easier to guess in people over the age of forty. The young are supposed to be influenced mainly by their Ascendant which characterizes the body and physical personality as a whole.

It should be clearly understood that it is nonsense to assume that all people born at a certain time will exhibit the same characteristics, or that they will even behave in the same manner. It is quite obvious that, from the very moment of its birth, a child is subject to the effects of its environment, and that this in turn will influence its character and heritage to a decisive extent. Also to be taken into account are education and economic conditions, which play a very important part in the formation of one's character as well.

However, it is clearly established that people born under one sign of the Zodiac do have certain basic traits in their character which are different from those born under other signs. It is obvious to every thinking person that certain events produce different reactions in various people. For instance, if a man slips on a banana skin and falls heavily on the pavement, one passer-by may laugh and find this extremely amusing, while another may just walk on, thinking: "What a fool falling down like that. He should look where he is going." A third might also walk away saying to himself: "It's none of my business—I'm glad it wasn't me." A fourth might walk past and think: "I'm sorry for that man, but I haven't the time to be bothered with helping him." And a fifth might stop to help the fallen man to his feet, comfort him and take him home. Here is just one event which could produce entirely different reactions in different people. And, obviously, there are many more. One that comes to mind immediately is the violently opposed views to events such as wars, industrial strikes, and so on. The fact that people have different attitudes to the same event is simply another way of saying that they have different characters. And this is not something that can be put down to background, for people of the same race, religion, or class, very often express quite different reactions to happenings or events. Similarly, it is often the case that members of the same family, where there is clearly uniform background of economic and social standing, education, race and religion, often argue bitterly among themselves over political and social issues.

People have, in general, certain character traits and qualities which, according to their environment, develop in either a positive or a negative manner. Therefore, selfishness (inherent selfishness, that is) might emerge as unselfishness; kindness and consideration as cruelty and lack of consideration towards others. In the same way, a naturally constructive person, may, through frustration, become destructive, and so on. The latent characteristics with which people are born can, therefore, through environment and good or bad training, become something that would appear to be its opposite, and so give the lie to the astrologer's description of their character. But this is not the case. The true character is still there, but it is buried deep beneath these external superficialities.

Careful study of the character traits of different signs can be immeasurable help, and can render beneficial service to the intelligent person. Undoubtedly, the reader will already have discovered that, while he is able to get on very well with some people, he just "cannot stand" others. The causes sometimes seem inexplicable. At times there is intense dislike, at other times immediate sympathy. And there is, too, the phenomenon of love at first sight, which is also apparently inexplicable. People appear to be either sympathetic or unsympathetic towards each other for no apparent reason.

Now if we look at this in the light of the Zodiac, we find that people born under different signs are either compatible or incompatible with each other. In other words, there are good and bad interrelating factors among the various signs. This does not, of course, mean that humanity can be divided into groups of hostile camps. It would be quite wrong to be hostile or indifferent toward people who happen to be born under an incompatible sign. There is no reason why everybody should not, or cannot, learn to control and adjust their feelings and actions, especially after they are aware of the positive qualities of other people by studying their character analyses, among other things.

Every person born under a certain sign has both positive and negative qualities, which are developed more or less according to his free will. Nobody is entirely good or entirely bad, and it is up to each one of us to learn to control himself on the one hand, and at the same time to endeavor to learn about himself and others.

It cannot be repeated often enough that, though the intrinsic nature of man and his basic character traits are born in him, nevertheless it is his own free will that determines whether he will make really good use of his talents and abilities—whether, in other words, he will overcome his vices or allow them to rule him. Most of us are born with at least a streak of laziness, irritability, or some other fault in our nature, and it is up to each one of us to see that we exert sufficient willpower to control our failings so that they do not harm ourselves or others.

Astrology can reveal our inclinations and tendencies. Our weaknesses should not be viewed as shortcomings that are impossible to change. The horoscope of a man may show him to have criminal leanings, for instance, but this does not mean he will definitely become a criminal.

The ordinary man usually finds it difficult to know himself. He is often bewildered. Astrology can frequently tell him more about himself than the different schools of psychology are able to do. Knowing his failings and shortcomings, he will do his best to overcome them, and make himself a better and more useful member of society and a helpmate to his family and friends. It can also save him a great deal of unhappiness and remorse.

And yet it may seem absurd that an ancient philosophy, something that is known as a "pseudo-science," could be a prop to the men and women of the twentieth century. But below the materialistic surface of modern life, there are hidden streams of feeling and thought. Symbology is reappearing as a study worthy of the scholar; the psychosomatic factor in illness has passed from the writings of the crank to those of the specialist; spiritual healing in all its forms is no longer a pious hope but an accepted phenomenon. And it is into this context that we consider astrology, in the sense that it is an analysis of human types.

Astrology and medicine had a long journey together, and only parted company a couple of centuries ago. There still remain in medical language such astrological terms as "saturnine," "choleric," and "mercurial," used in the diagnosis of physical tendencies. The herbalist, for long the handyman of the medical profession, has been dominated by astrology since the days of the Greeks. Certain herbs traditionally respond to certain planetary influences, and diseases must therefore be treated to ensure harmony between the medicine and the disease.

No one expects the most eccentric of modern doctors to go back to the practices of his predecessors. We have come a long way since the time when phases of the moon were studied in illness. Those days were a medical nightmare, with epidemics that were beyond control, and an explanation of the Black Death sought in conjunction with the planets. Nowadays, astrological diagnosis of disease has literally no parallel in modern life. And yet, age-old symbols of types and of the vulnerability of, say, the Saturnian to chronic diseases or the choleric to apoplexy and blood pressure and so on, are still applicable.

But the stars are expected to foretell and not only to diagnose. The astrological forecaster has a counterpart on a highly conventional level in the shape of the weather prophet, racing tipster and stock market forecaster, to name just three examples. All in their own way are aiming at the same result. They attempt to look a little further into the pattern of life and also try to determine future patterns accurately.

Astrological forecasting has been remarkably accurate, but often it is wide of the mark. The brave man who cares to predict world events takes dangerous chances. Individual forecasting is less clear cut; it can be a help or a disillusionment. Then welcome to the nagging question: if it is possible to foreknow, is it right to foretell? A complex point of ethics on which it is hard to pronounce judgment. The doctor faces the same dilemma if he finds that symptoms of a mortal disease are present in his patient and that he can only prognosticate a steady decline. How much to tell an individual in a crisis is a problem that has perplexed many distinguished scholars. Honest and conscientious astrologers in this modern world, where so many people are seeking guidance, face the same problem.

The ancient cults, the symbols of old religions, are eclipsed for the moment. They may return with their old force within a decade or two. But at present the outlook is dark. Human beings badly need assurance, as they did in the past, that all is not chaos. Somewhere, somehow, there is a pattern that must be worked out. As to the why and wherefore, the astrologer is not expected to give judgment. He is just someone who, by dint of talent and training, can gaze into the future.

Five hundred years ago it was customary to call in a learned man who was an astrologer who was probably also a doctor and a philosopher. By his knowledge of astrology, his study of planetary influences, he felt himself qualified to guide those in distress. The world has moved forward at a fantastic rate since then, and in this twentieth century speed has been the keyword everywhere. Tensions have increased, the spur of ambition has been applied indiscriminately. People are uncertain of themselves. At first sight it seems fantastic in the light of modern thinking that they turn to the most ancient of all studies, and get someone to calculate a horoscope for them. But is it *really* so fantastic if you take a second look? For astrology is concerned with tomorrow, with survival. And in a world such as ours, those two things are the keywords of the time in which we live.

HOW TO USE THESE PREDICTIONS

A person reading the predictions in this book should understand that they are produced from the daily position of the planets for a group of people and are not, of course, individually specialized. To get the full benefit of them he should relate the predictions to his own character and circumstances, co-ordinate them, and draw his own conclusions from them.

If he is a serious observer of his own life he should find a definite pattern emerge that will be a helpful and reliable guide.

The point is that we always retain our free will. The stars indicate certain directional tendencies but we are not compelled to follow. We can do or not do, and wisdom must make the choice.

We all have our good and bad days. Sometimes they extend into cycles of weeks. It is therefore advisable to study daily predictions in a span ranging from the day before to several days ahead; also to re-read the monthly predictions for similar cycles.

Daily predictions should be taken very generally. The word "difficult" does not necessarily indicate a whole day of obstruction or inconvenience. It is a warning to you to be cautious. Your caution will often see you around the difficulty before you are involved. This is the correct use of astrology.

In another section, detailed information is given about the influence of the moon as it passes through the various signs of the Zodiac. It includes instructions on how to use the Moon Tables. This information should be used in conjunction with the daily forecasts to give a fuller picture of the astrological trends.

THE MOON

Moon is the nearest planet to the earth. It exerts more observable influence on us from day to day than any other planet. The effect is very personal, very intimate, and if we are not aware of how it works it can make us quite unstable in our ideas. And the annoying thing is that at these times we often see our own instability but can do nothing about it. A knowledge of what can be expected may help considerably. We can then be prepared to stand strong against the moon's negative influences and use its positive ones to help us to get ahead. Who has not heard of going with the tide?

Moon reflects, has no light of its own. It reflects the sun—the life giver—in the form of vital movement. Moon controls the tides, the blood rhythm, the movement of sap in trees and plants. Its nature is inconstancy and change so it signifies our moods, our superficial behavior—walking, talking and especially thinking. Being a true reflector of other forces, moon is cold, watery like the surface of a still lake, brilliant and scintillating at times, but easily ruffled and disturbed by the winds of change.

The moon takes 28½ days to circle the earth and the Zodiac. It spends just over 2¼ days in each sign. During that time it reflects the qualities, energies and characteristics of the sign and, to a degree, the planet which rules the sign. While the moon in its transit occupies a sign incompatible with our own birth sign, we can expect to feel a vague uneasiness, perhaps a touch of irritableness. We should not be discouraged nor let the feeling get us down, or, worse still, allow ourselves to take the discomfort out on others. Try to remember that the moon has to change signs within 55 hours and, provided you are not physically ill, your mood will probably change with it. It is amazing how frequently depression lifts with the shift in the moon's position. And, of course, when the moon is transiting a sign compatible or sympathetic to yours you will probably feel some sort of stimulation or just plain happy to be alive.

In the horoscope, the moon is such a powerful indicator that competent astrologers often use the sign it occupied at birth as the birth sign of the person. This is done particularly when the sun is on the cusp, or edge, of two signs. Most experienced astrologers, however, coordinate both sun and moon signs by reading and confirming from one to the other and secure a far more accurate and personalized analysis.

For these reasons, the moon tables which follow this section (see pages 28–35) are of great importance to the individual. They show the days and the exact times the moon will enter each sign of the Zodiac for the year. Remember, you have to adjust the indicated times to local time. The corrections, already calculated for most of the main cities, are at the beginning of the tables. What follows now is a guide to the influences that will be reflected to the earth by the moon while it transits each of the twelve signs. The influence is at its peak about 26 hours after the moon enters a sign.

MOON IN ARIES

This is a time for action, for reaching out beyond the usual self-imposed limitations and faint-hearted cautions. If you have plans in your head or on your desk, put them into practice. New ventures, applications, new jobs, new starts of any kind—all have a good chance of success. This is the period when original and dynamic impulses are being reflected onto the earth. The energies are extremely vital and favor the pursuit of pleasure and adventure in practically every form. Sick people should feel an improvement. Those who are well will probably find themselves exuding confidence and optimism. People fond of physical exercise should find their bodies growing with tone and well-being. Boldness, strength, determination should characterize most of your activities with a readiness to face up to old challenges. Yesterday's problems may seem petty and exaggerated—so deal with them. Strike out alone. Self-reliance will attract others to you. This is a good time for making friends. Business and marriage partners are more likely to be impressed with the man and woman of action. Opposition will be overcome or thrown aside with much less effort than usual. CAUTION: Be dominant but not domineering.

MOON IN TAURUS

The spontaneous, action-packed person of yesterday gives way to the cautious, diligent, hardworking "thinker." In this period ideas will probably be concentrated on ways of improving finances. A great deal of time may be spent figuring out and going over schemes and plans. It is the right time to be careful with detail. People will find themselves working longer than usual at their desks. Or devoting more time to serious thought about the future. A strong desire to put order into business and financial arrangements may cause extra work. Loved ones may complain of being neglected and may fail to appreciate that your efforts are for their ultimate benefit. Your desire for system may extend to criticism of arrangements in the home and lead to minor upsets. Health may be affected through overwork. Try to secure a reasonable amount of rest and relaxation, although the tendency will be to "keep going" despite good advice. Work done conscientiously in this period should result in a solid contribution to your future security. CAUTION: Try not to be as serious with people as the work you are engaged in.

MOON IN GEMINI

The humdrum of routine and too much work should suddenly end. You are likely to find yourself in an expansive, quicksilver world of change and self-expression. Urges to write, to paint, to experience the freedom of some sort of artistic outpouring, may be very strong. Take full advantage of them. You may find yourself finishing something you began and put aside long ago. Or embarking on something new which could easily be prompted by a chance meeting, a new acquaintance, or even an advertisement. There may be a yearning for a change of scenery, the feeling to visit another country (not too far away), or at least to get away for a few days. This may result in short, quick journeys. Or, if you are planning a single visit, there may be some unexpected changes or detours on the way. Familiar activities will seem to give little satisfaction unless they contain a fresh element of excitement or expectation. The inclination will be towards untried pursuits, particularly those that allow you to express your inner nature. The accent is on new faces, new places. CAUTION: Do not be too quick to commit yourself emotionally.

MOON IN CANCER

Feelings of uncertainty and vague insecurity are likely to cause problems while the moon is in Cancer. Thoughts may turn frequently to the warmth of the home and the comfort of loved ones. Nostalgic impulses could cause you to bring out old photographs and letters and reflect on the days when your life seemed to be much more rewarding and less demanding. The love and understanding of parents and family may be important, and, if it is not forthcoming you may have to fight against a bit of self-pity. The cordiality of friends and the thought of good times with them that are sure to be repeated will help to restore you to a happier frame of mind. The feeling to be alone may follow minor setbacks or rebuffs at this time, but solitude is unlikely to help. Better to get on the telephone or visit someone. This period often causes peculiar dreams and up-surges of imaginative thinking which can be very helpful to authors of occult and mystical works. Preoccupation with the more person-al world of simple human needs should overshadow any material strivings. CAUTION: Do not spend too much time thinking—seek the company of loved ones or close friends.

MOON IN LEO

New horizons of exciting and rather extravagant activity open up. This is the time for exhilarating entertainment, glamorous and lavish parties, and expensive shopping sprees. Any merrymaking that relies upon your generosity as a host has every chance of being a spectacular success. You should find yourself right in the center of the fun, either as the life of the party or simply as a person whom happy people like to be with. Romance thrives in this heady at-mosphere and friendships are likely to explode unexpectedly into serious attachments. Children and younger people should be at-tracted to you and you may find yourself organizing a picnic or a visit to a fun-fair, the cinema or the seaside. The sunny company and vitality of youthful companions should help you to find some unsuspected energy. In career, you could find an opening for pro-motion or advancement. This should be the time to make a direct approach. The period favors those engaged in original research. CAUTION: Bask in popularity but not in flattery.

MOON IN VIRGO

Off comes the party cap and out steps the busy, practical worker. He wants to get his personal affairs straight, to rearrange them, if necessary, for more efficiency, so he will have more time for more work. He clears up his correspondence, pays outstanding bills, makes numerous phone calls. He is likely to make inquiries, or sign up for some new insurance and put money into gilt-edged invest-ment. Thoughts probably revolve around the need for future secur-ity—to tie up loose ends and clear the decks. There may be a ten-dency to be "finicky," to interfere in the routine of others, particu-larly friends and family members. The motive may be a genuine desire to help with suggestions for updating or streamlining their affairs, but these will probably not be welcomed. Sympathy may be felt for less fortunate sections of the community and a flurry of some sort of voluntary service is likely. This may be accompanied by strong feelings of responsibility on several fronts and health may suffer from extra efforts made. CAUTION: Everyone may not want your help or advice.

MOON IN LIBRA

These are days of harmony and agreement and you should find yourself at peace with most others. Relationships tend to be smooth and sweet-flowing. Friends may become closer and bonds deepen in mutual understanding. Hopes will be shared. Progress by cooperation could be the secret of success in every sphere. In business, established partnerships may flourish and new ones get off to a good start. Acquaintances could discover similar interests that lead to congenial discussions and rewarding exchanges of some sort. Love, as a unifying force, reaches its optimum. Marriage partners should find accord. Those who wed at this time face the prospect of a happy union. Cooperation and tolerance are felt to be stronger than dissension and impatience. The argumentative are not quite so loud in their bellowings, nor as inflexible in their attitudes. In the home, there should be a greater recognition of the other point of view and a readiness to put the wishes of the group before selfish insistence. This is a favorable time to join an art group. CAUTION: Do not be too independent—let others help you if they want to.

MOON IN SCORPIO

Driving impulses to make money and to economize are likely to cause upsets all round. No area of expenditure is likely to be spared the axe, including the household budget. This is a time when the desire to cut down on extravagance can become near fanatical. Care must be exercised to try to keep the aim in reasonable perspective. Others may not feel the same urgent need to save and may retaliate. There is a danger that possessions of sentimental value will be sold to realize cash for investment. Buying and selling of stock for quick profit is also likely. The attention may turn to having a good clean up round the home and at the office. Neglected jobs could suddenly be done with great bursts of energy. The desire for solitude may intervene. Self-searching thoughts could disturb. The sense of invisible and mysterious energies at work could cause some excitability. The reassurance of loves ones may help. CAUTION: Be kind to the people you love.

MOON IN SAGITTARIUS

These are days when you are likely to be stirred and elevated by discussions and reflections of a religious and philosophical nature. Ideas of far-away places may cause unusual response and excitement. A decision may be made to visit someone overseas, perhaps a person whose influence was important to your earlier character development. There could be a strong resolution to get away from present intellectual patterns, to learn new subjects and to meet more interesting people. The superficial may be rejected in all its forms. An impatience with old ideas and unimaginative contacts could lead to a change of companions and interests. There may be an upsurge of religious feeling and metaphysical inquiry. Even a new insight into the significance of astrology and other occult studies is likely under the curious stimulus of the moon in Sagittarius. Physically, you may express this need for fundamental change by spending more time outdoors: sports, gardening or going for long walks. CAUTION: Try to channel any restlessness into worthwhile study.

MOON IN CAPRICORN

Life in these hours may seem to pivot around the importance of gaining prestige and honor in the career, as well as maintaining a spotless reputation. Ambitious urges may be excessive and could be accompanied by quite acquisitive drives for money. Effort should be directed along strictly ethical lines where there is no possibility of reproach or scandal. All endeavors are likely to be characterized by great earnestness, and an air of authority and purpose which should impress those who are looking for leadership or reliability. The desire to conform to accepted standards may extend to sharp criticism of family members. Frivolity and unconventional actions are unlikely to amuse while the moon is in Capricorn. Moderation and seriousness are the orders of the day. Achievement and recognition in this period could come through community work or organizing for the benefit of some amateur group. CAUTION: Dignity and esteem are not always self-awarded.

MOON IN AQUARIUS

Moon in Aquarius is in the second last sign of the Zodiac where ideas can become disturbingly fine and subtle. The result is often a mental "no-man's land" where imagination cannot be trusted with the same certitude as other times. The dangers for the individual are the extremes of optimism and pessimism. Unless the imgination is held in check, situations are likely to be misread, and rosy conclusions drawn where they do not exist. Consequences for the unwary can be costly in career and business. Best to think twice and not speak or act until you think again. Pessimism can be a cruel self-inflicted penalty for delusion at this time. Between the two extremes are strange areas of self-deception which, for example, can make the selfish person think he is actually being generous. Eerie dreams which resemble the reality and even seem to continue into the waking state are also possible. CAUTION: Look for the fact and not just for the image in your mind.

MOON IN PISCES

Everything seems to come to the surface now. Memory may be crystal clear, throwing up long-forgotten information which could be valuable in the career or business. Flashes of clairvoyance and intuition are possible along with sudden realizations of one's own nature, which may be used for self-improvement. A talent, never before suspected, may be discovered. Qualities not evident before in friends and marriage partners are likely to be noticed. As this is a period in which the truth seems to emerge, the discovery of false characteristics is likely to lead to disenchantment or a shift in attachments. However, where qualities are realized it should lead to happiness and deeper feeling. Surprise solutions could bob up for old problems. There may be a public announcement of the solving of a crime or mystery. People with secrets may find someone has "guessed" correctly. The secrets of the soul or the inner self also tend to reveal themselves. Religious and philosophical groups may make some interesting discoveries. CAUTION: Not a time for activities that depend on secrecy.

MOON TABLES

TIME CORRECTIONS FOR
GREENWICH MOON TABLES

London, Glasgow, Dublin, Dakar...Same time

Vienna, Prague, Rome, Kinshasa, Frankfurt,
  Stockholm, Brussels, Amsterdam, Warsaw,
  Zurich...Add 1 hour

Bucharest, Istanbul, Beirut, Cairo, Johannesburg,
  Athens, Cape Town, Helsinki, Tel Aviv.............................Add 2 hours

Dhahran, Baghdad, Moscow, Leningrad, Nairobi,
  Addis Ababa, Zanzibar...Add 3 hours

Delhi, Calcutta, Bombay, Colombo....................................Add 5½ hours

Rangoon...Add 6½ hours

Saigon, Bangkok, Chungking..Add 7 hours

Canton, Manila, Hong Kong, Shanghai, Peking....................Add 8 hours

Tokyo, Pusan, Seoul, Vladivostok, Yokohama.......................Add 9 hours

Sydney, Melbourne, Guam, Port Moresby............................Add 10 hours

Azores, Reykjavik..Deduct 1 hour

Rio de Janeiro, Montevideo, Buenos Aires,
  Sao Paulo, Recife...Deduct 3 hours

LaPaz, San Juan, Santiago, Bermuda, Caracas,
  Halifax..Deduct 4 hours

New York, Washington, Boston, Detroit, Lima,
  Havana, Miami, Bogota..Deduct 5 hours

Mexico, Chicago, New Orleans, Houston.........................Deduct 6 hours

San Francisco, Seattle, Los Angeles, Hollywood,
  Ketchikan, Juneau..Deduct 8 hours

Honolulu, Fairbanks, Anchorage, Papeete.......................Deduct 10 hours

1995 MOON TABLES—GREENWICH TIME

JANUARY Day Moon Enters		FEBRUARY Day Moon Enters		MARCH Day Moon Enters	
1. Capric.		1. Pisces	8:06 am	1. Pisces	
2. Aquar.	6:40 pm	2. Pisces		2. Aries	11:31 pm
3. Aquar.		3. Aries	2:13 pm	3. Aries	
4. Pisces	9:50 pm	4. Aries		4. Aries	
5. Pisces		5. Aries		5. Taurus	8:51 am
6. Pisces		6. Taurus	0:10 am	6. Taurus	
7. Aries	4:57 am	7. Taurus		7. Gemini	8:56 pm
8. Aries		8. Gemini	0:45 pm	8. Gemini	
9. Taurus	3:59 pm	9. Gemini		9. Gemini	
10. Taurus		10. Gemini		10. Cancer	9:41 am
11. Taurus		11. Cancer	1:18 am	11. Cancer	
12. Gemini	4:58 am	12. Cancer		12. Leo	8:29 pm
13. Gemini		13. Leo	11:32 am	13. Leo	
14. Cancer	5:21 pm	14. Leo		14. Leo	
15. Cancer		15. Virgo	6:53 pm	15. Virgo	3:55 am
16. Cancer		16. Virgo		16. Virgo	
17. Leo	3:37 am	17. Virgo		17. Libra	8:19 am
18. Leo		18. Libra	0:01 am	18. Libra	
19. Virgo	11:40 am	19. Libra		19. Scorpio	10:53 am
20. Virgo		20. Scorpio	3:56 am	20. Scorpio	
21. Libra	5:55 pm	21. Scorpio		21. Sagitt.	0:58 pm
22. Libra		22. Sagitt.	7:14 am	22. Sagitt.	
23. Scorpio	10:33 pm	23. Sagitt.		23. Capric.	3:32 pm
24. Scorpio		24. Capric.	10:12 am	24. Capric.	
25. Scorpio		25. Capric.		25. Aquar.	7:11 pm
26. Sagitt.	1:38 am	26. Aquar.	1:15 pm	26. Aquar.	
27. Sagitt.		27. Aquar.		27. Aquar.	
28. Capric.	3:27 am	28. Pisces	5:17 pm	28. Pisces	0:19 am
29. Capric.				29. Pisces	
30. Aquar.	5:04 am			30. Aries	7:27 am
31. Aquar.				31. Aries	

Summer time to be considered where applicable.

1995 MOON TABLES—GREENWICH TIME

APRIL Day Moon Enters		MAY Day Moon Enters		JUNE Day Moon Enters	
1. Taurus	5:00 pm	1. Gemini	11:54 am	1. Cancer	
2. Taurus		2. Gemini		2. Leo	7:18 pm
3. Taurus		3. Gemini		3. Leo	
4. Gemini	4:50 am	4. Cancer	0:46 am	4. Leo	
5. Gemini		5. Cancer		5. Virgo	5:47 am
6. Cancer	5:41 pm	6. Leo	0:56 pm	6. Virgo	
7. Cancer		7. Leo		7. Libra	1:14 pm
8. Cancer		8. Virgo	10:34 pm	8. Libra	
9. Leo	5:16 am	9. Virgo		9. Scorpio	5:04 pm
10. Leo		10. Virgo		10. Scorpio	
11. Virgo	1:40 pm	11. Libra	4:31 am	11. Sagitt.	5:51 pm
12. Virgo		12. Libra		12. Sagitt.	
13. Libra	6:21 pm	13. Scorpio	6:54 am	13. Capric.	5:06 pm
14. Libra		14. Scorpio		14. Capric.	
15. Scorpio	8:14 pm	15. Sagitt.	6:59 am	15. Aquar.	4:53 pm
16. Scorpio		16. Sagitt.		16. Aquar.	
17. Sagitt.	8:52 pm	17. Capric.	6:37 am	17. Pisces	7:14 pm
18. Sagitt.		18. Capric.		18. Pisces	
19. Capric.	9:55 pm	19. Aquar.	7:40 am	19. Pisces	
20. Capric.		20. Aquar.		20. Aries	1:30 am
21. Capric.		21. Pisces	11:41 am	21. Aries	
22. Aquar.	0:39 am	22. Pisces		22. Taurus	11:36 am
23. Aquar.		23. Aries	7:14 pm	23. Taurus	
24. Pisces	5:52 am	24. Aries		24. Taurus	
25. Pisces		25. Aries		25. Gemini	0:03 am
26. Aries	1:42 pm	26. Taurus	5:47 am	26. Gemini	
27. Aries		27. Taurus		27. Cancer	0:57 pm
28. Taurus	11:54 pm	28. Gemini	6:08 pm	28. Cancer	
29. Taurus		29. Gemini		29. Cancer	
30. Taurus		30. Gemini		30. Leo	1:03 am
		31. Cancer	7:00 am		

Summer time to be considered where applicable.

1995 MOON TABLES—GREENWICH TIME

JULY		AUGUST		SEPTEMBER	
Day Moon Enters		**Day Moon Enters**		**Day Moon Enters**	
1. Leo		1. Libra	1:24 am	1. Sagitt.	4:58 pm
2. Virgo	11:36 am	2. Libra		2. Sagitt.	
3. Virgo		3. Scorpio	7:30 am	3. Capric.	7:46 pm
4. Libra	7:56 pm	4. Scorpio		4. Capric.	
5. Libra		5. Sagitt.	11:15 am	5. Aquar.	9:48 pm
6. Libra		6. Sagitt.		6. Aquar.	
7. Scorpio	1:20 am	7. Capric.	0:53 pm	7. Aquar.	
8. Scorpio		8. Capric.		8. Pisces	0:09 am
9. Sagitt.	3:38 am	9. Aquar.	1:29 pm	9. Pisces	
10. Sagitt.		10. Aquar.		10. Aries	4:15 am
11. Capric.	3:44 am	11. Pisces	2:47 pm	11. Aries	
12. Capric.		12. Pisces		12. Taurus	11:22 am
13. Aquar.	3:22 am	13. Aries	6:42 pm	13. Taurus	
14. Aquar.		14. Aries		14. Gemini	9:49 pm
15. Pisces	4:38 am	15. Aries		15. Gemini	
16. Pisces		16. Taurus	2:26 am	16. Gemini	
17. Aries	9:24 am	17. Taurus		17. Cancer	10:17 am
18. Aries		18. Gemini	1:41 pm	18. Cancer	
19. Taurus	6:21 pm	19. Gemini		19. Leo	10:20 pm
20. Taurus		20. Gemini		20. Leo	
21. Taurus		21. Cancer	2:25 am	21. Leo	
22. Gemini	6:24 am	22. Cancer		22. Virgo	8:02 am
23. Gemini		23. Leo	2:14 pm	23. Virgo	
24. Cancer	7:17 pm	24. Leo		24. Libra	2:51 pm
25. Cancer		25. Virgo	11:51 pm	25. Libra	
26. Cancer		26. Virgo		26. Scorpio	7:21 pm
27. Leo	7:08 am	27. Virgo		27. Scorpio	
28. Leo		28. Libra	7:16 am	28. Sagitt.	10:31 pm
29. Virgo	5:13 pm	29. Libra		29. Sagitt.	
30. Virgo		30. Scorpio	0:52 pm	30. Sagitt.	
31. Virgo		31. Scorpio			

Summer time to be considered where applicable.

1995 MOON TABLES—GREENWICH TIME

OCTOBER			NOVEMBER			DECEMBER		
Day	Moon	Enters	Day	Moon	Enters	Day	Moon	Enters
1.	Capric.	1:11 am	1.	Pisces	1:18 pm	1.	Aries	0:52 am
2.	Capric.		2.	Pisces		2.	Aries	
3.	Aquar.	4:00 am	3.	Aries	7:22 pm	3.	Taurus	9:41 am
4.	Aquar.		4.	Aries		4.	Taurus	
5.	Pisces	7:36 am	5.	Aries		5.	Gemini	8:36 pm
6.	Pisces		6.	Taurus	3:36 am	6.	Gemini	
7.	Aries	0:43 pm	7.	Taurus		7.	Gemini	
8.	Aries		8.	Gemini	1:56 pm	8.	Cancer	8:45 am
9.	Taurus	8:06 pm	9.	Gemini		9.	Cancer	
10.	Taurus		10.	Gemini		10.	Leo	9:25 pm
11.	Taurus		11.	Cancer	1:58 am	11.	Leo	
12.	Gemini	6:11 am	12.	Cancer		12.	Leo	
13.	Gemini		13.	Leo	2:38 pm	13.	Virgo	9:27 am
14.	Cancer	6:21 pm	14.	Leo		14.	Virgo	
15.	Cancer		15.	Leo		15.	Libra	7:10 pm
16.	Cancer		16.	Virgo	2:03 am	16.	Libra	
17.	Leo	6:47 am	17.	Virgo		17.	Libra	
18.	Leo		18.	Libra	10:19 am	18.	Scorpio	1:08 am
19.	Virgo	5:12 pm	19.	Libra		19.	Scorpio	
20.	Virgo		20.	Scorpio	2:41 pm	20.	Sagitt.	3:14 am
21.	Virgo		21.	Scorpio		21.	Sagitt.	
22.	Libra	0:16 am	22.	Sagitt.	3:57 pm	22.	Capric.	2:47 am
23.	Libra		23.	Sagitt.		23.	Capric.	
24.	Scorpio	4:07 am	24.	Capric.	3:49 pm	24.	Aquar.	1:53 am
25.	Scorpio		25.	Capric.		25.	Aquar.	
26.	Sagitt.	5:57 am	26.	Aquar.	4:16 pm	26.	Pisces	2:46 am
27.	Sagitt.		27.	Aquar.		27.	Pisces	
28.	Capric.	7:16 am	28.	Pisces	7:00 pm	28.	Aries	7:07 am
29.	Capric.		29.	Pisces		29.	Aries	
30.	Aquar.	9:24 am	30.	Pisces		30.	Taurus	3:22 pm
31.	Aquar.					31.	Taurus	

Summer time to be considered where applicable.

1995 PHASES OF THE MOON—GREENWICH TIME

New Moon	First Quarter	Full Moon	Last Quarter
Jan. 1	Jan. 8	Jan. 16	Jan. 24
Jan. 30	Feb. 7	Feb. 15	Feb. 22
Mar. 1	Mar. 9	Mar. 17	Mar. 23
Mar. 31	Apr. 8	Apr. 15	Apr. 22
Apr. 29	May 7	May 14	May 21
May 29	June 6	June 13	June 19
June 28	July 5	July 12	July 19
July 27	Aug. 4	Aug. 10	Aug. 18
Aug. 26	Sep. 2	Sep. 9	Sep. 16
Sep. 24	Oct. 1	Oct. 8	Oct. 16
Oct. 24	Oct. 30	Nov. 7	Nov. 15
Nov. 22	Nov. 29	Dec. 7	Dec. 15
Dec. 22	Dec. 28		

Each phase of the Moon lasts approximately seven to eight days, during which the Moon's shape gradually changes as it comes out of one phase and goes into the next.

There will be a partial solar eclipse during the New Moon phase on April 29 and October 24. There will be a lunar eclipse during the Full Moon phase on April 15.

1995 PLANTING GUIDE

	Aboveground Crops	Root Crops	Pruning	Weeds Pests
January	1-5-6-10-11-15	22-23-24-25-28-29	24-25	17-18-19-20-26-27-30
February	1-2-6-7-11-12	18-19-20-21-25	20-21	16-17-22-23-27
March	2-5-6-10-11	17-18-19-20-24-28-29	20-28-29	22-26-27-30
April	2-3-7-8-14-30	16-20-21-24-25	16-24-25	18-22-23-27-28
May	4-5-11-12-13-31	17-18-22-26-27	22	15-16-19-20-24-25
June	1-8-9-10-28-29	14-18-19-23-24	18-19	16-20-21-25-26
July	5-6-7-8-11	15-16-20-21-25-26	15-16-25-26	13-14-17-18-22-23
August	1-2-3-4-8-28-29-30-31	12-16-17-21-22	12-21-22	14-15-19-20-24-25
September	4-8-25-26-27-28	9-13-18-19-22-23	9-18-19	10-11-15-16-20-21-22-23
October	1-2-5-6-24-25-28-29	10-11-15-16-22-23	15-16	12-13-17-18-19-20-21
November	2-6-25-29-30	7-11-12-19-20-21	11-12-21	9-10-14-15-16-17
December	3-4-22-23-26-27-31	8-9-16-17-18-19	8-9-18-19	7-11-12-13-14-20-21

1995 FISHING GUIDE

	Good	Best
January	4-8-13-14-17-18-19-30	1-15-16-24
February	13-14-15-16-17-22	7-12-18
March	9-14-15-16-19-23-31	1-17-18-20
April	12-13-15-17-18-22	8-14-16-29
May	7-15-16-21-29	11-12-13-14-17
June	6-11-12-13-15-16	10-14-19-28
July	9-10-13-14-19-27	5-11-12-15
August	7-9-10-11-13-18-26	4-8-12
September	2-6-7-10-11-12-16-24	8-9
October	7-8-9-30	1-5-6-10-11-16-24
November	4-5-8-9-10-15-22	6-7-29
December	5-6-7-10-15-28	4-8-9-22

MOON'S INFLUENCE OVER DAILY AFFAIRS

The Moon makes a complete transit of the Zodiac every 27 days 7 hours and 43 minutes. In making this transit the Moon forms different aspects with the planets and consequently has favorable or unfavorable bearings on affairs and events for persons according to the sign of the Zodiac under which they were born. Whereas the Sun exclusively represents fire, the Moon rules water. The action of the Moon may be described as fluctuating, variable, absorbent and receptive.

When the Moon is in conjunction with the Sun it is called a New Moon; when the Moon and Sun are in opposition it is called a Full Moon. From New Moon to Full Moon, first and second quarter—which takes about two weeks—the Moon is increasing or waxing. From Full Moon to New Moon, third and fourth quarter, the Moon is decreasing or waning. The Moon Table indicates the New Moon and Full Moon and the quarters.

ACTIVITY	MOON IN
Business:	
buying and selling	Sagittarius, Aries, Gemini, Virgo
new, requiring public support	1st and 2nd quarter
meant to be kept quiet	3rd and 4th quarter
Investigation	3rd and 4th quarter
Signing documents	1st & 2nd quarter, Cancer, Scorpio, Pisces
Advertising	2nd quarter, Sagittarius
Journeys and trips	1st & 2nd quarter, Gemini, Virgo
Renting offices, etc.	Taurus, Leo, Scorpio, Aquarius
Painting of house/apartment	3rd & 4th quarter, Taurus, Scorpio, Aquarius
Decorating	Gemini, Libra, Aquarius
Buying clothes and accessories	Taurus, Virgo
Beauty salon or barber shop visit	1st & 2nd quarter, Taurus, Leo, Libra, Scorpio, Aquarius
Weddings	1st & 2nd quarter

MOON'S INFLUENCE OVER YOUR HEALTH

ARIES   Head, brain, face, upper jaw
TAURUS   Throat, neck, lower jaw
GEMINI   Hands, arms, lungs, shoulders, nervous system
CANCER   Esophagus, stomach, breasts, womb, liver
LEO   Heart, spine
VIRGO   Intestines, liver
LIBRA   Kidneys, lower back
SCORPIO   Sex and eliminative organs
SAGITTARIUS   Hips, thighs, liver
CAPRICORN   Skin, bones, teeth, knees
AQUARIUS   Circulatory system, lower legs
PISCES   Feet, tone of being

Try to avoid work being done on that part of the body
when the Moon is in the sign governing that part.

MOON'S INFLUENCE OVER PLANTS

Centuries ago it was established that seeds planted when the Moon is
in certain signs and phases called Fruitful will produce more growth
than seeds planted when the Moon is in a Barren sign.

FRUITFUL SIGNS	BARREN SIGNS	DRY SIGNS
Taurus	Aries	Aries
Cancer	Gemini	Gemini
Libra	Leo	Sagittarius
Scorpio	Virgo	Aquarius
Capricorn	Sagittarius	
Pisces	Aquarius	

ACTIVITY	MOON IN
Mow lawn, trim plants	**Fruitful sign:** 1st & 2nd quarter
Plant flowers	**Fruitful sign:** 2nd quarter; best in Cancer and Libra
Prune	**Fruitful sign:** 3rd & 4th quarter
Destroy pests; spray	**Barren sign:** 4th quarter
Harvest potatoes, root crops	**Dry sign:** 3rd & 4th quarter; Taurus, Leo, and Aquarius

THE SIGNS: DOMINANT CHARACTERISTICS

March 21–April 20

The Positive Side of Aries

The Arien has many positive points to his character. People born under this first sign of the Zodiac are often quite strong and enthusiastic. On the whole, they are forward-looking people who are not easily discouraged by temporary setbacks. They know what they want out of life and they go out after it. Their personalities are strong. Others are usually quite impressed by the Arien's way of doing things. Quite often they are sources of inspiration for others traveling the same route. Aries men and women have a special zest for life that is often contagious; for others, they are often the example of how life should be lived.

The Aries person usually has a quick and active mind. He is imaginative and inventive. He enjoys keeping busy and active. He generally gets along well with all kinds of people. He is interested in mankind, as a whole. He likes to be challenged. Some would say he thrives on opposition, for it is when he is set against that he often does his best. Getting over or around obstacles is a challenge he generally enjoys. All in all, the Arien is quite positive and young-thinking. He likes to keep abreast of new things that are happening in the world. Ariens are often fond of speed. They like things to be done quickly and this sometimes aggravates their slower colleagues and associates.

The Aries man or woman always seems to remain young. Their whole approach to life is youthful and optimistic. They never say die, no matter what the odds. They may have an occasional setback, but it is not long before they are back on their feet again.

The Negative Side of Aries

Everybody has his less positive qualities—and Aries is no exception. Sometimes the Aries man or woman is not very tactful in communicating with others; in his hurry to get things done he is apt to

be a little callous or inconsiderate. Sensitive people are likely to find him somewhat sharp-tongued in some situations. Often in his eagerness to achieve his aims, he misses the mark altogether. At times the Arien is too impulsive. He can occasionally be stubborn and refuse to listen to reason. If things do not move quickly enough to suit the Aries man or woman, he or she is apt to become rather nervous or irritable. The uncultivated Arien is not unfamiliar with moments of doubt and fear. He is capable of being destructive if he does not get his way. He can overcome some of his emotional problems by steadily trying to express himself as he really is, but this requires effort.

April 21–May 20

The Positive Side of Taurus

The Taurus person is known for his ability to concentrate and for his tenacity. These are perhaps his strongest qualities. The Taurus man or woman generally has very little trouble in getting along with others; it's his nature to be helpful toward people in need. He can always be depended on by his friends, especially those in trouble.

The Taurean generally achieves what he wants through his ability to persevere. He never leaves anything unfinished but works on something until it has been completed. People can usually take him at his word; he is honest and forthright in most of his dealings. The Taurus person has a good chance to make a success of his life because of his many positive qualities. The Taurean who aims high seldom falls short of his mark. He learns well by experience. He is thorough and does not believe in short-cuts of any kind. The Taurean's thoroughness pays off in the end, for through his deliberateness he learns how to rely on himself and what he has learned. The Taurus person tries to get along with others, as a rule. He is not overly critical and likes people to be themselves. He is a tolerant person and enjoys peace and harmony—especially in his home life.

The Taurean is usually cautious in all that he does. He is not a person who believes in taking unnecessary risks. Before adopting any one line of action, he will weigh all of the pros and cons. The

Taurus person is steadfast. Once his mind is made up it seldom changes. The person born under this sign usually is a good family person—reliable and loving.

The Negative Side of Taurus

Sometimes the Taurus man or woman is a bit too stubborn. He won't listen to other points of view if his mind is set on something. To others, this can be quite annoying. The Taurean also does not like to be told what to do. He becomes rather angry if others think him not too bright. He does not like to be told he is wrong, even when he is. He dislikes being contradicted.

Some people who are born under this sign are very suspicious of others—even of those persons close to them. They find it difficult to trust people fully. They are often afraid of being deceived or taken advantage of. The Taurean often finds it difficult to forget or forgive. His love of material things sometimes makes him rather avaricious and petty.

May 21–June 20

The Positive Side of Gemini

The person born under this sign of the Heavenly Twins is usually quite bright and quick-witted. Some of them are capable of doing many different things. The Gemini person very often has many different interests. He keeps an open mind and is always anxious to learn new things.

The Geminian is often an analytical person. He is a person who enjoys making use of his intellect. He is governed more by his mind than by his emotions. He is a person who is not confined to one view: he can often understand both sides to a problem or question. He knows how to reason; how to make rapid decisions if need be.

He is an adaptable person and can make himself at home almost anywhere. There are all kinds of situations he can adapt to. He is a person who seldom doubts himself; he is sure of his talents and his

ability to think and reason. The Geminian is generally most satisfied when he is in a situation where he can make use of his intellect. Never short of imagination, he often has strong talents for invention. He is rather a modern person when it comes to life; the Geminian almost always moves along with the times—perhaps that is why he remains so youthful throughout most of his life.

Literature and art appeal to the person born under this sign. Creativity in almost any form will interest and intrigue the Gemini man or woman.

The Geminian is often quite charming. A good talker, he often is the center of attraction at any gathering. People find it easy to like a person born under this sign because he can appear easygoing and usually has a good sense of humor.

The Negative Side of Gemini

Sometimes the Gemini person tries to do too many things at one time—and as a result, winds up finishing nothing. Some Geminians are easily distracted and find it rather difficult to concentrate on one thing for too long a time. Sometimes they give in to trifling fancies and find it rather boring to become too serious about any one thing. Some of them are never dependable, no matter what they promise.

Although the Gemini man or woman often appears to be well-versed on many subjects, this is sometimes just a veneer. His knowledge may be only superficial, but because he speaks so well he gives people the impression of erudition. Some Geminians are sharp-tongued and inconsiderate; they think only of themselves and their own pleasure.

June 21–July 20

The Positive Side of Cancer

The Cancerians's most positive point is his understanding nature. On the whole, he is a loving and sympathetic person. He would never go out of his way to hurt anyone. The Cancer man or woman

is often very kind and tender; they give what they can to others. They hate to see others suffering and will do what they can to help someone in less fortunate circumstances than themselves. They are often very concerned about the world. Their interest in people generally goes beyond that of just their own families and close friends; they have a deep sense of brotherhood and respect humanitarian values. The Cancerian means what he says, as a rule; he is honest about his feelings.

The Cancer man or woman is a person who knows the art of patience. When something seems difficult, he is willing to wait until the situation becomes manageable again. He is a person who knows how to bide his time. The Cancerian knows how to concentrate on one thing at a time. When he has made his mind up he generally sticks with what he does, seeing it through to the end.

The Cancerian is a person who loves his home. He enjoys being surrounded by familiar things and the people he loves. Of all the signs, Cancer is the most maternal. Even the men born under this sign often have a motherly or protective quality about them. They like to take care of people in their family—to see that they are well loved and well provided for. They are usually loyal and faithful. Family ties mean a lot to the Cancer man or woman. Parents and in-laws are respected and loved. The Cancerian has a strong sense of tradition. He is very sensitive to the moods of others.

The Negative Side of Cancer

Sometimes the Cancerian finds it rather hard to face life. It becomes too much for him. He can be a little timid and retiring, when things don't go too well. When unfortunate things happen, he is apt to just shrug and say, "Whatever will be will be." He can be fatalistic to a fault. The uncultivated Cancerian is a bit lazy. He doesn't have very much ambition. Anything that seems a bit difficult he'll gladly leave to others. He may be lacking in initiative. Too sensitive, when he feels he's been injured, he'll crawl back into his shell and nurse his imaginary wounds. The Cancer woman often is given to crying when the smallest thing goes wrong.

Some Cancerians find it difficult to enjoy themselves in environments outside their homes. They make heavy demands on others, and need to be constantly reassured that they are loved.

July 21–August 21

The Positive Side of Leo

Often Leos make good leaders. They seem to be good organizers and administrators. Usually they are quite popular with others. Whatever group it is that he belongs to, the Leo man is almost sure to be or become the leader.

The Leo person is generous most of the time. It is his best characteristic. He or she likes to give gifts and presents. In making others happy, the Leo person becomes happy himself. He likes to splurge when spending money on others. In some instances it may seem that the Leo's generosity knows no boundaries. A hospitable person, the Leo man or woman is very fond of welcoming people to his house and entertaining them. He is never short of company.

The Leo person has plenty of energy and drive. He enjoys working toward some specific goal. When he applies himself correctly, he gets what he wants most often. The Leo person is almost never unsure of himself. He has plenty of confidence and aplomb. He is a person who is direct in almost everything he does. He has a quick mind and can make a decision in a very short time.

He usually sets a good example for others because of his ambitious manner and positive ways. He knows how to stick to something once he's started. Although the Leo person may be good at making a joke, he is not superficial or glib. He is a loving person, kind and thoughtful.

There is generally nothing small or petty about the Leo man or woman. He does what he can for those who are deserving. He is a person others can rely upon at all times. He means what he says. An honest person, generally speaking, he is a friend that others value.

The Negative Side of Leo

Leo, however, does have his faults. At times, he can be just a bit too arrogant. He thinks that no one deserves a leadership position except him. Only he is capable of doing things well. His opinion of himself is often much too high. Because of his conceit, he is sometimes rather unpopular with a good many people. Some Leos are too materialistic; they can only think in terms of money and profit.

Some Leos enjoy lording it over others—at home or at their place of business. What is more, they feel they have the right to. Egocentric to an impossible degree, this sort of Leo cares little about how others think or feel. He can be rude and cutting.

August 22–September 22

The Positive Side of Virgo

The person born under the sign of Virgo is generally a busy person. He knows how to arrange and organize things. He is a good planner. Above all, he is practical and is not afraid of hard work.

The person born under this sign, Virgo, knows how to attain what he desires. He sticks with something until it is finished. He never shirks his duties, and can always be depended upon. The Virgo person can be thoroughly trusted at all times.

The man or woman born under this sign tries to do everything to perfection. He doesn't believe in doing anything half-way. He always aims for the top. He is the sort of a person who is constantly striving to better himself—not because he wants more money or glory, but because it gives him a feeling of accomplishment.

The Virgo man or woman is a very observant person. He is sensitive to how others feel, and can see things below the surface of a situation. He usually puts this talent to constructive use.

It is not difficult for the Virgoan to be open and earnest. He believes in putting his cards on the table. He is never secretive or under-handed. He's as good as his word. The Virgo person is generally plain-spoken and down-to-earth. He has no trouble in expressing himself.

The Virgo person likes to keep up to date on new developments in his particular field. Well-informed, generally, he sometimes has a keen interest in the arts or literature. What he knows, he knows well. His ability to use his critical faculties is well-developed and sometimes startles others because of its accuracy.

The Virgoan adheres to a moderate way of life; he avoids excesses. He is a responsible person and enjoys being of service.

The Negative Side of Virgo

Sometimes a Virgo person is too critical. He thinks that only he can do something the way it should be done. Whatever anyone else does is inferior. He can be rather annoying in the way he quibbles over insignificant details. In telling others how things should be done, he can be rather tactless and mean.

Some Virgos seem rather emotionless and cool. They feel emo-

tional involvement is beneath them. They are sometimes too tidy, too neat. With money they can be rather miserly. Some try to force their opinions and ideas on others.

September 23–October 22

The Positive Side of Libra

Librans love harmony. It is one of their most outstanding character traits. They are interested in achieving balance; they admire beauty and grace in things as well as in people. Generally speaking, they are kind and considerate people. Librans are usually very sympathetic. They go out of their way not to hurt another person's feelings. They are outgoing and do what they can to help those in need.

People born under the sign of Libra almost always make good friends. They are loyal and amiable. They enjoy the company of others. Many of them are rather moderate in their views; they believe in keeping an open mind, however, and weighing both sides of an issue fairly before making a decision.

Alert and often intelligent, the Libran, always fair-minded, tries to put himself in the position of the other person. They are against injustice; quite often they take up for the underdog. In most of their social dealings, they try to be tactful and kind. They dislike discord and bickering, and most Libras strive for peace and harmony in all their relationships.

The Libra man or woman has a keen sense of beauty. They appreciate handsome furnishings and clothes. Many of them are artistically inclined. Their taste is usually impeccable. They know how to use color. Their homes are almost always attractively arranged and inviting. They enjoy entertaining people and see to it that their guests always feel at home and welcome.

The Libran gets along with almost everyone. He is well-liked and socially much in demand.

The Negative Side of Libra

Some people born under this sign tend to be rather insincere. So eager are they to achieve harmony in all relationships that they will even go so far as to lie. Many of them are escapists. They find facing

the truth an ordeal and prefer living in a world of make-believe.

In a serious argument, some Librans give in rather easily even when they know they are right. Arguing, even about something they believe in, is too unsettling for some of them.

Librans sometimes care too much for material things. They enjoy possessions and luxuries. Some are vain and tend to be jealous.

October 23–November 22

The Positive Side of Scorpio

The Scorpio man or woman generally knows what he or she wants out of life. He is a determined person. He sees something through to the end. The Scorpion is quite sincere, and seldom says anything he doesn't mean. When he sets a goal for himself he tries to go about achieving it in a very direct way.

The Scorpion is brave and courageous. They are not afraid of hard work. Obstacles do not frighten them. They forge ahead until they achieve what they set out for. The Scorpio man or woman has a strong will.

Although the Scorpion may seem rather fixed and determined, inside he is often quite tender and loving. He can care very much for others. He believes in sincerity in all relationships. His feelings about someone tend to last; they are profound and not superficial.

The Scorpio person is someone who adheres to his principles no matter what happens. He will not be deterred from a path he believes to be right.

Because of his many positive strengths, the Scorpion can often achieve happiness for himself and for those that he loves.

He is a constructive person by nature. He often has a deep understanding of people and of life, in general. He is perceptive and unafraid. Obstacles often seem to spur him on. He is a positive person who enjoys winning. He has many strengths and resources; challenge of any sort often brings out the best in him.

The Negative Side of Scorpio

The Scorpio person is sometimes hypersensitive. Often he imagines injury when there is none. He feels that others do not bother to

recognize him for his true worth. Sometimes he is given to excessive boasting in order to compensate for what he feels is neglect

The Scorpio person can be rather proud and arrogant. They can be rather sly when they put their minds to it and they enjoy outwitting persons or institutions noted for their cleverness.

Their tactics for getting what they want are sometimes devious and ruthless. They don't care too much about what others may think. If they feel others have done them an injustice, they will do their best to seek revenge. The Scorpion often has a sudden, violent temper; and this person's interest in sex is sometimes quite unbalanced or excessive.

November 23–December 20

The Positive Side of Sagittarius

People born under this sign are often honest and forthright. Their approach to life is earnest and open. The Sagittarian is often quite adult in his way of seeing things. They are broadminded and tolerant people. When dealing with others the person born under the sign of Sagittarius is almost always open and forthright. He doesn't believe in deceit or pretension. His standards are high. People who associate with the Sagittarian, generally admire and respect him.

The Sagittarian trusts others easily and expects them to trust him. He is never suspicious or envious and almost always thinks well of others. People always enjoy his company because he is so friendly and easy-going. The Sagittarius man or woman is often good-humored. He can always be depended upon by his friends, family, and co-workers.

The person born under this sign of the Zodiac likes a good joke every now and then; he is keen on fun and this makes him very popular with others.

A lively person, he enjoys sports and outdoor life. The Sagittarian is fond of animals. Intelligent and interesting, he can begin an animated conversation with ease. He likes exchanging ideas and discussing various views.

He is not selfish or proud. If someone proposes an idea or plan that is better than his, he will immediately adopt it. Imaginative yet practical, he knows how to put ideas into practice.

He enjoys sport and game, and it doesn't matter if he wins or loses. He is a forgiving person, and never sulks over something that has not worked out in his favor.

He is seldom critical, and is almost always generous.

The Negative Side of Sagittarius

Some Sagittarians are restless. They take foolish risks and seldom learn from the mistakes they make. They don't have heads for money and are often mismanaging their finances. Some of them devote much of their time to gambling.

Some are too outspoken and tactless, always putting their feet in their mouths. They hurt others carelessly by being honest at the wrong time. Sometimes they make promises which they don't keep. They don't stick close enough to their plans and go from one failure to another. They are undisciplined and waste a lot of energy.

December 21–January 19

The Positive Side of Capricorn

The person born under the sign of Capricorn is usually very stable and patient. He sticks to whatever tasks he has and sees them through. He can always be relied upon and he is not averse to work.

An honest person, the Capricornian is generally serious about whatever he does. He does not take his duties lightly. He is a practical person and believes in keeping his feet on the ground.

Quite often the person born under this sign is ambitious and knows how to get what he wants out of life. He forges ahead and never gives up his goal. When he is determined about something, he almost always wins. He is a good worker—a hard worker. Although things may not come easy to him, he will not complain, but continue working until his chores are finished.

He is usually good at business matters and knows the value of money. He is not a spendthrift and knows how to put something away for a rainy day; he dislikes waste and unnecessary loss.

The Capricornian knows how to make use of his self-control. He

can apply himself to almost anything once he puts his mind to it. His ability to concentrate sometimes astounds others. He is diligent and does well when involved in detail work.

The Capricorn man or woman is charitable, generally speaking, and will do what is possible to help others less fortunate. As a friend, he is loyal and trustworthy. He never shirks his duties or responsibilities. He is self-reliant and never expects too much of the other fellow. He does what he can on his own. If someone does him a good turn, then he will do his best to return the favor.

The Negative Side of Capricorn

Like everyone, the Capricornian, too, has his faults. At times, he can be over-critical of others. He expects others to live up to his own high standards. He thinks highly of himself and tends to look down on others.

His interest in material things may be exaggerated. The Capricorn man or woman thinks too much about getting on in the world and having something to show for it. He may even be a little greedy.

He sometimes thinks he knows what's best for everyone. He is too bossy. He is always trying to organize and correct others. He may be a little narrow in his thinking.

January 20–February 18

The Positive Side of Aquarius

The Aquarius man or woman is usually very honest and forthright. These are his two greatest qualities. His standards for himself are generally very high. He can always be relied upon by others. His word is his bond.

The Aquarian is perhaps the most tolerant of all the Zodiac personalities. He respects other people's beliefs and feels that everyone is entitled to his own approach to life.

He would never do anything to injure another's feelings. He is never unkind or cruel. Always considerate of others, the Aquarian is always willing to help a person in need. He feels a very strong tie between himself and all the other members of mankind.

The person born under this sign is almost always an individualist. He does not believe in teaming up with the masses, but prefers going his own way. His ideas about life and mankind are often quite advanced. There is a saying to the effect that the average Aquarian is fifty years ahead of his time.

He is broadminded. The problems of the world concern him greatly. He is interested in helping others no matter what part of the globe they live in. He is truly a humanitarian sort. He likes to be of service to others.

Giving, considerate, and without prejudice, Aquarians have no trouble getting along with others.

The Negative Side of Aquarius

The Aquarian may be too much of a dreamer. He makes plans but seldom carries them out. He is rather unrealistic. His imagination has a tendency to run away with him. Because many of his plans are impractical, he is always in some sort of a dither.

Others may not approve of him at all times because of his unconventional behavior. He may be a bit eccentric. Sometimes he is so busy with his own thoughts, that he loses touch with the realities of existence.

Some Aquarians feel they are more clever and intelligent than others. They seldom admit to their own faults, even when they are quite apparent. Some become rather fanatic in their views. Their criticism of others is sometimes destructive and negative.

February 19–March 20

The Positive Side of Pisces

The Piscean can often understand the problems of others quite easily. He has a sympathetic nature. Kindly, he is often dedicated in the way he goes about helping others. The sick and the troubled often turn to him for advice and assistance.

He is very broadminded and does not criticize others for their faults. He knows how to accept people for what they are. On the whole, he is a trustworthy and earnest person. He is loyal to his

friends and will do what he can to help them in time of need. Generous and good-natured, he is a lover of peace; he is often willing to help others solve their differences. People who have taken a wrong turn in life often interest him and he will do what he can to persuade them to rehabilitate themselves.

He has a strong intuitive sense and most of the time he knows how to make it work for him; the Piscean is unusually perceptive and often knows what is bothering someone before that person, himself, is aware of it. The Pisces man or woman is an idealistic person, basically, and is interested in making the world a better place in which to live. The Piscean believes that everyone should help each other. He is willing to do more than his share in order to achieve cooperation with others.

The person born under this sign often is talented in music or art. He is a receptive person; he is able to take the ups and downs of life with philosophic calm.

The Negative Side of Pisces

Some Pisceans are often depressed; their outlook on life is rather glum. They may feel that they have been given a bad deal in life and that others are always taking unfair advantage of them. The Piscean sometimes feel that the world is a cold and cruel place. He is easily discouraged. He may even withdraw from the harshness of reality into a secret shell of his own where he dreams and idles away a good deal of his time.

The Piscean can be rather lazy. He lets things happen without giving the least bit of resistance. He drifts along, whether on the high road or on the low. He is rather short on willpower.

Some Pisces people seek escape through drugs or alcohol. When temptation comes along they find it hard to resist. In matters of sex, they can be rather permissive.

THE SIGNS AND
THEIR KEY WORDS

		POSITIVE	NEGATIVE
ARIES	self	courage, initiative, pioneer instinct	brash rudeness, selfish impetuosity
TAURUS	money	endurance, loyalty, wealth	obstinacy, gluttony
GEMINI	mind	versatility	capriciousness, unreliability
CANCER	family	sympathy, homing instinct	clannishness, childishness
LEO	children	love, authority, integrity	egotism, force
VIRGO	work	purity, industry, analysis	fault-finding, cynicism
LIBRA	marriage	harmony, justice	vacillation, superficiality
SCORPIO	sex	survival, regeneration	vengeance, discord
SAGITTARIUS	travel	optimism, higher learning	lawlessness
CAPRICORN	career	depth	narrowness, gloom
AQUARIUS	friends	human fellowship, genius	perverse unpredictability
PISCES	confine-ment	spiritual love, universality	diffusion, escapism

THE ELEMENTS AND QUALITIES OF THE SIGNS

ELEMENT	SIGN	QUALITY	SIGN
FIRE....................	ARIES LEO SAGITTARIUS	CARDINAL.........	ARIES LIBRA CANCER CAPRICORN
EARTH................	TAURUS VIRGO CAPRICORN	FIXED.................	TAURUS LEO SCORPIO AQUARIUS
AIR.....................	GEMINI LIBRA AQUARIUS		
WATER..............	CANCER SCORPIO PISCES	MUTABLE.........	GEMINI VIRGO SAGITTARIUS PISCES

Every sign has both an element and a quality associated with it. The element indicates the basic makeup of the sign, and the quality describes the kind of activity associated with each.

Signs can be grouped together according to their *element* and *quality*. Signs of the same element share many basic traits in common. They tend to form stable configurations and ultimately harmonious relationships. Signs of the same quality are often less harmonious, but they share many dynamic potentials for growth as well as profound fulfillment.

THE FIRE SIGNS

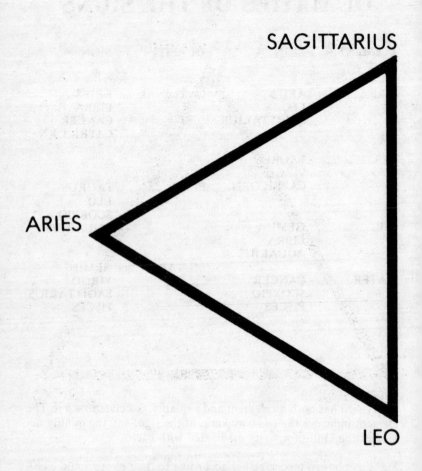

SAGITTARIUS

ARIES

LEO

This is the fire group. On the whole these are emotional, volatile types, quick to anger, quick to forgive. They are adventurous, powerful people and act as a source of inspiration for everyone. They spark into action with immediate exuberant impulses. They are intelligent, self-involved, creative and idealistic. They all share a certain vibrancy and glow that outwardly reflects an inner flame and passion for living.

THE EARTH SIGNS

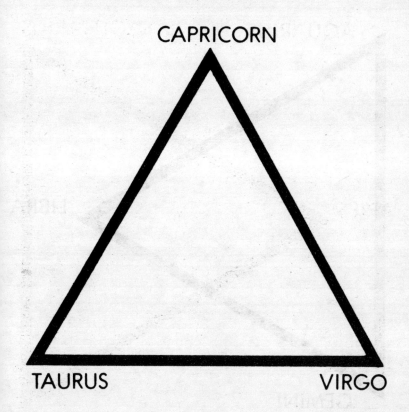

This is the earth group. They are in constant touch with the material world and tend to be conservative. Although they are all capable
of spartan self-discipline, they are earthy, sensual people who are
stimulated by the tangible, elegant and luxurious. The thread of
their lives is always practical, but they do fantasize and are often
attracted to dark, mysterious, emotional people. They are like great
cliffs overhanging the sea, forever married to the ocean but always
resisting erosion from the dark, emotional forces that thunder at
their feet.

THE AIR SIGNS

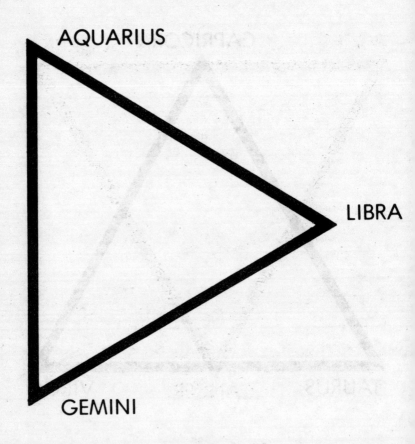

This is the air group. They are light, mental creatures desirous of contact, communication and relationship. They are involved with people and the forming of ties on many levels. Original thinkers, they are the bearers of human news. Their language is their sense of word, color, style and beauty. They provide an atmosphere suitable and pleasant for living. They add change and versatility to the scene, and it is through them that we can explore new territory of human intelligence and experience.

THE WATER SIGNS

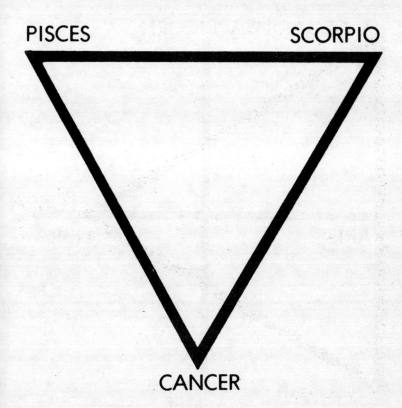

PISCES   SCORPIO

CANCER

This is the water group. Through the water people, we are all joined together on emotional, non-verbal levels. They are silent, mysterious types whose magic hypnotizes even the most determined realist. They have uncanny perceptions about people and are as rich as the oceans when it comes to feeling, emotion or imagination. They are sensitive, mystical creatures with memories that go back beyond time. Through water, life is sustained. These people have the potential for the depths of darkness or the heights of mysticism and art.

THE CARDINAL SIGNS

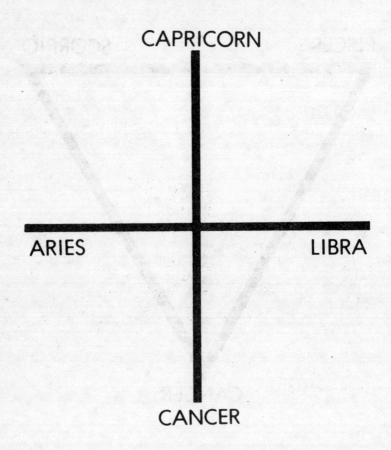

Put together, this is a clear-cut picture of dynamism, activity, tremendous stress and remarkable achievement. These people know the meaning of great change since their lives are often characterized by significant crises and major successes. This combination is like a simultaneous storm of summer, fall, winter and spring. The danger is chaotic diffusion of energy; the potential is irrepressible growth and victory.

THE FIXED SIGNS

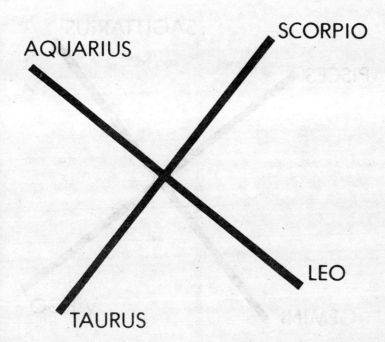

Fixed signs are always establishing themselves in a given place or area of experience. Like explorers who arrive and plant a flag, these people claim a position from which they do not enjoy being deposed. They are staunch, stalwart, upright, trusty, honorable people, although their obstinacy is well-known. Their contribution is fixity, and they are the angels who support our visible world.

THE MUTABLE SIGNS

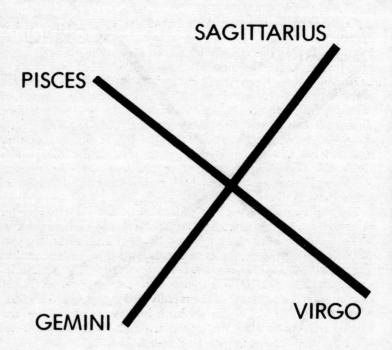

SAGITTARIUS

PISCES

GEMINI

VIRGO

Mutable people are versatile, sensitive, intelligent, nervous and deeply curious about life. They are the translators of all energy. They often carry out or complete tasks initiated by others. Combinations of these signs have highly developed minds; they are imaginative and jumpy and think and talk a lot. At worst their lives are a Tower of Babel. At best they are adaptable and ready creatures who can assimilate one kind of experience and enjoy it while anticipating coming changes.

HOW TO APPROXIMATE YOUR RISING SIGN

Apart from the month and day of birth, the exact *time* of birth is another vital factor in the determination of an accurate horoscope. Not only do the planets move with great speed, but one must know how far the Earth has turned during the day. That way you can determine exactly where the planets are located with respect to the precise birthplace of an individual. This makes *your* horoscope *your* horoscope. In addition to these factors, another grid is laid upon that of the Zodiac and the planets: the houses. After all three have been considered, specific planetary relationships can be measured and analyzed in accordance with certain ordered procedures. It is the skillful translation of all this complex astrological language that a serious astrologer strives for in his attempt at coherent astrological synthesis. Keep this in mind.

The horoscope sets up a kind of framework around which the life of an individual grows like wild ivy, this way and that, weaving its way around the trellis of the natal positions of the planets. The year of birth tells us the positions of the distant, slow-moving planets like Jupiter, Saturn, Uranus and Pluto. The month of birth indicates the Sun sign, or birth sign as it is commonly called, as well as indicating the positions of the rapidly moving planets like Venus, Mercury and Mars. The day of birth locates the position of our Moon, and the moment of birth determines the houses through what is called the Ascendant, or Rising Sign.

As the Earth rotates on its axis once every 24 hours, each one of the twelve signs of the Zodiac appears to be "rising" on the horizon, with a new one appearing about every two hours. Actually it is the turning of the Earth that exposes each sign to view, but you will remember that in much of our astrological work we are discussing "apparent" motion. This *Rising Sign* marks the Ascendant and it colors the whole orientation of a horoscope. It indicates the sign governing the first house of the chart, and will thus determine which signs will govern all the other houses. The idea is a bit complicated at first, and we needn't dwell on complications in this introduction, but if you can imagine two color wheels with twelve divisions superimposed upon each other, one moving slowly and the other remaining still, you will have some idea of how the signs keep shifting the "color" of the houses as the Rising Sign continues to change every two hours.

The important point is that the birth chart, or horoscope, actually does define specific factors of a person's makeup. It contains a picture of being, much the way the nucleus of a tiny cell contains the potential for an entire elephant, or a packet of seeds contains a rosebush. If there were no order or continuity to the world, we could plant roses and get elephants. This same order that gives continuous flow to our lives often annoys people if it threatens to determine too much of their lives. We must grow from what we were planted, and there's no reason why we can't do that magnificently. It's all there in the horoscope. Where there is limitation, there is breakthrough; where there is crisis, there is transformation. Accurate analysis of a horoscope can help you find these points of breakthrough and transformation, and it requires knowledge of subtleties and distinctions that demand skillful judgment in order to solve even the simplest kind of personal question.

It is still quite possible, however, to draw some conclusions based upon the sign occupied by the Sun alone. In fact, if you're just being introduced to this vast subject, you're better off keeping it simple. Otherwise it seems like an impossible jumble, much like trying to read a novel in a foreign language without knowing the basic vocabulary. As with anything else, you can progress in your appreciation and understanding of astrology in direct proportion to your interest. To become really good at it requires study, experience, patience and above all—and maybe simplest of all—a fundamental understanding of what is actually going on right up there in the sky over your head. It is a vital living process you can observe, contemplate and ultimately understand. You can start by observing sunrise, or sunset, or even the full Moon.

In fact you can do a simple experiment after reading this introduction. You can erect a rough chart by following the simple procedure below:

1. Draw a circle with twelve equal segments.

2. Starting at what would be the nine o'clock position on a clock, number the segments, or houses, from 1 to 12 in a *counterclockwise direction*.

3. Label house number 1 in the following way: 4 A.M.-6 A.M.

4. In a counterclockwise direction, label the rest of the houses: 2 A.M.-4 A.M., MIDNIGHT-2 A.M., 10 P.M-MIDNIGHT, 8 P.M.-10 P.M., 6 P.M.-8 P.M., 4 P.M.-6 P.M., 2 P.M.-4 P.M., NOON-2 P.M., 10 A.M.-NOON, 8 A.M.-10 A.M., and 6 A.M.-8 A.M.

5. Now find out what time you were born and place the sun in the appropriate house.

6. Label the edge of that house with your Sun sign. You now have a description of your basic character and your fundamental drives. You can also see in what areas of life on Earth you will be most likely to focus your constant energy and center your activity.

7. If you are really feeling ambitious, label the rest of the houses with the signs, starting with your Sun sign, in order, still in a *counterclockwise direction.* When you get to Pisces, start over with Aries and keep going until you reach the house behind the Sun.

8. Look to house number 1. The sign that you have now labeled and attached to house number 1 is your Rising sign. It will color your self-image, outlook, physical constitution, early life and whole orientation to life. Of course this is a mere approximation, since there are many complicated calculations that must be made with respect to adjustments for birth time, but if you read descriptions of the sign preceding and the sign following the one you have calculated in the above manner, you may be able to identify yourself better. In any case, when you get through labeling all the houses, your drawing should look something like this:

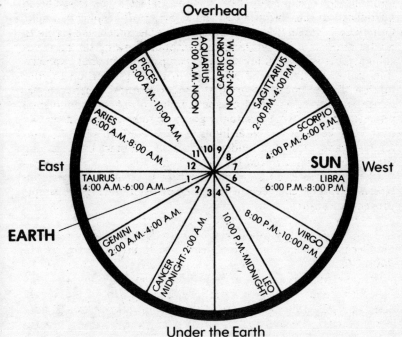

Basic chart illustrating the position of the Sun in Scorpio, with the Ascendant Taurus as the Rising Sign.

This individual was born at 5:15 P.M. on October 31 in New York City. The Sun is in Scorpio and is found in the 7th house. The Rising sign, or the sign governing house number 1, is Taurus, so this person is a blend of Scorpio and Taurus.

Any further calculation would necessitate that you look in an ephemeris, or table of planetary motion, for the positions of the rest of the planets for your particular birth year. But we will take the time to define briefly all the known planets of our Solar System and the Sun to acquaint you with some more of the astrological vocabulary that you will be meeting again and again. (See page 21 for a full explanation of the Moon in all the Signs.)

THE PLANETS AND SIGNS THEY RULE

The signs of the Zodiac are linked to the planets in the following way. Each sign is governed or ruled by one or more planets. No matter where the planets are located in the sky at any given moment, they still rule their respective signs, and when they travel through the signs they rule, they have special dignity and their effects are stronger.

Following is a list of the planets and the signs they rule. After looking at the list, go back over the definitions of the planets and see if you can determine how the planet ruling *your* Sun sign has affected your life.

SIGNS	RULING PLANETS
Aries	Mars, Pluto
Taurus	Venus
Gemini	Mercury
Cancer	Moon
Leo	Sun
Virgo	Mercury
Libra	Venus
Scorpio	Mars, Pluto
Sagittarius	Jupiter
Capricorn	Saturn
Aquarius	Saturn, Uranus
Pisces	Jupiter, Neptune

THE PLANETS
OF THE
SOLAR SYSTEM

Here are the planets of the Solar System. They all travel around the Sun at different speeds and different distances. Taken with the Sun, they all distribute individual intelligence and ability throughout the entire chart.

The planets modify the influence of the Sun in a chart according to their own particular natures, strengths and positions. Their positions must be calculated for each year and day, and their function and expression in a horoscope will change as they move from one area of the Zodiac to another.

Following, you will find brief statements of their pure meanings.

THE SUN

SUN

This is the center of existence. Around this flaming sphere all the planets revolve in endless orbits. Our star is constantly sending out its beams of light and energy without which no life on Earth would be possible. In astrology it symbolizes everything we are trying to become, the center around which all of our activity in life will always revolve. It is the symbol of our basic nature and describes the natural and constant thread that runs through everything that we do from birth to death on this planet.

To early astrologers, the sun seemed to be another planet because it crossed the heavens every day, just like the rest of the bodies in the sky.

It is the only star near enough to be seen well—it is, in fact, a dwarf star. Approximately 860,000 miles in diameter, it is about ten times as wide as the giant planet Jupiter. The next nearest star is nearly 300,000 times as far away, and if the Sun were located as far away as most of the bright stars, it would be too faint to be seen without a telescope.

Everything in the horoscope ultimately revolves around this singular body. Although other forces may be prominent in the charts of some individuals, still the Sun is the total nucleus of being and symbolizes the complete potential of every human being alive. It is vitality and the life force. Your whole essence comes from the position of the Sun.

You are always trying to express the Sun according to its position by house and sign. Possibility for all development is found in the Sun, and it marks the fundamental character of your personal radiations all around you.

It is the symbol of strength, vigor, wisdom, dignity, ardor and generosity, and the ability for a person to function as a mature individual. It is also a creative force in society. It is consciousness of the gift of life.

The underdeveloped solar nature is arrogant, pushy, undependable and proud, and is constantly using force.

MERCURY

Mercury is the planet closest to the Sun. It races around our star, gathering information and translating it to the rest of the system. Mercury represents your capacity to understand the desires of your own will and to translate those desires into action.

In other words it is the planet of Mind and the power of communication. Through Mercury we develop an ability to think, write, speak and observe—to become aware of the world around us. It colors our attitudes and vision of the world, as well as our capacity to communicate our inner responses to the outside world. Some people who have serious disabilities in their power of verbal communication have often wrongly been described as people lacking intelligence.

Although this planet (and its position in the horoscope) indicates your power to communicate your thoughts and perceptions to the world, intelligence is something deeper. Intelligence is distributed throughout all the planets. It is the relationship of the planets to each other that truly describes what we call intelligence. Mercury rules speaking, language, mathematics, draft and design, students, messengers, young people, offices, teachers and any pursuits where the mind of man has wings.

VENUS

Venus is beauty. It symbolizes the harmony and radiance of a rare and elusive quality: beauty itself. It is refinement and delicacy, softness and charm. In astrology it indicates grace, balance and the aesthetic sense. Where Venus is we see beauty, a gentle drawing in of energy and the need for satisfaction and completion. It is a special touch that finishes off rough edges. It is sensitivity, and affection, and it is always the place for that other elusive phenomenon: love. Venus describes our sense of what is beautiful and loving. Poorly developed, it is vulgar, tasteless and self-indulgent. But its ideal is the flame of spiritual love—Aphrodite, goddess of love, and the sweetness and power of personal beauty.

MARS

This is raw, crude energy. The planet next to Earth but outward from the Sun is a fiery red sphere that charges through the horoscope with force and fury. It represents the way you reach out for new adventure and new experience. It is energy and drive, initiative, courage and daring. The power to start something and see it through. It can be thoughtless, cruel and wild, angry and hostile, causing cuts, burns, scalds and wounds. It can stab its way through a chart, or it can be the symbol of healthy spirited adventure, well-channeled constructive power to begin and keep up the drive. If you have trouble starting things, if you lack the get-up-and-go to start the ball rolling, if you lack aggressiveness and self-confidence, chances are there's another planet influencing your Mars. Mars rules soldiers, butchers, surgeons, salesmen—any field that requires daring, bold skill, operational technique or self-promotion.

JUPITER

This is the largest planet of the Solar System. Scientists have recently learned that Jupiter reflects more light than it receives from the Sun. In a sense it is like a star itself. In astrology it rules good luck and good cheer, health, wealth, optimism, happiness, success and joy. It is the symbol of opportunity and always opens the way for new possibilities in your life. It rules exuberance, enthusiasm, wisdom, knowledge, generosity and all forms of expansion in general. It rules actors, statesmen, clerics, professional people, religion, publishing and the distribution of many people over large areas.

Sometimes Jupiter makes you think you deserve everything, and you become sloppy, wasteful, careless and rude, prodigal and lawless, in the illusion that nothing can ever go wrong. Then there is the danger of over-confidence, exaggeration, undependability and over-indulgence.

Jupiter is the minimization of limitation and the emphasis on spirituality and potential. It is the thirst for knowledge and higher learning.

SATURN

Saturn circles our system in dark splendor with its mysterious rings, forcing us to be awakened to whatever we have neglected in the past. It will present real puzzles and problems to be solved, causing delays, obstacles and hindrances. By doing so, Saturn stirs our own sensitivity to those areas where we are laziest.

Here we must patiently develop *method,* and only through painstaking effort can our ends be achieved. It brings order to a horoscope and imposes reason just where we are feeling least reasonable. By creating limitations and boundary, Saturn shows the consequences of being human and demands that we accept the changing cycles inevitable in human life. Saturn rules time, old age and sobriety. It can bring depression, gloom, jealousy and greed, or serious acceptance of responsibilities out of which success will develop. With Saturn there is nothing to do but face facts. It rules laborers, stones, granite, rocks and crystals of all kinds.

The Outer Planets

The following three are the outer planets. They liberate human beings from cultural conditioning, and in that sense are the law breakers. In early times it was thought that Saturn was the last planet of the system—the outer limit beyond which we could never go. The discovery of the next three planets ushered in new phases of human history, revolution and technology.

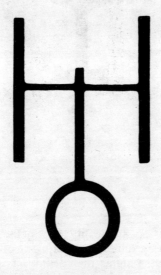

URANUS

Uranus rules unexpected change, upheaval, revolution. It is the symbol of total independence and asserts the freedom of an individual from all restriction and restraint. It is a breakthrough planet and indicates talent, originality and genius in a horoscope. It usually causes last-minute reversals and changes of plan, unwanted separations, accidents, catastrophes and eccentric behavior. It can add irrational rebelliousness and perverse bohemianism to a personality or a streak of unaffected brilliance in science and art. It rules technology, aviation and all forms of electrical and electronic advancement. It governs great leaps forward and topsy-turvy situations, and *always* turns things around at the last minute. Its effects are difficult to ever really predict, since it rules sudden last-minute decisions and events that come like lightning out of the blue.

NEPTUNE

Neptune dissolves existing reality the way the sea erodes the cliffs beside it. Its effects are subtle like the ringing of a buoy's bell in the fog. It suggests a reality higher than definition can usually describe. It awakens a sense of higher responsibility often causing guilt, worry, anxieties or delusions. Neptune is associated with all forms of escape and can make things seem a certain way so convincingly that you are absolutely sure of something that eventually turns out to be quite different.

It is the planet of illusion and therefore governs the invisible realms that lie beyond our ordinary minds, beyond our simple factual ability to prove what is "real." Treachery, deceit, disillusionment and disappointment are linked to Neptune. It describes a vague reality that promises eternity and the divine, yet in a manner so complex that we cannot really fathom it at all. At its worst Neptune is a cheap intoxicant; at its best it is the poetry, music and inspiration of the higher planes of spiritual love. It has dominion over movies, photographs and much of the arts.

PLUTO

Pluto lies at the outpost of our system and therefore rules finality in a horoscope—the final closing of chapters in your life, the passing of major milestones and points of development from which there is no return. It is a final wipeout, a closeout, an evacuation. It is a distant, subtle but powerful catalyst in all transformations that occur. It creates, destroys, then recreates. Sometimes Pluto starts its influence with a minor event or insignificant incident that might even go unnoticed. Slowly but surely, little by little, everything changes, until at last there has been a total transformation in the area of your life where Pluto has been operating. It rules mass thinking and the trends that society first rejects, then adopts and finally outgrows.

Pluto rules the dead and the underworld—all the powerful forces of creation and destruction that go on all the time beneath, around and above us. It can bring a lust for power with strong obsessions.

It is the planet that rules the metamorphoses of the caterpillar into a butterfly, for it symbolizes the capacity to change totally and forever a person's life style, way of thought and behavior.

FAMOUS PERSONALITIES

ARIES: Hans Christian Andersen, Pearl Bailey, Marlon Brando, Wernher Von Braun, Charlie Chaplin, Joan Crawford, Da Vinci, Bette Davis, Doris Day, W. C. Fields, Alec Guinness, Adolf Hitler, William Holden, Thomas Jefferson, Nikita Khrushchev, Elton John, Arturo Toscanini, J. P. Morgan, Paul Robeson, Gloria Steinem, Lowell Thomas, Vincent van Gogh, Tennessee Williams

TAURUS: Fred Astaire, Charlote Brontë, Carol Burnett, Irving Berlin, Bing Crosby, Salvador Dali, Tchaikovsky, Queen Elizabeth II, Duke Ellington, Ella Fitzgerald, Henry Fonda, Sigmund Freud, Orson Welles, Joe Louis, Lenin, Karl Marx, Golda Meir, Eva Peron, Bertrand Russell, Shakespeare, Kate Smith, Benjamin Spock, Barbra Streisand, Shirley Temple, Harry Truman

GEMINI: Mikhail Baryshnikov, Boy George, Igor Stravinsky, Carlos Chavez, Walt Whitman, Bob Dylan, Ralph Waldo Emerson, Judy Garland, Paul Gauguin, Allen Ginsberg, Benny Goodman, Bob Hope, Burl Ives, John F. Kennedy, Peggy Lee, Marilyn Monroe, Joe Namath, Cole Porter, Laurence Olivier, Harriet Beecher Stowe, Queen Victoria, John Wayne, Frank Lloyd Wright

CANCER: "Dear Abby," David Brinkley, Yul Brynner, Pearl Buck, Marc Chagall, Jack Dempsey, Mildred (Babe) Zaharias, Mary Baker Eddy, Henry VIII, John Glenn, Ernest Hemingway, Lena Horne, Oscar Hammerstein, Helen Keller, Ann Landers, George Orwell, Nancy Reagan, Rembrandt, Richard Rodgers, Ginger Rogers, Rubens, Jean-Paul Sartre, O. J. Simpson

LEO: Neil Armstrong, Russell Baker, James Baldwin, Emily Brontë, Wilt Chamberlain, Julia Child, Cecil B. De Mille, Ogden Nash, Amelia Earhart, Edna Ferber, Arthur Goldberg, Dag Hammarskjöld, Alfred Hitchcock, Mick Jagger, George Meany, George Bernard Shaw, Napoleon, Jacqueline Onassis, Henry Ford, Francis Scott Key, Andy Warhol, Mae West, Orville Wright

VIRGO: Ingrid Bergman, Warren Burger, Maurice Chevalier, Agatha Christie, Sean Connery, Lafayette, Peter Falk, Greta Garbo, Althea Gibson, Arthur Godfrey, Goethe, Buddy Hackett, Michael Jackson, Lyndon Johnson, D. H. Lawrence, Sophia Loren, Grandma Moses, Arnold Palmer, Queen Elizabeth I, Walter Reuther, Peter Sellers, Lily Tomlin, George Wallace

LIBRA: Brigitte Bardot, Art Buchwald, Truman Capote, Dwight D. Eisenhower, William Faulkner, F. Scott Fitzgerald, Gandhi, George Gershwin, Micky Mantle, Helen Hayes, Vladimir Horowitz, Doris Lessing, Martina Navratalova, Eugene O'Neill, Luciano Pavarotti, Emily Post, Eleanor Roosevelt, Bruce Springsteen, Margaret Thatcher, Gore Vidal, Barbara Walters, Oscar Wilde

SCORPIO: Vivien Leigh, Richard Burton, Art Carney, Johnny Carson, Billy Graham, Grace Kelly, Walter Cronkite, Marie Curie, Charles de Gaulle, Linda Evans, Indira Gandhi, Theodore Roosevelt, Rock Hudson, Katherine Hepburn, Robert F. Kennedy, Billie Jean King, Martin Luther, Georgia O'Keeffe, Pablo Picasso, Jonas Salk, Alan Shepard, Robert Louis Stevenson

SAGITTARIUS: Jane Austen, Louisa May Alcott, Woody Allen, Beethoven, Willy Brandt, Mary Martin, William F. Buckley, Maria Callas, Winston Churchill, Noel Coward, Emily Dickinson, Walt Disney, Benjamin Disraeli, James Doolittle, Kirk Douglas, Chet Huntley, Jane Fonda, Chris Evert Lloyd, Margaret Mead, Charles Schulz, John Milton, Frank Sinatra, Steven Spielberg

CAPRICORN: Muhammad Ali, Isaac Asimov, Pablo Casals, Dizzy Dean, Marlene Dietrich, James Farmer, Ava Gardner, Barry Goldwater, Cary Grant, J. Edgar Hoover, Howard Hughes, Joan of Arc, Gypsy Rose Lee, Martin Luther King, Jr., Rudyard Kipling, Mao Tse-tung, Richard Nixon, Gamal Nasser, Louis Pasteur, Albert Schweitzer, Stalin, Benjamin Franklin, Elvis Presley

AQUARIUS: Marian Anderson, Susan B. Anthony, Jack Benny, Charles Darwin, Charles Dickens, Thomas Edison, John Barrymore, Clark Gable, Jascha Heifetz, Abraham Lincoln, John McEnroe, Yehudi Menuhin, Mozart, Jack Nicklaus, Ronald Reagan, Jackie Robinson, Norman Rockwell, Franklin D. Roosevelt, Gertrude Stein, Charles Lindbergh, Margaret Truman

PISCES: Edward Albee, Harry Belafonte, Alexander Graham Bell, Frank Borman, Chopin, Adelle Davis, Albert Einstein, Jackie Gleason, Winslow Homer, Edward M. Kennedy, Victor Hugo, Mike Mansfield, Michelangelo, Edna St. Vincent Millay, Liza Minelli, John Steinbeck, Linus Pauling, Ravel, Diana Ross, William Shirer, Elizabeth Taylor, George Washington

LEO

CHARACTER ANALYSIS

The person born under the sign of Leo usually knows how to handle a position of authority well. Others have a deep respect for the decisions he makes. The Leo man or woman generally has something aristocratic about him that commands respect. The person born under this fifth sign of the Zodiac generally knows how to stand on his own two feet. He is independent in many things that he does. He knows how to direct his energies so that he will be able to achieve his ends. He seldom wastes time; he is to the point. In love matters, the Leo is quite passionate. He doesn't stint when it comes to romance and is capable of deep emotions. The Leo is a stable person; he has the ability to see things through to the end without wavering on his standpoint.

Leo people are quite generous in all that they do. They give themselves fully to every situation. To others they often appear quite lordly; they are often at the helm of organizations, running things.

The Leo person does not believe in being petty or small. Quite often he goes out of his way to make others happy. He would never stoop to doing anything which he felt was beneath his dignity. He has a deep feeling of self-respect. He would never treat others badly. He is kind-hearted, sometimes to a fault. Although he does his best not to hurt others, he is apt to have his moments of irritation when he feels that it is better to speak outright than to give a false impression of his attitudes.

Leo people generally learn to shoulder certain responsibilities at an early age. They have an understanding of life that others sometimes never attain. They do not shy away from conflict or troubles. They believe in dealing with opposition directly. They are quite active in their approach to problems. Life, to them, should be attacked with zest and vigor. There is nothing lazy or retiring about a person born under this sign. He is outgoing, often fond of strenuous sports; keenly interested in having a good time. Everything about his attitudes is likely to be king-sized.

When the Leo man or woman knows what he wants in life, he goes out after it. He is not a person who gives up easily. He perseveres until he wins. He is not interested in occupying a position where he has to be told what to do. He is too independent for that sort of thing. He wants to be the person who runs things and he seems almost naturally suited for an authoritative position. His bearing is that of someone who expects others to listen to him when he speaks. He is a forceful person; he knows how to command respect. He is seldom unsure of himself, but when he is, he sees to it that others do not notice. He is quite clever at organizing things. He is a person who likes order. He knows how to channel his creative talents in such a way that the results of whatever he does are always constructive and original. Leadership positions bring out the best in a person born under this sign.

The Leo person is generally quite tolerant and open-minded. He believes in live-and-let-live so long as the other person does not infringe on what he believes to be his natural rights. In most things, he is fair. He believes in being frank and open. On the whole, the Leo person is active and high-strung. If something irritates him or runs against his grain, he will let it be known. He can be short-tempered if the occasion calls for it.

He is a person who believes in sticking to his principles. He is not interested in making compromises—especially if he feels that his standpoint is the correct one. He can become angry if opposed. But, all in all, his bad temper does not last for a long time. He is the kind of person who does not hold grudges.

The Leo person often has a flair for acting. Some of the best actors in the world have been people born under this sign. Their dramatic talents are often considerable; even as children Leo people have a strong understanding of drama. There is also something poetic about them. They can be quite romantic at times. They have a deep love and appreciation of beauty. They are fond of display and have a love of luxury that often startles modest people.

On the whole, he is a rather proud person. His head is easily turned by a compliment. The cultivated Leo, however, knows how to take flattery in his stride. Others may try to get around him by flattering him—they generally succeed with the weaker Leos, for they are quite caught up with themselves and feel that no compliment is too great. This should not be interpreted as pure vanity. The Leo person has a clear understanding of his own superiority and worth.

In spite of the fact that he is generous in most things, the person born under this sign may not appreciate others making demands of him. He may not mind offering favors, but he does not like them to be asked of him.

The person born under this sign feels that it is important to be your own boss. He does not like others to tell him what to do. He is quite capable, he feels, of handling his own affairs—and quite well. If he has to work with others, he may become rather impatient, especially if they are somewhat slow or unsure. He does not like to be kept waiting. Team work for him is sometimes a very frustrating experience. He likes to be on his own.

Health

The Leo person is generally well built. He is a sturdy person, capable of taking a lot of stress and strain if necessary. Still, he may take on more than he can manage from time to time, and this is likely to exhaust him physically. He enjoys challenge, however, and finds it difficult to turn down a proposition which gives him a chance to demonstrate his worth—even if it is beyond his real capabilities. Although he is basically an active person, he does have his limits. If he refuses to recognize them, he may become the victim of a nervous disorder. Some people born under this sign are fond of keeping late hours—in pursuit of pleasure or fame. They can keep this up for some time, but in the end it does have a telling effect on their health. People born under this sign often wear themselves out by going from one extreme to the other.

The weak parts of the Leo are his spine and heart. He should see to it that he does nothing that might affect these areas of his body. In many instances, the Leo has to restrain himself in order to protect his health. Heart disease or rheumatic fever sometimes strikes people born under this sign. In spite of this, the Leo generally has a strong resistance to disease. His constitution is good; whenever he does fall ill, he generally recovers rather quickly. The Leo man or woman cannot stand being sick. He has to be up and around; lying in bed is quite bothersome for him.

On the whole, the Leo is a brave person. However, he may have to learn the art of being physically courageous. This is generally not one of his natural attributes. If ideas or principles are at stake he is not afraid to stand up and let others know his opinion; but where physical dangers are involved he may be somewhat fearful.

The Leo man or woman has a deep love of life. He can be quite pleasure-oriented. He likes the good things that life has to offer. Sometimes he is over-enthusiastic in his approach to things, and as a result accidents occur. Under certain conditions he may take chances, that others wouldn't. It is important that the person born under this sign learn how to curb impulsiveness, as often it works against him.

The Leo woman is often charming and beautiful. She seldom has any trouble in finding a mate. Men are drawn to her almost automatically because of her grace and poise. They are known for their attractive eyes and regal bearing. Their features are often fine and delicate. There is seldom anything gross about a woman born under the sign of Leo, even when they tend to be heavy-set or large. There is always something fine that is easy to recognize in their build and carriage.

Even when they become older, Leo people remain energetic. Their zest for life never dies. They can prolong their lives, by avoiding excesses in drinking or in general life-style.

Occupation

The Leo seems to gravitate to jobs where he will have a chance to exercise his ability to manage. He is best suited to positions of authority; people respect the decisions he makes. He seems to be a natural-born leader. He knows how to take command of any situation in which he finds himself. The decisions he makes are usually just. He is direct in the way he handles his business affairs. When dealing with others he is open. He says what he means—even if he runs the danger of being blunt or offensive. He is the kind of person who believes that honesty is the best policy. Lies don't go down well with him. The truth—even if it is painful—is better than a kind lie.

In spite of the fact that the Leo person is sometimes critical to a fault, the people who work under him generally respect him and try to understand him. They seldom have reason to question his authority.

In work situations, the Leo always tries to do his best. His interest in being the top person has considerable motivational force. He is not interested in second place; only the top position is good enough for him. He will strive until he gets the position he feels is his due. The Leo person generally has a good understanding of the way things work and how to improve work situations so that better results can be obtained. He knows how to handle people—how they think and how they behave. His understanding of human nature is considerable. He is not the kind of person to rest on his laurels. He is always in search of ways to better an existing situation. He knows how to move along with the times and always tries to keep abreast of new developments in his field.

He is a proud person. In every struggle—be it physical or intellectual—he fights to win. Failure is something he finds difficult to accept. He seldom considers the possibility; success is the only thing he keeps in mind as he works. He coordinates all of his energies and efforts so that success is almost guaranteed. Dull, routine work he is glad to leave to others. His interest lies in the decision-making area of business. He wants to discuss important issues and have a hand in making policies.

He leads things well; there can be no question of that. He is deeply interested in others, and he would never abuse his position as supervisor or manager, but use it to help those working under him.

On the whole, he is a responsible person. He handles his duties capably. He does not, however, enjoy being told what to do. When others try to lord it over him, he is likely to resent it—sometimes quite violently. He feels that no one is in a position to lead him. He often finds fault with the way others try to run things; sometimes he is quite just in his criticism.

The person born under this sign usually does well in a position where he has to deal with the public. He knows how to be persuasive in his argument. Others seldom have reason to doubt his word, for he is usually sure of what he has to say. A Leo person is likely to do well in any kind of business where he is given an opportunity to make use of his managerial skills. Politics is another area where the man or woman born under this sign is apt to do quite well.

As was mentioned before, many Leos seem to be natural-born actors. They have convincing ease when on the stage; they know how to immerse themselves completely in a dramatic role. They do well in almost any kind of creative work. They have the soul of an artist or poet. In whatever he does, theater work, politics, advertising, or industrial management, the Leo will do what he can to occupy the top position. If he does not have it in the beginning, you can be sure he is working toward it.

The Leo person is far from being stingy. He loves entertaining his friends and relatives in a royal manner. Generous, sometimes to a fault, he is far from being careless with his money. He has a deep-hidden fear of being poor. He'll do what he can to protect his interests. The Leo man or woman is generally fortunate enough to occupy a position that pays well. If he earns a lot, he is apt to spend a lot. He does not like to have to count pennies. Luxurious surroundings give him the feeling of success. Money is seldom a problem to the wise Leo man or woman. Some of them wind up considerably well-off early in life. They usually don't mind taking chances with their finances; quite often they are lucky in speculation or gambling.

If he feels that someone is in serious financial trouble he does not mind helping him out. He is generous and good-hearted when it comes to lending money; but he doesn't like to be taken advantage of. If someone makes unnecessary demands of him financially, he is apt to become disagreeable.

He likes giving people he cares for presents. The gifts he gives are usually expensive and in good taste. He likes to please others—to make them grateful for the gifts he has given them. He likes others to think well of him and that is perhaps why he is rather keen on giving presents. He likes to be the one others turn to when in trouble or lean on for support.

A show of wealth makes the Leo feel important. The cultivated Leo sees to it that his extravagance never becomes unreasonable or unbearable.

Home and Family

The Leo man or woman needs a place where he can relax in peace and quiet. His home is his castle. He likes to live in a place that radiates comfort and harmony. Home life is important to the Leo person. He likes to feel that his family needs him—financially as well as emotionally. He likes to be the one who runs things at home. He expects his standards to be upheld by the other members of his family. He is generally a good provider.

The Leo person makes an excellent host. He knows how to make his guests feel at home. He likes to entertain his close friends quite often. The Leo woman does everything she can to make her guests feel they are liked and cared for. She is usually a very attentive hostess.

When the Leo person spends money it is usually to show that he is capable of spending it. For him it is a display of power or success. It lets others know what he is worth. He sees to it that his home has all of the latest appliances and luxuries. He enjoys impressing others by his clothes and furnishings, even though this may encourage them to envy him.

The woman born under this sign usually enjoys dressing well. Her wardrobe is apt to be large. If she is able, she may not wear the same thing more than once or twice. She is very conscious of being in style. If her husband is not a big earner, she may be quite a burden, for her extravagance is sometimes boundless. If she is married to a man who is not in a top earning position, she will do what she can to help him achieve it.

The Leo person is fond of children. Leos enjoy taking care of them and seeing them grow up. Sometimes, however, they are too forceful as parents and don't give their children a chance to develop their own potential. They like to be proud of their offspring and appreciate it when others pay them compliments about their children's behavior. Some Leo parents love their children so much that they are blind to their faults. They become angry if others should accuse them of spoiling their children. They are anxious to see their children succeed and sometimes expect too much of them too soon. When the children reach adulthood and assert their own will, the Leo parent is apt to feel that his children are not appreciative for all that he has done for them. He may resent their show of independence.

Social Relationships

Leo people have no trouble making friends. People seem to gravitate to them. It is unusual for someone born under this sign not to be popular. They are warm, friendly, and considerate. People like them because of their sure, authoritative ways. Leo people know how to keep the friends they make. They are outgoing, open, and helpful. They never refuse someone in real need.

They usually have what is popularly known as "personality". They are never dull or retiring people. They are always out front where they can easily be seen. They like having a rich and active social life. Sometimes they make considerable gains in their business affairs, through social activities. For them, business and pleasure can mix. They are never short of important contacts.

Those who love Leos accept their leadership without having any qualms. They trust their good judgement; their ability to regulate things. They like mixing with people, but still, they may feel it necessary to keep some distance.

LOVE AND MARRIAGE

Love is an important area of the Leo's life. Leos are very emotional and apt to get carried away in love. They take all kinds of risks in order to win someone they are fond of. When amorous, Leos may lose all sense of what is wrong and what is right.

Leos are sentimental and easily moved. Every love affair is serious to them. They may flirt from time to time, but when earnest in love they do what they can to make it permanent. A Leo is very affectionate by nature and he displays this in private. He or she is not fond of being demonstrative in public places. Somehow Leo feels this is undignified. Love and affection should be kept between two people in private. When in love, Leos are faithful. They do not believe in cheating; constancy is important to them. Generally speaking, Leo people are attractive and are never at a loss for company. The opposite sex falls under the charm of a Leo person quite easily. When looking for a permanent mate, the wise and cultivated Leo chooses someone who is not jealous or possessive—someone who won't suspect him of infidelity if he finds someone else attractive and is quite frank about it.

Romance and the Leo Woman

The Leo woman is passionate by nature. She is very warm and giving when in love. Men find her a very desirable creature and are apt to lose their heads over her when in love. She has an undeniable charm for the opposite sex. Other women are not apt to care for her when men are in the vicinity, for she has no trouble in outshining them all. She is serious when it comes to love. She may have many love affairs before she settles down, but all of them will be serious; she almost never flirts. She doesn't like a jealous or possessive man; she wants the person she loves to trust her implicitly. She doesn't like her love to be doubted.

She likes to be active socially. She enjoys being catered to by the man who loves her. She is fond of parties and entertainment. The man who courts her may have to spend quite a bit of money in order to please her. Sometimes, she is rather dreamy when in love and chooses the wrong man for a partner.

She is the kind of woman who stands behind her man in all that she does. She does what she can to help him ascend the ladder of success. She is an intelligent conversationalist and can often entertain her husband's business associates in such a way that her husband can make important gains. She is a charming hostess.

The Leo mother is affectionate and understanding. She will do all she can to see to it that her children are brought up properly.

Romance and the Leo Man

The Leo man is considered a real Casanova by many. He is passionate when in love and will stop at nothing to please the object of his affection. Women love his fiery, sure nature. They feel safe and secure when they are with him. He is a difficult person for many a woman to resist. When romancing someone, the Leo does what he can to keep the affair exciting and happy. He lavishes gifts on the person he loves. Dining and dancing at the best places in town are something the Leo person is likely to be fond of when dating.

If the Leo person loves someone he is likely to be blind to her faults. He may be more in love with his idea of a person than with the person herself. So caught up is he in his passion that he is likely to forget all practical matters. Sometimes the Leo marries unluckily because of this. He idolizes his love to such an extent that he feels she is incapable of human faults and weaknesses.

The Leo man is a passionate lover. He woos the woman of his choice until he wins her. It is important for him to love, and to have that love returned. Women are easily attracted to him because of his charming ways. He knows how to make a woman feel important and wanted.

He is serious about love. He doesn't believe in meaningless flings. He is very concerned with appearance and is easily attracted to a goodlooking woman. He is apt to build a certain fantasy world around the woman he loves and set her on a high pedestal. He will do everything he can to make her happy. He is an attentive lover and is fond of presenting his loved one with presents. He does not like possessive or jealous women. He wants his sweetheart or wife to give him the freedom he feels he is entitled to. Although he may be attracted to other women after marriage, it is unlikely that he will ever be unfaithful.

As a parent and husband he is an excellent provider. He likes to be admired by his family. He may become rather irritable if he feels his family is not as loving and as affectionate as he is. He wants his family to be one he can be proud of.

Woman—Man

LEO WOMAN
ARIES MAN

The man born under the sign of Aries is often attracted to the Leo woman. In you he can find that mixture of intellect and charm that is often difficult to find in a woman.

In some ways, the Aries man resembles an intellectual mountain goat leaping from crag to crag. He has an insatiable thirst for knowledge. He is ambitious and is apt to have his finger in many pies. He can do with a woman like you—someone attractive, quick-witted, and smart.

He is not interested in a clinging vine kind of wife, but someone who is there when he needs her; someone who listens and understands what he says; someone who can give advice if he should ever have to ask for it—which is not likely to be often. The Aries man wants a woman who is a good companion and a good sport. He is looking for a woman who will look good on his arm without hanging on it too heavily. He is looking for a woman who has both feet on the ground and yet is mysterious and enticing—a kind of domestic Helen of Troy whose face or fine dinner can launch a thousand business deals if need be. That woman he is in search of sounds a little like you, doesn't it. If the shoe fits, wear it. It will make you feel like Cinderella.

The Aries man makes a good husband. He is faithful and attentive. He is an affectionate kind of man. He'll make you feel needed and loved. Love is a serious matter for the Aries man. He does not believe in flirting or playing the field—especially after he's found the woman of his dreams. He'll expect you to be as constant in your affection as he is in his. He'll expect you to be one hundred percent his; he won't put up with any nonsense while romancing you.

The Aries man may be pretty progressive and modern about

many things; however, when it comes to wearing the pants he's downright conventional; it's strictly male attire. The best position you can take in the relationship is a supporting one. He's the boss and that's that. Once you have learned to accept that, you'll find the going easy.

The Aries man, with his endless energy and drive, likes to relax in the comfort of his home at the end of the day. The good homemaker can be sure of holding his love. He's keen on slippers and pipe, and a comfortable armchair. If you see to it that everything in the house is where he expects to find it, you'll have no difficulty keeping the relationship on an even keel.

Life and love with an Aries man may be just the medicine you need. He'll be a good provider. He'll spoil you if he's financially able.

He's young at heart and can get along easily with children.

LEO WOMAN
TAURUS MAN

If you've got your heart set on a man born under the sign of Taurus, you'll have to learn the art of being patient. Taureans take their time about everything—even love.

The steady and deliberate Taurus man is a little slow on the draw; it may take him quite a while before he gets around to popping that question. For the Leo woman who doesn't mind twiddling her thumbs, the waiting and anticipating almost always pays off in the end. Taurus men want to make sure that every step they take is a good one—particularly, if they feel that the path they're on could lead to the altar.

If you are in the mood for a whirlwind romance, you had better cast your net in shallower waters. Moreover, most Taureans prefer to do the angling themselves. They are not keen on women taking the lead; once she does, he's liable to drop her like a dead fish. If you let yourself get caught on his terms, you'll find that he's fallen for you—hook, line, and sinker.

The Taurus man is fond of a comfortable homelife. It is very important to him. If you keep those home fires burning you will have no trouble keeping that flame in your Taurean's heart aglow. You have a talent for homemaking; use it. Your taste in furnishings is excellent. You know how to make a house come alive with inviting colors and decorations.

Taurus, the strong, steady, and protective Bull could be the answer to your prayers. Perhaps he could be the anchor for your dreams and plans. He could help you acquire a more balanced outlook and approach to your life. If you're given to impulsiveness, he could help you to curb it. He's the man who is always there when you need him.

When you tie the knot with a man born under Taurus, you can put away fears about creditors pounding on the front door. Taurueans are practical about everything including bill-paying. When he carries you over that threshold, you can be certain that the entire house is paid for, not only the doorsill.

As a housewife, you won't have to worry about putting aside your many interests for the sake of back-breaking house chores. Your Taurus husband will see to it that you have all the latest time-saving appliances and comforts.

You can forget about acquiring premature gray hairs due to unruly, ruckus-raising children under your feet. Papa Taurus is a master at keeping offspring in line. He's crazy about kids but he also knows what's good for them.

LEO WOMAN
GEMINI MAN

The Gemini man is quite a catch. Many a woman has set her cap for him and failed to bag him. Generally, Gemini men are intelligent, witty, and outgoing. Many of them tend to be rather versatile. The Gemini man could easily wind up being your better half.

One thing that causes a Twin's mind and affection to wander is a bore, and it is unlikely that an active Leo woman would ever allow herself to be accused of that. The Gemini man that has caught your heart will admire you for your ideas and intellect—perhaps even more than for your home-making talents and good looks.

The Leo woman needn't feel that once she's made her marriage vows that she'll have to store her interests and ambition in the attic somewhere. The Gemini man will admire you for your zeal and liveliness. He's the kind of guy who won't scowl if you let him shift for himself in the kitchen once in a while. In fact, he'll enjoy the challenge of wrestling with pots and pans himself for a change. Chances are, too, that he might turn out to be a better cook than you—that is, if he isn't already.

The man born under the sign of the Twins is a very active person. There aren't many women who have enough pep to keep up with him. But pep is no problem for the spry Leo woman. You are both dreamers, planners, and idealists. The strong Leo woman can easily fill the role of rudder for her Geminian's ship-without-a-sail. If you are a cultivated, purposeful Leo, he won't mind it at all. The intelligent Twin is often aware of his shortcomings and doesn't resent it if someone with better bearings gives him a shove in the right direction—when it's needed. The average Gemini does not have serious ego-hangups and will even accept a well-deserved chewing out from his mate quite gracefully.

When you and your Gemini man team up, you'll probably always have a houseful of people to entertain—interesting people, too; Geminians find it hard to tolerate sluggish minds and dispositions.

People born under Gemini generally have two sides to their natures, as different as night and day. It's very easy for them to be happy-go-lucky one minute, then down in the dumps the next. They hate to be bored and will generally do anything to make their lives interesting, vivid, and action-packed.

Gemini men are always attractive to the opposite sex. You'll perhaps have to allow him an occasional harmless flirt—it will seldom amount to more than that if you're his proper mate.

The Gemini father is a pushover for children. He loves them so much, he generally lets them do what they want.

LEO WOMAN
CANCER MAN

Chances are you won't hit it off too well with the man born under Cancer if love is your object, but then Cupid has been known to do some pretty unlikely things. The Cancerian is a very sensitive man—thin-skinned and occasionally moody. You've got to keep on your toes—and not step on his—if you're determined to make a go of the relationship.

The Cancer man may be lacking in many of the qualities you seek in a man, but when it comes to being faithful and being a good provider, he's hard to beat.

It is the perceptive Leo woman who will not mistake the Crab's quietness for sullenness or his thriftiness for pennypinching. In some respects, he is like that wise old owl out on a limb; he may look like he's dozing but actually he hasn't missed a thing. Cancerians often possess a well of knowledge about human behavior; they can come across with some pretty helpful advice to those in trouble. He can certainly guide you in making investments both in time and in money. He may not say much, but he's always got his wits about him.

The Crab may not be the match or the catch for many a Leo woman; in fact, he is likely to seem downright dull to the on-the-move Leo girl. True to his sign, he can be fairly cranky and crabby when handled the wrong way. He is perhaps more sensitive than he should be.

Leo people are usually as smart as a whip. If you're clever, you will never in any way convey the idea that you consider your Cancerian a little short on brain power. Browbeating is a sure-fire way of sending the Crab angrily scurrying back to his shell—and it's quite possible that all of that lost ground will never be recovered.

The Crab is most himself at home. Once settled down for the night or the weekend, wild horses couldn't drag him any farther than the gatepost—that is, unless those wild horses were dispatched by his mother. The Crab is sometimes a Momma's boy. If his mate doesn't put her foot down, he will see to it that his mother always comes first. No self-respecting Leo would ever allow herself to play second fiddle—even if it's to her old gray-haired mother-in-law. If she's tactful, she'll discover that slipping into number one position is as easy as pie (that legendary one his mother used to bake).

If you pamper your Cancer man, you'll find that "mother" turns up increasingly less—at the front door as well as in conversations.

Cancerians make protective, proud, and patient fathers.

LEO WOMAN
LEO MAN

You probably won't have any trouble understanding the Leo man as you were born under the same sign. Still, some conflict is possible due to the fact that you both are very much alike. Be tactful and tolerant in a Leo-Leo relationship.

For many women, Leo is the sign of love. When the Lion puts his mind to romance, he doesn't stint. If he has it his way, it will be all wining, dining, and dancing till the wee hours of the morning.

The Leo man is all heart and knows how to make his woman feel like a woman. More often than not, he is a man a woman can look up to. He's a man who manages to have full control of just about any situation he finds himself in. He's a winner.

The Leo man may not look like Tarzan, but he knows how to roar and beat his chest if he has to. He's the kind of man you can lean upon. He'll also give you support in your plans and projects. He's often capable of giving advice that pays off. Leo men are direct. They don't pussyfoot around.

Leo men often rise to the top of their profession and through their examples, prove to be great sources of inspiration to others.

Although he's a ladies' man, the Leo man is very particular about his ladies. His standards are high when it comes to love interests. He believes that romance should be played on a fair give-and-take basis. He won't put up with any monkey-shines in a love relationship. It's all or nothing.

You'll find him a frank, off-the-shoulder person; he generally says what is on his mind.

If you decide that a Leo man is the one for you, be prepared to stand behind him full-force. He expects it—and usually deserves it. He's the head of the house and can handle that position without a hitch. He knows how to go about breadwinning and, if he has his way (and most Leos do have their own way), he'll see to it that you'll have all the luxuries you crave and the comforts you need.

It's unlikely that the romance in your marriage will ever die out. Lions need love like flowers need sunshine. They're ever-amorous and generally expect like attention and affection from their mate. Lions are fond of going out on the town; they love to give parties as well as go to them. You should encounter no difficulties in sharing his interests in this direction.

Leos make strict fathers, generally. You'll have to do your best to smooth down your children's roughed-up feelings.

LEO WOMAN
VIRGO MAN

The Virgo man is all business—or he may seem so to you. He is usually very cool, calm, and collected. He's perhaps too much of a fuss-budget to wake up deep romantic interests in a Leo woman. Torrid romancing to him is just so much sentimental mush. He can do without it and can make that quite evident in short order. He's keen on chastity and, if necessary, he can lead a sedentary, sexless life without caring too much about the fun others think he's missing. In short, you are liable to find him a first-class dud. He doesn't have much of an imagination; flights of fancy don't interest him. He is always correct and likes to be handled correctly. Almost everything about him is orderly. "There's a place for everything" is likely to be an adage he'll fall upon quite regularly.

He does have an honest-to-goodness heart, believe it or not. The Leo woman who finds herself strangely attracted to his cool, feet-flat-on-the-ground ways, will discover that his is a constant heart, not one that goes in for flings or sordid affairs. Virgos take an awfully long time to warm up to someone. A practical man, even in matters of the heart, he wants to know just what kind of a person you are before he takes a chance on you.

The impulsive Leo girl had better not make the mistake of kissing her Virgo friend on the street—even if it's only a peck on the cheek. He's not at all demonstrative and hates public displays of affection. Love, according to him, should be kept within the confines of one's home—with the curtains drawn. Once he believes that you are on the level with him as far as your love is concerned, you'll see how fast he can lose his cool. Virgos are considerate, gentle lovers. He'll spend a long time, though, getting to know you. He'll like you before he loves you.

A Leo-Virgo romance can be a sometime—or, rather, a one-time thing. If the bottom ever falls out, don't bother reaching for the adhesive tape. Nine times out of ten he won't care about patching up. He's a once-burnt-twice-shy guy. When he crosses your telephone number out of his address book, he's crossing you out of his life for good.

Neat as a pin, he's thumbs-down on what he considers "sloppy" housekeeping. An ashtray with just one stubbed-out cigarette in it can annoy him even if it's just two seconds old. Glassware should always sparkle and shine.

If you marry him, keep your kids spic-and-span, at least by the time he gets home from work. Train them to be kind and courteous.

LEO WOMAN
LIBRA MAN

If there's a Libran in your life, you are most likely a very happy woman. Men born under this sign have a way with women. You'll always feel at ease in a Libran's company; you can be yourself when you're with him.

Like you, he can be moody at times. His moodiness, though, is more puzzling. One moment he comes on hard and strong with declarations of his love, the next moment you find that he's left you like yesterday's mashed potatoes. He'll come back, though; don't worry. Librans are like that. Deep down inside he really knows what he wants even though he may not appear to.

You'll appreciate his admiration of beauty and harmony. If you're dressed to the teeth and never looked lovelier, you'll get a ready compliment—and one that's really deserved. Librans don't indulge in idle flattery. If they don't like something, they are tactful enough to remain silent.

Librans will go to great lengths to preserve peace and harmony—even tell a fat lie if necessary. They don't like show-downs or disagreeable confrontations. The frank Leo woman is all for getting whatever is bothering her off her chest and out into the open, even if it comes out all wrong. To the Libran, making a clean breast of everything seems like sheer folly sometimes.

You may lose your patience while waiting for your Libra friend to make up his mind. It takes him ages sometimes to make a decision. He weighs both sides carefully before committing himself to anything. You seldom dillydally—at least about small things—and so it's likely that you will find it difficult to see eye to eye with a hesitating Libra when it comes to decision-making methods.

All in all, though, he is kind, gentle, and fair. He is interested in the "real" truth; he'll try to balance everything out until he has all the correct answers. It is not difficult for him to see both sides of a story.

He's a peace-loving man. The sight of blood is apt to turn his stomach.

Librans are not showoffs. Generally, they are well-balanced people. Honest, wholesome, and affectionate, they are serious about every love encounter they have. If he should find that the girl he's dating is not really suited to him, he will end the relationship in such a tactful manner that no hard feelings will come about.

The Libra father is firm, gentle, and patient.

LEO WOMAN
SCORPIO MAN

Many people have a hard time understanding a man born under the sign of Scorpio. Few, however, are able to resist his fiery charm.

When angered, he can act like an overturned wasps' nest; his sting is capable of leaving an almost permanent mark. If you find yourself interested in a man born under this sign, you'd better learn how to keep on the good side of him. If he's in love with you, you'll know about it. Scorpio men let no one get in their way when they are out to win a certain heart. When it comes to romance, they never take "no" for an answer.

The Scorpio man can be quite blunt when he chooses; at times, he'll strike you as being a brute. His touchiness may get on your nerves after a while and if it does, you'd better tiptoe away from the scene rather than chance an explosive confrontation. He's capable of giving you a sounding-out that will make you pack your bags and go back to mother—for good.

You're the kind of woman who can put up with almost anything once you put your mind and heart to it. A stormy Scorpio relationship may be worth its ups and downs. Scorpio men are all quite perceptive and intelligent. In some respects, they know how to use their brains more effectively than others. They believe in winning in whatever they do—and in business, they usually achieve the position they want through drive and intellect.

He doesn't give a hoot for homelife, generally. He doesn't like being tied down. He would rather be out on the battlefield of life, belting away at what he feels is a just and worthy cause.

Many women are easily attracted to him. You are perhaps no exception. Know what you're getting into, before you go making any promises to him. Women who allow themselves to be swept off their feet by a Scorpio man, shortly find that they're dealing with a pepper pot of seething excitement. He's passion with a capital P, make no mistake about that.

Scorpios are straight to the point. They can be as sharp as a razor blade and just as cutting. Don't give him cause to find fault with you and you'll do just fine.

If you decide to marry him and take the bitter with the sweet, prepare yourself for a challenging relationship. Chances are you won't have as much time for your own interests as you'd like. Your Scorpio man may keep you at his beck and call.

In spite of the ins and outs of his difficult character, the Scorpio man makes an acceptable father.

LEO WOMAN
SAGITTARIUS MAN

If you've set your cap for a man born under the sign of Sagittarius, you may have to apply an awful lot of strategy before you can persuade him to get down on bended knee. Although some Sagittarians may be marriage-shy, they're not ones to skitter away from romance. You'll find a love relationship with a Sagittarian—whether a fling or "the real thing"—a very enjoyable experience.

As a rule, Sagittarians are bright, happy, and healthy people. They have a strong sense of fair play. Often they are a source of inspiration to others. They are full of drive and ideas.

You'll be taken by the Sagittarian's infectious grin and his light-hearted friendly nature. If you do wind up being the woman in his life, you'll find that he's apt to treat you more like a buddy than the love of his life. It's just his way. Sagittarians are often more chummy than romantic.

You'll admire his broadmindedness in most matters—including those of the heart. If, while dating you, he claims that he still wants to play the field, he'll expect you to enjoy the same liberty. Once he's promised to love, honor, and obey, however, he does just that. Marriage for him, once he's taken that big step, is very serious business.

The Sagittarius man is quick-witted. He has a genuine interest in equality. He hates prejudice and injustice. Generally, Sagittarians are good at sports. They love the great out-of-doors and respect wildlife in all its forms.

He's not much of a homebody. Quite often he's occupied with

far away places either in his daydreams or in reality. He enjoys being on-the-move. He's got ants in his pants and refuses to sit still for long stretches at a time. Humdrum routine—especially at home—bores him. At the drop of a hat, he may ask you to whip off your apron and dine out for a change. He likes surprising people. He'll take great pride in showing you off to his friends. He'll always be a considerate mate; he will never embarrass or disappoint you intentionally.

His friendly, sun-shiny nature is capable of attracting many people. Like you, he's very tolerant when it comes to friends and you'll most likely spend a great deal of time entertaining people.

Sagittarians are all thumbs when it comes to little shavers. They develop an interest in children as they get older and wiser.

LEO WOMAN
CAPRICORN MAN

A with-it girl like you is likely to find the average Capricorn man a bit of a drag. The man born under the sign of the Goat is often a closed person and difficult to get to know. Even if you do get to know him, you may not find him very interesting.

In romance, Capricorn men are a little on the rusty side. You'll probably have to make all the passes.

You may find his plodding manner, irritating, and his conservative, traditional ways downright maddening. He's not one to take chances on anything. "If it was good enough for my father, it's good enough for me" may be his motto. He follows a way that is tried and true.

Whenever adventure rears its tantalizing head, the Goat will turn the other way; he's just not interested.

He may be just as ambitious as you are—perhaps even more so—but his ways of accomplishing his aims are more subterranean or, at least, seem so. He operates from the background a good deal of the time. At a gathering you may never even notice him but he's there, taking in everything and sizing up everyone—planning his next careful move.

Although Capricorns may be intellectual to a degree, it is generally not the kind of intelligence you appreciate. He may not be as quick or as bright as you; it may take ages for him to understand a simple joke.

If you decide to take up with a man born under this sign, you ought to be pretty good in the "cheering up" department. The Capricorn man often acts as though he's constantly being followed by a cloud of gloom.

The Capricorn man is most himself when in the comfort and

privacy of his own home. The security possible within four walls can make him a happy man. He'll spend as much time as he can at home. If he is loaded down with extra work, he'll bring it home instead of working overtime at the office.

You'll most likely find yourself frequently confronted by his relatives. Family is very important to the Capricorn—*his* family that is. They had better take a pretty important place in your life, too, if you want to keep your home a happy one.

Although his caution in most matters may all but drive you up the wall, you'll find his concerned way with money justified most of the time. He'll plan everything right down to the last penny.

He can be quite a scold when it comes to disciplining children. You'll have to step in and soften things.

LEO WOMAN
AQUARIUS MAN

Aquarians love everybody—even their worst enemies, sometimes. Through your relationship with an Aquarian you'll find yourself running into all sorts of people, ranging from near-genius to downright insane—and they're all friends of his.

As a rule, Aquarians are extremely friendly and open. Of all the signs, they are perhaps the most tolerant. In the thinking department, they are often miles ahead of others.

You'll most likely find your relationship with this man a challenging one. Your high respect for intelligence and imagination may be reason enough for you to settle your heart on a Water Bearer. You'll find that you can learn a lot from him.

In the holding-hands phase of your romance, you may find that your Water Bearing friend has cold feet. Aquarians take quite a bit of warming up before they are ready to come across with that first goodnight kiss. More than likely, he'll just want to be your pal in the beginning. For him, that's an important first step in any relationship—love, included. The "poetry and flowers" stage—if it ever comes—will be later. The Aquarian is all heart; still, when it comes to tying himself down to one person and for keeps, he is liable to hesitate. He may even try to get out of it if you breath down his neck too heavily.

The Aquarius man is no Valentino and wouldn't want to be. The kind of love-life he's looking for is one that's made up mainly for companionship. Although he may not be very romantic, the memory of his first romance will always hold an important position in his heart. Sometimes Aquarians wind up marrying their childhood sweethearts.

You won't find it difficult to look up to a man born under the sign of the Water Bearer, but you may find the challenge of trying to keep up with him dizzying. He can pierce through the most complicated problem as if it were a matter of $2 + 2$. You may find him a little too lofty and high-minded—but don't judge him too harshly if that's the case; he's way ahead of his time—your time, too, most likely.

If you marry this man, he'll stay true to you. Don't think that once the honeymoon is over, you'll be chained to the kitchen sink forever. Your Aquarius husband will encourage you to keep active in your own interests and affairs. You'll most likely have a minor tiff now and again but never anything serious.

Kids love him and vice-versa. He'll be as tolerant with them as he is with adults.

LEO WOMAN
PISCES MAN

The man born under Pisces is quite a dreamer. Sometimes he's so wrapped up in his dreams that he's difficult to reach. To the average ambitious woman, he may seem a little sluggish.

He's easy-going most of the time. He seems to take things in his stride. He'll entertain all kinds of views and opinions from just about anyone, nodding or smiling vaguely, giving the impression that he's with them one hundred percent while that may not be the case at all. His attitude may be "why bother" when he is confronted with someone wrong who thinks he's right. The Pisces man will seldom speak his mind if he thinks he'll be rigidly opposed.

The Pisces man is oversensitive at times—he's afraid of getting his feelings hurt. He'll sometimes imagine a personal injury when none's been made at all. Chances are you'll find this complex of his maddening; at times you may feel like giving him a swift kick where it hurts the most. It wouldn't do any good, though. It would just add fuel to the fire of his persecution complex.

One thing you will admire about this man is his concern for people who are sickly or troubled. He'll make his shoulder available to anyone in the mood for a good cry. He can listen to one hard-luck story after another without seeming to tire. When his advice is asked, he is capable of coming across with some pretty important words of wisdom. He often knows what is bugging someone before that person is aware of it himself. It's almost intuitive with Pisceans, it seems. Still, at the end of the day, he looks forward to some peace and quiet. If you've got a problem on your mind when he comes home, don't unload it in his lap. If you do, you're liable to find him short-tempered. He's a good listener, but he can only take so much.

Pisces men are not aimless although they may seem so at times. The positive sort of Pisces man is quite often successful in his profession and is likely to wind up rich and influential. Material gain, however, is not a direct goal for a man born under this sign.

The weaker Piscean is usually content to stay put on the level where he finds himself. He won't complain too much if the roof leaks and the fence is in need of repair. He'll just shrug it off as a minor inconvenience.

Because of their seemingly laissez-faire manner, people under this sign—needless to say—are immensely popular with children. For tots they play the double role of confidant and playmate. It will never enter his mind to discipline a child, no matter how spoiled or incorrigible that child becomes.

Man—Woman

LEO MAN
ARIES WOMAN

The Aries woman is quite a charmer. When she tugs at the strings of your heart, you'll know it. She's a woman who's in search of a knight in shining armor. She is a very particular person with very high ideals. She won't accept anyone but the man of her dreams.

The Aries woman never plays around with passion; she means business when it comes to love.

Don't get the idea that she's a dewy-eyed Miss. She isn't. In fact, she can be pretty practical and to-the-point when she wants. She's a girl with plenty of drive and ambition. With an Aries woman behind you, you are liable to go far in life. She knows how to help her man get ahead. She's full of wise advice; you only have to ask. In some cases, the Aries woman has a keen business sense; many of them become successful career women. There is nothing backward or retiring about her. She is equipped with a good brain and she knows how to use it.

Your union with her could be something strong, secure, and romantic. If both of you have your sights fixed in the same direction, there is almost nothing that you could not accomplish.

The Aries woman is proud and capable of being quite jealous. While you're with her, never cast your eye in another woman's direction. It could spell disaster for your relationship. The Aries woman won't put up with romantic nonsense when her heart is at stake.

If the Aries woman backs you up in your business affairs, you can be sure of succeeding. However, if she only is interested in advancing her own career and puts her interests before yours, she can be sure of rocking the boat. It will put a strain on the relationship. The over-ambitious Aries woman can be a pain in the neck and make you forget that you were in love with her once.

The cultivated Aries woman makes a wonderful wife and mother. She has a natural talent for home-making. With a pot of paint and some wallpaper, she can transform the dreariest domicile into an abode of beauty and snug comfort. The perfect hostess—even when friends just happen by —she knows how to make guests feel at home.

You'll also admire your Arien because she knows how to stand on her own two feet. Hers is of an independent nature. She won't break down and cry when things go wrong, but pick herself up and try to patch matters.

The Aries woman makes a fine, affectionate mother.

LEO MAN
TAURUS WOMAN

The woman born under the sign of Taurus may lack a little of the sparkle and bubble you often like to find in a woman. The Taurus woman is generally down-to-earth and never flighty. It's important to her that she keep both feet flat on the ground. She is not fond of bounding all over the place, especially if she's under the impression that there's no profit in it.

On the other hand, if you hit it off with a Taurus woman, you won't be disappointed at all in the romance area. The Taurus woman is all woman and proud of it, too. She can be very devoted and loving once she decides that her relationship with you is no fly-by-night romance. Basically, she's a passionate person. In sex, she's direct and to-the-point. If she really loves you, she'll let you know she's yours—and without reservations. Better not flirt with other women once you've committed yourself to her. She is capable of being jealous and possessive.

She'll stick by you through thick and thin. It's almost certain that if the going ever gets rough, she'll not go running home to her mother. She can adjust to hard times just as graciously as she can to the good times.

Taureans are, on the whole, pretty even-tempered. They like to be treated with kindness. Pretty things and soft things make them purr like kittens.

You may find her a little slow and deliberate. She likes to be safe and sure about everything. Let her plod along if she likes; don't coax her but just let her take her own sweet time. Everything she does is done thoroughly and, generally, without mistakes. Don't deride her for being a kind of slow-poke. It could lead to flying pots and pans and a fireworks display that would put Bastille Day to shame. The Taurus woman doesn't anger readily but when prodded often enough, she's capable of letting loose with a cyclone of ill-will. If you treat her with kindness and consideration, you'll have no cause for complaint.

The Taurean loves doing things for her man. She's a whiz in the kitchen and can whip up feasts fit for a king if she thinks they'll be royally appreciated. She may not fully understand you, but she'll adore you and be faithful to you if she feels you're worthy of it.

The woman born under Taurus will make a wonderful mother. She knows how to keep her children well-loved, cuddled, and warm. She may find them difficult to manage, however, when they reach the teenage stage.

LEO MAN
GEMINI WOMAN

You may find a romance with a woman born under the sign of the Twins a many-splendoured thing. In her you can find the intellectual companionship you often look for in a friend or mate. A Gemini girl friend can appreciate your aims and desires because she travels pretty much the same road as you do intellectually —that is, at least part of the way. She may share your interest but she will lack your tenacity.

She suffers from itchy feet. She can be here, there . . . all over the place and at the same time, or so it would seem. Her eagerness to move about may make you dizzy, still you'll enjoy and appreciate her liveliness and mental agility.

Geminians often have sparkling personalities; you'll be attracted by her warmth and grace. While she's on your arm you'll probably notice that many male eyes are drawn to her—she may even return a gaze or two, but don't let that worry you. All women born under this sign have nothing against a harmless flirt once in a while. They enjoy this sort of attention; if she feels she is already spoken for, however, she will never let it get out of hand.

Although she may not be as handy as you'd like in the kitchen, you'll never go hungry for a filling and tasty meal. She's as much in a hurry as you are, and won't feel like she's cheating by breaking out the instant mashed potatoes or the frozen peas. She may not be much of a cook but she is clever; with a dash of this and a suggestion of that, she can make an uninteresting TV dinner taste like something out of a Jim Beard cookbook. Then, again, maybe you've struck it rich and have a Gemini girl friend who finds complicated recipes a challenge to her intellect. If so, you'll find every meal a tantalizing and mouth-watering surprise.

When you're beating your brains out over the Sunday crossword puzzle and find yourself stuck, just ask your Gemini girlie; she'll give you all the right answers without batting an eyelash.

Like you, she loves all kinds of people. You may even find that you're a bit more particular than she. Often all that a Geminian requires is that her friends be interesting . . . and stay interesting. One thing she's not able to abide is a dullard.

Leave the party-organizing to your Gemini sweetheart or mate and you'll never have a chance to know what a dull moment is. She'll bring the swinger out in you if you give her half a chance.

A Gemini mother enjoys her children. Like them, she's often restless, adventurous, and easily bored.

LEO MAN
CANCER WOMAN

If you fall in love with a Cancer woman, be prepared for anything. Cancerians are sometimes difficult to understand when it comes to love. In one hour, she can unravel a whole gamut of emotions that will leave you in a tizzy. She'll keep you guessing, that's for sure.

You may find her a little too uncertain and sensitive for your liking. You'll most likely spend a good deal of time encouraging her—helping her to erase her foolish fears. Tell her she's a living doll a dozen times a day and you'll be well loved in return.

Be careful of the jokes you make when in her company—don't let any of them revolve around her, her personal interests, or her family. If you do, you'll most likely reduce her to tears. She can't stand being made fun of. It will take bushels of roses and tons of chocolates—not to mention the apologies—to get her to come back out of her shell.

In matters of money-managing, she may not easily come around to your way of thinking. Money will never burn a hole in her pocket. You may get the notion that your Cancerian sweetheart or mate is a direct descendent of Scrooge. If she has her way, she'll hang onto that first dollar you earned. She's not only that way with money, but with everything right on up from bakery string to jelly jars. She's a saver; she never throws anything away, no matter how trivial.

Once she returns your "I love you", you'll find you have an affectionate, self-sacrificing, and devoted woman on your hands. Her love for you will never alter unless you want it to. She'll put you high upon a pedestal and will do everything—even if it's against your will—to keep you up there.

Cancer women love home life. For them, marriage is an easy step. They're domestic with a capital D. She'll do her best to make your home comfortable and cozy. She is more at ease at home than anywhere else. She makes an excellent hostess. The best in her comes out when she is in her own environment.

Cancer women make the best mothers of all the signs of the Zodiac. She'll consider every complaint of her child a major catastrophe. With her, children always come first. If you're lucky, you'll run a close second. You'll perhaps see her as too devoted to the children. You may have a hard time convincing her that her apron strings are a little too long.

LEO MAN
LEO WOMAN

If you can manage a girl who likes to kick up her heels every now and again, then the Leo woman was made for you. You'll have to learn to put away jealous fears—or at least forget about them—when you take up with a woman born under this sign, because she's often the kind that makes heads turn and tongues wag. You don't necessarily have to believe any of what you hear—it's most likely just jealous gossip. Take up with a Leo woman and you'll be taking off on a romance full of fire and ice; be prepared to take the good things with the bad—the bitter with the sweet.

The Leo girl has more than a fair share of grace and glamour. She is aware of her charms and knows how to put them to good use. Needless to say, other women in her vicinity turn green with envy and will try anything short of shoving her into the nearest lake, in order to put her out of commission.

If she's captured your heart and fancy, woo her full-force if your intention is to eventually win her. Shower her with expensive gifts and promise her the moon—if you're in a position to go that far—then you'll find her resistance beginning to weaken. It's not that she's such a difficult cookie—she'll probably make a lot over you once she's decided you're the man for her—but she does enjoy a lot of attention. What's more, she feels she's entitled to it. Her mild arrogance, though, is becoming. The Leo woman knows how to transform the crime of excessive pride into a very charming misdemeanor. It sweeps most men right off their feet. Those who do not succumb to her leonine charm are few and far between.

If you've got an important business deal to clinch and you have doubts as to whether or not it will go over, bring your Leo girl along to that business luncheon and it's a cinch that that contract will be yours. She won't have to do or say anything—just be there at your side. The grouchiest oil magnate can be transformed into a gushing, obedient schoolboy if there's a Leo woman in the room.

If you're rich and want to stay that way, don't give your Leo mate a free hand with the charge accounts and credit cards. If you're poor, the luxury-loving Leo will most likely never enter your life.

She makes a strict yet easy-going mother. She loves to pal around with her children.

LEO MAN
VIRGO WOMAN

The Virgo woman may be a little too difficult for you to understand at first. Her waters run deep. Even when you think you know her, don't take any bets on it. She's capable of keeping things hidden in the deep recesses of her womanly soul—things she'll only release when she's sure that you're the man she's been looking for. It may take her some time to come around to this decision. Virgo girls are finnicky about almost everything; everything has to be letter-perfect before they're satisfied. Many of them have the idea that the only people who can do things correctly are Virgos.

Nothing offends a Virgo woman more than slovenly dress, sloppy character, or a careless display of affection. Make sure your tie is not crooked and your shoes sport a bright shine before you go calling on this lady. Keep your off-color jokes for the locker-room; she'll have none of that. Take her arm when crossing the street. Don't rush the romance. Trying to corner her in the back of a cab may be one way of striking out. Never criticize the way she looks; in fact, the best policy would be to agree with her as much as possible. Still, there's just so much a man can take; all those dos and don'ts you'll have to observe if you want to get to first base with a Virgo may be just a little too much to ask of you. After a few dates, you may come to the conclusion that she just isn't worth all that trouble. However, the Virgo woman is mysterious enough, generally speaking, to keep her men running back for more. Chances are you'll be intrigued by her airs and graces.

If love-making means a lot to you, you'll be disappointed at first in the cool ways of your Virgo girl. However, under her glacial facade there lies a hot cauldron of seething excitement. If you're patient and artful in your romantic approach, you'll find that all that caution was well worth the trouble. When Virgos love, they don't stint. It's all or nothing as far as they're concerned. Once they're convinced that they love you, they go all the way, right off the bat—tossing all cares to the wind.

One thing a Virgo woman can't stand in love is hypocrisy.

They don't give a hoot about what the neighbors say, if their hearts tell them, "go ahead". They're very concerned with human truths—so much so that if their hearts stumble upon another fancy, they're liable to be true to that new heart-throb and leave you standing in the rain.

She's honest to her heart and will be as true to you as you are with her, generally. Do her wrong once, however, and it's farewell.

She's both strict and tender with children. As a mother she'll try to bring out the best in her children.

LEO MAN
LIBRA WOMAN

You'll probably find that the girl born under the sign of Libra is worth more than her weight in gold. She's a woman after your own heart.

With her, you'll always come first—make no mistake about that. She'll always be behind you 100 percent, no matter what you do. When you ask her advice about almost anything, you'll most likely get a very balanced and realistic opinion. She is good at thinking things out and never lets her emotions run away with her when clear logic is called for.

As a homemaker she is hard to beat. She is very concerned with harmony and balance. You can be sure she'll make your house a joy to live in; she'll see to it that the house is tastefully furnished and decorated. A Libran cannot stand filth or disarray—it gives her goose-bumps. Anything that does not radiate harmony, in fact, runs against her orderly grain.

She is chock-full of charm and womanly ways. She can sweep just about any man off his feet with one winning smile. When it comes to using her brains, she can out-think almost anyone and, sometimes, with half the effort. She is diplomatic enough, though, never to let this become glaringly apparent. She may even turn the conversation around so that you think you were the one who did all the brain-work. She couldn't care less, really, just as long as you wind up doing what is right.

The Libra woman will put you up on a pretty high pedestal. You are her man and her idol. She'll leave all the decision-making, large or small, up to you. She's not interested in running things and will only offer her assistance if she feels you really need it.

Some find her approach to reason masculine; however, in the areas of love and affection the Libra woman is *all* woman. She'll literally shower you with love and kisses during your romance with her. She doesn't believe in holding out. You shouldn't, either, if you want to hang onto her.

She is the kind of girl who likes to snuggle up to you in front of the fire on chilly autumn nights—the kind of girl who will bring you breakfast in bed Sunday. She'll be very thoughtful about anything that concerns you. If anyone dares suggest you're not the grandest guy in the world, she'll give that person what-for. She'll defend you till her dying breath. The Libra woman will be everything you want her to be.

She'll be a sensitive and loving mother. Still, you'll always come before the children.

LEO MAN
SCORPIO WOMAN

The Scorpio woman can be a whirlwind of passion—perhaps too much passion to really suit you. When her temper flies, you'd better lock up the family heirlooms and take cover. When she chooses to be sweet, you're apt to think that butter wouldn't melt in her mouth—but, of course, it would.

The Scorpio woman can be as hot as a tamale or as cool as a cucumber, but whatever mood she's in, she's in it for real. She does not believe in posing or putting on airs.

The Scorpio woman is often sultry and seductive—her femme fatale charm can pierce through the hardest of hearts like a laser beam. She may not look like Mata Hari (quite often Scorpios resemble the tomboy next door) but once she's fixed you with her tantalizing eyes, you're a goner.

Life with the Scorpio woman will not be all smiles and smooth-sailing; when prompted, she can unleash a gale of venom. Generally, she'll have the good grace to keep family battles within the walls of your home. When company visits, she's apt to give the impression that married life with you is one great big joy-ride. It's just one of her ways of expressing her loyalty to you—at least in front of others. She may fight you tooth and nail in the confines of your livingroom, but at a ball or during an evening out, she'll hang onto your arm and have stars in her eyes.

Scorpio women are good at keeping secrets. She may even keep a few buried from you if she feels like it.

Never cross her up on even the smallest thing. When it comes to revenge, she's an eye-for-an-eye woman. She's not too keen on forgiveness—especially if she feels she's been wronged unfairly. You'd be well-advised not to give her any cause to be jealous, either. When the Scorpio woman sees green, your life will be made far from rosy. Once she's put you in the dog-house, you can be sure that you're going to stay there a while.

You may find life with a Scorpio woman too draining. Although she may be full of the old paprika, it's quite likely that she's not the kind of girl you'd like to spend the rest of your natural life with. You'd prefer someone gentler and not so hot-tempered; someone who can take the highs with the lows and not bellyache; someone who is flexible and understanding. A woman born under Scorpio can be heavenly, but she can also be the very devil when she chooses.

As a mother, a Scorpio is protective and encouraging.

LEO MAN
SAGITTARIUS WOMAN

You'll most likely never come across a more good-natured girl than the one born under the sign of Sagittarius. Generally, they're full of bounce and good cheer. Their sunny disposition seems almost permanent and can be relied upon even on the rainiest of days.

Women born under this sign are almost never malicious. If ever they seem to be it is only seeming. Sagittarians are often a little short on tact and say literally anything that comes into their pretty little heads—no matter what the occasion. Sometimes the words that tumble out of their mouths seem downright cutting and cruel. Still, no matter what she says, she means well. The Sagittarius woman is quite capable of losing some of her friends—and perhaps even some of yours—through a careless slip of the lip.

On the other hand, you are liable to appreciate her honesty and good intentions. To you, qualities of this sort play an important part in life. With a little patience and practice, you can probably help cure your Sagittarian of her loose tongue; in most cases, she'll give into your better judgement and try to follow your advice to the letter.

Chances are she'll be the outdoors type of girl friend. Long hikes, fishing trips, and white-water canoeing will most likely appeal to her. She's a busy person; no one could ever call her a slouch. She sets great store in mobility. Her feet are itchy and she won't sit still for a minute if she doesn't have to.

She is great company most of the time and, generally, lots of fun. Even if your buddies drop by for poker and beer, she won't have any trouble fitting in.

On the whole, she is a very kind and sympathetic woman. If she feels she's made a mistake, she'll be the first to call your attention to it. She's not afraid to own up to her faults and shortcomings.

You might lose your patience with her once or twice. After she's seen how upset her shortsightedness or tendency to blabbermouth has made you, she'll do her best to straighten up.

The Sagittarian woman is not the kind who will pry into your business affairs. But she'll always be there, ready to offer advice if you need it. If you come home with red stains on your collar and you say it's paint and not lipstick, she'll believe you.

She'll seldom be suspicious; your word will almost always be good enough for her.

She is a wonderful and loving friend to her children.

LEO MAN
CAPRICORN WOMAN

If you are not a successful businessman, or at least on your way to success, it's quite possible that a Capricorn woman will have no interest in entering your life. Generally speaking, she is a very security-minded female; she'll see to it that she invests her time only in sure things. Men who whittle away their time with one unsuccessful scheme or another, seldom attract a Capricorn. Men who are interested in getting somewhere in life and keep their noses close to the grindstone quite often have a Capricorn woman behind them, helping them to get ahead.

Although she is a kind of "climber" she is not what you could call cruel or hard-hearted. Beneath that cool, seemingly calculating, exterior, there's a warm and desirable woman. She just happens to think that it is just as easy to fall in love with a rich or ambitious man as it is with a poor or lazy one. She's practical.

The Capricorn woman may be keenly interested in rising to the top, but she'll never be aggressive about it. She'll seldom step on someone's feet or nudge competitors away with her elbows. She's quiet about her desires. She sits, waits, and watches. When an opening or opportunity does appear, she'll latch onto it lickety-split. For an on-the-move man, an ambitious Capricorn wife or girlfriend can be quite an asset. She can probably give you some very good advice about business matters. When you invite the boss and his wife for dinner, she'll charm them both right off the ground.

The Capricorn woman is thorough in whatever she does: cooking, cleaning, making a success out of life—Capricorns make excellent hostesses as well as guests. Generally, they are very well mannered and gracious, no matter what their backgrounds are. They seem to have a built-in sense of what is right. Crude behavior or a careless faux-pas can offend them no end.

If you should marry a woman born under Capricorn you need never worry about her going on a wild shopping spree. Capricorns are careful with every cent that comes into their hands. They understand the value of money better than most women and have no room in their lives for careless spending.

Capricorn girls are usually very fond of family—their own, that is. With them, family ties run very deep. Don't make jokes about her relatives; she won't stand for it. You'd better check her family out before you get down on bended knee; after your marriage you'll undoubtedly be seeing lots of them.

Capricorn mothers train their children to be polite and kind.

LEO MAN
AQUARIUS WOMAN

If you find that you've fallen head over heels for a woman born under the sign of the Water Bearer, you'd better fasten your safety belt. It may take you quite a while to actually discover what this girl is like—and even then, you may have nothing to go on but a string of vague hunches. The Aquarian is like a rainbow, full of bright and shining hues; she's like no other girl you've ever known. There is something elusive about her—something delightfully mysterious. You'll most likely never be able to put your finger on it. It's nothing calculated, either; Aquarians don't believe in phony charm.

There will never be a dull moment in your life with this Water Bearing woman; she seems to radiate adventure and magic. She'll most likely be the most open-minded and tolerant woman you've ever met. She has a strong dislike for injustice and prejudice. Narrow-mindedness runs against her grain.

She is very independent by nature and quite capable of shifting for herself if necessary. She may receive many proposals for marriage from all sorts of people without ever really taking them seriously. Marriage is a very big step for her; she wants to be sure she knows what she's getting into. If she thinks that it will seriously curb her independence and love of freedom, she's liable to shake her head and give the man his engagement ring back—if indeed she's let the romance get that far.

The line between friendship and romance is a pretty fuzzy one for an Aquarian. It's not difficult for her to remain buddy-buddy with an ex-lover. She's tolerant, remember? So, if you should see her on the arm of an old love, don't jump to any hasty conclusions.

She's not a jealous person herself and doesn't expect you to be, either. You'll find her pretty much of a free spirit most of the time. Just when you think you know her inside-out, you'll discover that you don't really know her at all.

She's a very sympathetic and warm person; she can be helpful to people in need of assistance and advice.

She'll seldom be suspicious even if she has every right to be. If the man she loves slips and allows himself a little fling, chances are she'll just turn her head the other way. Her tolerance does have its limits, however, and her man should never press his luck at hanky-panky.

She makes a big-hearted mother; her good qualities rub off on her children.

LEO MAN
PISCES WOMAN

Many a man dreams of a Piscean kind of a girl. You're perhaps no exception. She's soft and cuddly—very domestic. She'll let you be the brains of the family; she's contented to just lean on your shoulder and let you be the master of the household.

She can be very ladylike and proper. Your business associates and friends will be dazzled by her warmth and femininity. Although she's a charmer, there is a lot more to her than just a pretty face. There is a brain ticking away behind that soft, womanly facade. You may never become aware of it—that is, until you're married to her. It's no cause for alarm, however; she'll most likely never use it against you.

If she feels you're botching up your married life through careless behavior or if she feels you could be earning more money than you do, she'll tell you about it. But any wife would, really. She will never try to usurp your position as head of the family.

No one had better dare say one uncomplimentary word about you in her presence. It's liable to cause her to break into tears. Pisces women are usually very sensitive beings. Their reaction to adversity, frustration, or anger is just a plain, good, old-fashioned cry. They can weep buckets when inclined.

She'll have an extra-special dinner waiting for you when you come home from an important business meeting. Don't bother to go into any of the details about the meeting, though, at the dinner table; she doesn't have much of a head for business matters, usually, and is only too happy to leave that up to you.

She can do wonders with a house. She is very fond of soft and beautiful things. There will always be plenty of fresh-cut flowers around the house. She'll see that you always have plenty of socks and underwear in that top drawer of your dresser.

Treat her with tenderness and your relationship will be an enjoyable one. She's most likely fond of chocolates. A bunch of beautiful roses will never fail to make her eyes light up. See to it that you never forget her birthday or your anniversary. She won't.

If you are patient and kind, you can keep a Pisces woman happy for a lifetime. She is, however, not without her faults. Her "sensitivity" may get on your nerves after a while. You may find her lacking in imagination and zest. You may even feel that she only uses her tears as a method of getting her own way.

She makes a strong, self-sacrificing mother. She'll find it difficult to refuse her children anything.

LEO

YEARLY FORECAST: 1995

*Forecast for 1995 Concerning Business
and Financial Matters, Job Prospects,
Travel, Health, Romance and Marriage
for Those Born with the Sun
in the Zodiacal Sign of Leo.
July 21–August 21*

For those of you born under the influence of the Sun in the
zodiacal sign of Leo, which is ruled by the Sun itself, brightest of
all the celestial bodies and symbol of success and brilliance, this
can be an especially fortunate year. Lady Luck will tend to be very
much on your side both in personal and professional matters. And
yet it will be more important than ever for you not to get carried
away on winning streaks, or press your good fortune too far.
Success in business and career affairs will come from finding the
right balance between speculation and practical common sense.
Timing will be of the essence, especially in getting new ventures
off the ground. Where finances are concerned, you will tend to
find that your earnings fluctuate more than usual, going up and
down in spurts. Taxation matters can create problems if you do not
take the trouble to look well ahead and obtain professional advice
or assistance when appropriate. Job prospects are unsettled. You
may need to accept a greater degree of uncertainty and insecurity
with regard to occupational affairs. But keep your eye on your
long-term goals; perseverance will win out in the end and bring
you the prospects you deserve.

Travel can provide a welcome break in your routine. Other than
one vacation period in 1995, however, you are likely to find that
pressures and commitments keep you tied closer to your home
base. Health may not be quite as stable and resilient as usual for
Leo men and women. Certain sensitivities and allergies can become accentuated. And there is likely to be a greater psychological

component in any ailment you do experience, so it is important to make the extra effort to understand yourself. This is a year when your powerful romantic urges will tend to be stronger than ever. For those of you who are single, this can be especially lucky; you may meet the partner of a lifetime. But for all Leos it is clear that emotional and physical security will be a greater consideration now. Setting up a home and putting down roots is likely to be a major priority. And for those of you who do not yet have children, this may be just the right time to start a family through birth or adoption.

For Leo business and professional people, there can be little doubt that a more flamboyant style will be much to your liking. Highlight your natural charm. Be yourself, even in formal situations. People will tend to accept you more and also be attracted by your charisma if you are simply what you are. You are a natural gambler, although this does not necessarily mean putting your own money, let alone other people's, on the line. What it does mean is knowing instinctively when things are going your way and taking full advantage of favorable situations and circumstances. Throughout this year it is essential that you base all decisions and moves on thorough and detailed research work. Extra hours, or even days, devoted to investigating the finer details of plans and transactions will be well worth the investment. Do not bluff your way through subjects you do not understand; take the trouble to find out about them. This is also a sensitive year with regard to staffing and work forces. A greater degree of coming and going on the part of employees may require you to reconsider arrangements. There is no point spending time and money training individuals who are likely to decide to move on after a few months or even weeks. Working out more attractive incentive schemes can be the ideal solution. Try to channel and use the creativity and inventiveness of your work force; if you do so, the chances of them becoming dissatisfied and moving on to greener pastures will be radically reduced. Between the start of April and the first week of June you may be in for a few surprises involving cooperative teamwork. Partners can be unreliable, and may even desert you completely. Deciding whether to treat people as colleagues and equals or as helpers and subordinates can be tricky and deserves some very careful thought. Between January 23 and May 24 avoid becoming too argumentative; there is a greater risk of antagonizing potentially helpful people who are put off by your ruthless or aggressive style. Between July 21 and September 6 can be good for initiating dynamic new campaigns. From September 7 to October 19, avoid the temptation to put off jobs until the last moment. If you wait too long and then make a last-minute rush to meet deadlines, you are unlikely to produce work up to your usual high standard.

Where financial matters are concerned, take advantage of good fortune when it comes your way but do not push your luck too far. And beware of any gambling urges. You may make a few surprise wins on the horses or elsewhere, but remember that Leos have a real weakness for gambling which can easily turn into an addiction. This is a year when caution is called for with regard to shared funds and joint accounts. Marital funds, in particular, can prove a major asset, especially if you or your mate fall temporarily out of work. On the other hand, such money sources also need to be replenished as much as possible. During times of rich earnings, remember to put that extra share aside for a rainy day. This can be an especially good year for investing in property. Real estate can be a sound investment, which will also have the added advantage of tying up your funds so that you are not able to get at them on some of your wilder impulses. Legacy or alimony matters may take longer than you had anticipated before a satisfactory settlement is reached. Legal costs in any dispute are likely to be somewhat higher than you had expected. During the first three weeks of the year, put in a little extra overtime so you start off with a useful bonus or overtime pay. Throughout the year, but especially during December, think twice before throwing away good money on supposed health cures or treatments which might actually have little or no positive effect.

This should be an unusual year where work and employment are concerned. Employers are more likely to keep you in the dark about your future prospects. The major reason for this is probably that they themselves do not know what is just around the corner. On the other hand, possibly not everyone is being completely honest with you about occupational matters, and there is even a risk of deception on the part of someone you have grown to trust. Heed the very wise adage about not putting all your eggs in one basket. Especially if you are self-employed, or only working on a part-time basis, avoid becoming overly dependent on one particular source of work and income. Stretch your net wider; diversify. It can be surprising where you are able to find work, and with whom. Be prepared for the unexpected, and use your intuition. Even if you are working for only one employer, chances are that there will be frequent changes in routines and tasks. Again, be flexible. This can be a good year for starting to work from your own home base.

This is not a year when travel is especially important. You may have your sights set on that attractive vacation you have been promising yourself, or which someone else has promised you. And a holiday in a distant location can be particularly enjoyable if it is paid for at someone else's expense or if you are invited to stay at the home of acquaintances or friends. But otherwise, money problems may rear their ugly head at the most inconvenient moments. And matters closer to home will tend to absorb your attention, especially from the end of April all the way through December. If you are not able to relax completely in some distant place, however attractive or idyllic it is, there is little point in your making such a long journey.

Good health is easier to maintain this year provided you allow yourself plenty of time for rest and tranquillity. Too much rushing around, too much change of scenery, and too much emotional and mental pressure are likely to take their toll. If you do not deal with problems in the appropriate way, they could start to manifest physically in allergies, exhaustion, or other peculiar symptoms whose real cause is not just in the body. Meditation and creative visualization can be ideal ways of maintaining physical and emotional stability and equilibrium. If traveling abroad, watch out for those foreign foods. Also check to ensure that any water supply you use is sanitary. It would be a shame to spoil a vacation due to failing to take obvious precautions. Try to take things extra easy throughout December. If you overwork or push yourself too hard in other ways, you will be too tired and exhausted to enjoy the end-of-year break.

Single Leo men and women are likely to be more attractive than ever to others. Your own romantic urges are also guaranteed to be stronger. You never need much romantic encouragement, so there is nothing to be lost by going all out for what you want. However, if you are looking for a partner, choose someone who is unattached; otherwise the problems could become enormous for everyone involved. For Leos who are already married, or involved in a long-term relationship, this is a year when you are likely to feel a greater need to settle down. Try to understand the emotional needs and wishes of your partner. On closer examination you will probably discover that their greatest wishes are actually yours as well. There is a certain amount of emotional maturing and growing up which even adult Leos now need to do. Once you have started, you will be amazed at how much you have been missing.

DAILY FORECAST

January–December 1995

JANUARY

1. SUNDAY. Quiet. This is likely to be a quiet start to the new year. Make the most of the opportunity to relax at home, especially if you are returning to work tomorrow. Focus on New Year's resolutions centering around health issues. You are ready to give up something which you know is bad for you, such as cigarettes or sugar. It is a good time to join a health club or recreation center in your area. For Leos who are unemployed at the moment, this is a favorable time for preparing a new resume and writing cover letters; this way you can make an immediate start. If you are thinking of a career change, discuss preliminary plans with your family or partner.

2. MONDAY. Lucky. Be prepared for some minor problems this morning, which probably involve having to sort out someone else's mistakes from the tail end of last year. For Leo business people, the afternoon is the best time for staff meetings. Conditions favor new advertising for the coming months. Employing an agency to produce professional artwork or a marketing slogan could be money well spent. If you are looking for rented accommodations this is a good time for asking around; you may hear of a place by word of mouth. Enjoy an evening out with your partner or that special someone. Together you can chart a new course that will keep you close as you reach for a dream.

3. TUESDAY. Demanding. Leo employees need to stay flexible. Someone in authority is expecting a great deal of you. Try not to let anybody force changes on you without having your say first. Take extra care with written work. It might be worth typing job applications; this way it should be easier to spot spelling or grammar mistakes. If you use a word processor in your work or at

127

home, guard against the risk of losing your work by making a backup disk. For Leos in permanent relationships there is a greater danger of an argument this evening. Although this is unlikely to be serious, you need to clear the air to keep a minor issue from escalating to something serious. Fatigue can be a sign of an oncoming cold. Go to bed early tonight.

4. WEDNESDAY. Stressful. For Leo business people this is likely to be a frustrating day. A new client may cancel an appointment at the last moment, which could be difficult to reschedule. Your best policy is to be patient; there is nothing to be gained from forcing the issue. A personal relationship has reached the make-or-break stage. You need to decide now between further commitment or making a clean break. Guard against making any hasty financial decisions. Seek out expert advice on long-term investment plans before signing a contract on the dotted line. If you are house hunting you may have to lower your sights to avoid going into debt beyond your means.

5. THURSDAY. Easygoing. If you have a spare room at home, this is a good time for taking in a lodger; the extra income could make the difference in balancing your personal budget. Do not forget to ask for references and for a deposit against breakage or unpaid bills. If your job does not supply you with a pension, consider setting up one of your own; be prepared to shop around for the best deal. Start with an affordable monthly or yearly allotment; you can always increase your deposits at a later date. This is a good evening for catching up with personal correspondence, which should include writing thank-you letters for gifts received at Christmas as well as making contact with old friends you missed over the holidays.

6. FRIDAY. Enjoyable. This is a pleasant end to the working week. You will be busy but not under intense pressure. If you are expecting a cost-of-living pay raise, you may get the good news today. Do not hesitate to ask about a bonus or other payments that are owed to you; there may have been an administrative error which could be easy to sort out. This is a good day for Leos who work from home; business should show signs of picking up again after the Christmas break. If you have been unable to cure a minor ailment through over-the-counter medicine, this is a good time to make an appointment with your family physician. If you do not have one, try to make an appointment with a recommended practitioner rather than picking a name out of the telephone book.

7. SATURDAY. Happy. For Leo students who are still on vacation, this is a good day for getting down to some studying; it should be easier to get back in the groove than you had thought. For Leo parents, this is a favorable time to spend a day out with your children. Something educational, such as a science museum or historical exhibition, could prove fun as well as instructive. This is an auspicious day for new romance for Leos who are single. You may meet someone new, but probably you will be making a date with someone you already know. This is a starred evening for a trip to the movies or the theater. There is a good possibility of picking up last-minute tickets at a bargain price.

8. SUNDAY. Deceptive. Although you may be actively revising your long-term aims and goals, this is unlikely to be a favorable day for making firm decisions. Make sure that you are clear in your own mind about where your real interests lie; only then should you begin to map out your future career. You may have to put duty before pleasure; this might mean having to entertain relatives or in-laws with whom you feel you have little in common. Make an extra effort to be sociable. If you are driving, guard against drinking over the legal limit; there is a greater danger of being stopped at a checkpoint. It would probably be safer and easier to use public transportation or call a taxi if out late tonight.

9. MONDAY. Disconcerting. If you are attending an interview today either for a promotion or a new job, guard against being complacent. The questions you are asked may be more searching than you had anticipated, but your thorough preparation should pay off. This is a good day for Leo salespeople who work on commission; some hard-won business could prove to be worth all the effort you have put in. Leo parents may have to fork out extra cash for a school trip or gym equipment. Teenagers may request more pocket money; do not hesitate to negotiate for household chores to be done in return. Avoid unnecessary risks in sport; there is a greater danger of personal injury.

10. TUESDAY. Pleasant. This promises to be a productive day for Leo business people. Meetings with new clients should prove successful. Take a valued customer out for lunch; this will probably feel more like pleasure than work. For Leos in managerial roles, this is a good day for departmental meetings; your powers of motivation should be at their strongest. It is also an auspicious day for new creative projects, especially for Leos who make a living from writing or crafts. If you are seeking to extend your social circle, this is a good time for joining a sports club or an evening class related to a hobby where you can be certain of meeting like-minded people. It is time to broaden your cultural horizons.

11. WEDNESDAY. Changeable. Leo employers should not put off interviewing potential candidates for vacancies. You may have to offer substantial relocation expenses in order to fill a top position. If you are looking for rented accommodations for yourself or your business, it may be more productive to place your own advertisement rather than replying to others; this way you can avoid viewing places which are unsuitable. Married Leos have to concentrate on dividing your time more equally between work and home. Partners are complaining that you do not spend enough time together. Try to reach a compromise which is acceptable to both of you. Evening favors such mutual activities as catching up with routine tasks at home.

12. THURSDAY. Sensitive. If you work as part of a team you may have a heavier workload than usual, probably as a result of someone else not pulling their weight. Try not to let this situation get out of hand. Being assertive about the problem now could save a lot of bad feeling in the future. Avoid making decisions without consulting others; a colleague may have the opposite viewpoint. This is unlikely to be a good day for fund-raising efforts. It may be time to revise your approaches and strategies. Do not hesitate to experiment with new ideas. A relationship which started as an innocent friendship may be developing into something much closer and deeper.

13. FRIDAY. Misleading. A colleague may be stirring up trouble at work. Try not to get involved in fighting their battles for them; there could be more to their grievances than meets the eye. This is a day when it is probably wisest to keep your own counsel in order to avoid confiding in the wrong person. Leos in managerial roles have to make decisions for the benefit of the group. Remind yourself that you cannot please everyone all of the time. This is also a good day for joining a club or society with a view to widening your circle of friends. For married Leos, this is a favorable evening for socializing with mutual friends either at home or at a favorite night spot.

14. SATURDAY. Good. If you have recently moved into a new home, this is a good day for shopping for household items. Do not overlook local outlets and antique shops. There is a greater chance now of picking up some beautiful furniture at a reasonable cost. You may also need to buy electrical goods, especially labor-saving devices such as a dishwasher or microwave oven. An ailing friend should be making a rapid recovery; a visit from you today would be greatly appreciated. For Leo parents, there may be a generous offer from a friend or relative to babysit this evening. Make the most of the opportunity to spend some uninterrupted time enjoying each other's company.

15. SUNDAY. Buoyant. Leos approaching retirement should be putting your financial affairs in order. Endowment policies designed to mature at this time are likely to yield healthy profits. No matter what your age, this is a favorable time for drafting a will; this way you can be sure that your estate will be divided as you want. If you have regrets about a recent split with your partner, this is a good day for attempting a reconciliation. Be prepared to talk through the problems; patience is your best policy in working toward a solution. Nostalgic feelings should be indulged. This is a good evening for sorting through old photographs and preserving your favorites in an album.

16. MONDAY. Worrisome. There may be cause for concern over a partner's health. It might be up to you to insist on a doctor's appointment or at least a day of rest. If you are at work today be prepared for constant interruptions. You may find that the only way to get things done is to go off by yourself to a quiet corner. If you are under pressure, your best policy is to establish priorities. If you are trying to prepare a report, you might have to postpone or delegate nonessential matters. Leos who are unemployed at the moment should devote extra time to researching the advertised job openings which interest you; a professional attitude can never fail to impress a prospective employer.

17. TUESDAY. Pleasant. This is a day when everything seems to be going your way. Have confidence in your own abilities as you forge ahead in your career. If you spend your working life mostly sitting at a desk or in the car, this is a favorable time for taking up a sport. A certain level of fitness is essential to your general well-being. If you are at home with small children, make a point of changing your usual routine; variety is just as important for youngsters as it is for you. Romance could be in the air for single Leos. Try not to be shy when it comes to letting someone know that you care. That special person is waiting for you to make some sign of encouragement.

18. WEDNESDAY. Easygoing. This is a good day for taking a fresh look at your personal image. This may include treating yourself to a new suit in the latest fashion. You might also decide to change your hairstyle. It is a good day for buying jewelry or other fashion accessories such as a hat or scarf. This is a favorable time for furthering your own ambitions. If you are bored with your current job, it is up to you to push for early promotion or keep your eyes open for something completely new. Married Leos need to pay extra attention to your partner's needs. Be sure to share with them your dreams and schemes for the future. Listen more than you talk and you should gain valuable insight.

19. THURSDAY. Unsettling. If you are unemployed at the moment you may be feeling a financial pinch. Make sure that you have claimed all the benefits to which you are entitled; ask for more information if you are not sure of your rights. Working Leos need to take extra care not to overspend. Be realistic about what you actually purchase with your money. This might mean having to stick to a stricter budget for a while. A new romance may not be going as smoothly as you had hoped. You may be discovering that your interests in life are entirely different. Try to aim for a successful blending of opposites; this way you should be able to learn from each other.

20. FRIDAY. Fortunate. For Leos who are at home, this promises to be an enjoyable day. You should be able to get through household chores more quickly than usual, then use the free time for relaxing or pursuing your own creative interests. For Leo business people, this is a good day for entertaining or accepting an offer of lunch from a new contact. If you are thinking of becoming self-employed, research the financial aspects in more detail; cash flow projections or your tax situation could be affected. It is a good day for opening a savings account at your bank. Remember that saving even a little each month is better than not saving at all; pay yourself as well as your creditors.

21. SATURDAY. Good. If you want to start redecorating your home, this is a good day for shopping for materials. There is a greater chance of finding just the wallpaper or shade of paint that you have been looking for. There are several jobs which you can do yourself rather than going to the expense of hiring a professional, but do not attempt electrical work unless you are sure of what to do. This is a good day for taking a closer look at your home security; this could include taking out homeowner's insurance or fitting more secure locks to doors or windows. It is a good evening for entertaining at home. Do not hesitate to experiment with new recipes; they could turn out surprisingly well.

22. SUNDAY. Demanding. Catch up with personal telephone calls to friends or family this morning to keep in touch or to make arrangements for a visit in the near future. Take extra care when handling sharp instruments such as kitchen knives or work tools. A lapse of concentration could result in a minor injury. Do not leave potentially dangerous items lying around, especially if there are young children in the house. Leos who are tired of preparing meals and cleaning up afterward should make a date to go out for lunch for a change. If you are in the early stages of a relationship, this is a good day for you and your partner to be together, away from other friends or family members.

23. MONDAY. Tricky. If you are looking for a new car, shop around before making a decision. A secondhand vehicle may seem like a bargain; but it would be wise to get the advice of an expert before you part with any cash. There could be faults which only a trained mechanic would find. Leos who are on the road today have to allow extra time for getting to appointments; traffic is likely to be heavier than usual. Try to avoid the routes where you know that road repairs are in progress. Social arrangements for this evening might fall through at the last moment. Try to take the disappointment in stride even if you feel someone has inexcusably let you down.

24. TUESDAY. Important. If you are planning to buy your first house, this is a favorable day for submitting a mortgage application; the process should be more straightforward than you imagined. You may also want to refinance your current mortgage in order to carry out major home improvements such as installing a new bathroom or kitchen. Be sure to get several estimates for the work before committing yourself to a contractor. If you share rented accommodations, this is a good day for establishing house rules to ensure that everyone does their fair share of the work. Consider opening a joint bank account for communal bills such as electricity or basic telephone service.

25. WEDNESDAY. Variable. You might start off the day feeling under the weather. There is a greater risk of an argument with someone close to you this morning. Try not to harbor resentful feelings, even if it seems that they are deliberately being difficult. This should be a productive day at work. Superiors are happy to leave you to your own devices rather than breathing down your neck. A colleague may ask if you can give a home to a pet. Think carefully about the responsibilities involved before you agree; you might not feel ready to devote the necessary amount of time to its care. Evening favors cleaning out a closet at home; put still usable items aside for charity. Conditions are ideal for late travel.

26. THURSDAY. Changeable. This is likely to be a fun day for Leos who work with children. Concentrate on drawing out their natural creative and imaginative abilities, perhaps through painting or drama. Money worries may be weighing on your mind. Do not fall into the trap of ignoring bills in the hope that they will go away. Let those to whom you owe money know if you are having difficulty meeting payments in full. This way you should be able to come to a mutually acceptable arrangement for spreading the cost over a longer period of time. For single Leos, this could be a lucky day for starting a new romance with someone you meet through a mutual outside interest.

27. FRIDAY. Exciting. For Leo business people, the working week is likely to finish on a high note. Efforts made in the past to secure new customers should pay off. This is a good day for meetings with other staff; a certain individual is more willing than usual to go along with your suggestions. If you are looking for a new job, take the initiative; write directly to the decision-maker instead of relying on an employment agency. If your romantic relationship has been going through a rough patch, this evening could be the perfect time for a heart-to-heart talk. Cut through the side issues if you want to isolate the real problems. Aim for practical solutions which suit you both.

28. SATURDAY. Good. For Leos who work on weekends, there is a greater possibility that today's workload will be heavier than usual. This may include having to put in some overtime, but the extra pay should make it worth your while. If you are at home, catch up with household chores. Pitch in if you have roommates even though you may feel you are doing more than your fair share. It is up to you to point out any changes you would like in who does what. Begin today to look for rented accommodations with a partner; a joint income gives you a wider choice of affordable places. Evening favors starting a diet; try to reeducate your eating habits rather than just aiming for an immediate weight loss.

29. SUNDAY. Misleading. You may be troubled by a strange dream from last night. Write it down; you might be able to make better sense of it at a later date. If you have no definite social arrangements today you are likely to suffer from a bout of boredom. Try to keep busy with small jobs around the home rather than letting time slip through your fingers. Someone close to you may be out of sorts, but there is little point trying to cheer them up. There could be a problem that they feel they need to solve by themselves. Try not to take their moodiness personally. If you have an important day at work tomorrow, review and make last-minute preparations early tonight.

30. MONDAY. Enjoyable. This is a propitious day for starting a new job, especially if you are entering into a partnership. For single Leos, a new romance could be in the cards with someone you have known for quite a while as a friend or colleague. Friends may announce their engagement today, or there could be news of a baby on the way for someone close to you. If you have recently fallen out with a colleague, swallow your pride and make the peace; they should willingly follow your example. Leo parents should be encouraging children to take up a new interest such as learning a musical instrument or trying out for a sports team. You, too, will enjoy a new hobby.

31. TUESDAY. Fair. Think before you speak. Loved ones may be short-tempered and could easily take offense where none was intended. Remember to tread lightly in order to avoid confrontations. This promises to be a productive day for Leo salespeople, but do not rely on verbal agreements until they are confirmed in writing. Perfecting your telephone technique could improve your success rate, especially when it comes to handling objections in a calm manner. This is a good day for buying soft furnishings for your home such as curtains or luxury linen. At a local garden center you may be able to pick up a house plant at a bargain price. Find out its watering, nutrient, and light requirements so that it will thrive in a new environment.

FEBRUARY

1. WEDNESDAY. Changeable. If you are house hunting, be prepared for frustration when it comes to making financial arrangements. You may not be able to secure the necessary mortgage without paying interest about the prevailing rate. Be realistic about the cost of renovating an old property. It might be worth paying for a private inspection to get a clearer picture of just how much work would be involved. Shop for casual clothes, but resist the temptation to open a credit account. This is a good evening for getting some physical exercise by working out at the gym or swimming a few laps. Double-check social arrangements for later; someone may have the wrong date or time.

2. THURSDAY. Positive. There could be welcome news about money coming your way through an inheritance or as a gift from a relative. Be sure to take expert advice when it comes to investing a large sum. Do not allow yourself to be rushed into making binding decisions without investigating all of the options open to you. A personal problem could be resolved by seeking some professional counseling. There are times when an objective viewpoint is the only way to regain a sense of perspective. A colleague may come to you for advice on a private matter. If you have the confidence to trust your intuition, you may be able to offer some valuable insights. This is a good day for buying vintage wine as an investment as well as a special treat.

3. FRIDAY. Buoyant. If involved in litigation at the moment, you may be able to make great strides today. Information helpful to your case that has been withheld could now come to light just in the nick of time. For Leos who are being sued, this is a favorable day for reaching an amicable agreement concerning financial settlements. If there are children involved in a lawsuit, be sure that you make their welfare a priority; their immediate and long-term security could be affected by what is decided now. This is a good day for planning a vacation with someone close to you. A weekend away could be especially appealing if you are settling happily into a new relationship.

4. SATURDAY. Lucky. If your brain is feeling rusty, remind yourself that it is never too late to return to education. This is a good day for finding out about evening classes in your area.

Learning a second language or studying a purely academic subject could be just the challenge you need, and a good way of expanding your social circle at the same time. Current Leo students are likely to benefit from discussing your studies with classmates. Their suggestions might provide the necessary inspiration for finishing a report or dissertation. Put this evening aside for socializing with longtime friends, with or without your partner. Conversation at a dinner party should be anything but boring.

5. SUNDAY. Mixed. You may have been putting off writing back to friends who live in far-off places. Try to find time this morning to drop them a line and put your conscience at rest. This afternoon is good for helping out with an affair in your local community such as collecting for a charity or manning a booth offering information. It is a good day to browse in flea markets or antique shops; there is a greater chance of picking up a bargain if you are looking for a special item to add to your collection. Try to get to know your favorite work colleagues socially. Invite them over for brunch or lunch or supper with their mate or partner. Do not talk shop too much if there are others present.

6. MONDAY. Unpredictable. Be careful not to cross swords with a superior. You may just have to accept that their decision on work matters is final, even if it is at odds with your own way of thinking. Resist the temptation to voice criticisms to your co-workers; there is no guarantee of their discretion. This should be a productive day for Leos in journalism or public relations. Interviews should give you plenty of creative scope, but take extra care not to misquote somebody on a political issue. This is a good day for claiming a tax rebate or overtime pay owed to you. Leo parents may be in demand this evening for help with homework; encourage your children to think creatively in solving problems.

7. TUESDAY. Sensitive. Work more closely than usual with your immediate colleagues. Workplace efficiency requires that the right hand know what the left hand is doing. Try to improve communications at all levels. A new staff member may be feeling somewhat at sea; make an extra effort to take care of them until they find their feet. Guard against tampering with your professional reputation. Remind yourself that it does sometimes matter what other people think. Avoid incurring the disapproval of a superior; make an extra effort to carry out instructions to the letter. If your mate or partner has had a stressful day, offer to cook the evening meal and to clean up afterward.

8. WEDNESDAY. Demanding. You may feel that someone close to you is deliberately going against your wishes. Perhaps they are nursing a grievance over an issue which you had thought was resolved. A confrontation might be inevitable if you want to get to the bottom of the matter. There is a greater risk of social arrangements with a friend being canceled, but there is apt to be a sound reason for this, such as illness in the family or being let down by a babysitter. Offer to visit them at home if they need company or moral support. Your partner may insist on inviting over a friend you dislike; if you are worried that you cannot be sociable, make your own plans for the evening.

9. THURSDAY. Difficult. For Leos involved with fundraising, this is likely to be a day of frustration. Generous offers may be slow in materializing or might fail to be honored at all. It is a good time for revising your strategies. You might find that you are wasting a lot of time and energy approaching the wrong people. Be willing to take on extra responsibilities at work if you are short staffed. A positive attitude is sure to be noticed by your superiors as well as making for a more pleasant working environment for everyone else. A friend who is suffering from financial hardship may ask you for a loan. By all means lend what you can, but make sure that repayment terms are clear.

10. FRIDAY. Fortunate. If you have had a particularly difficult time at work this week, the tide should turn in your favor today. Decisive action on your part could lead to several problems being resolved all at once. Have confidence in your own abilities; do not be afraid to step into the limelight and use your initiative when others seem reluctant to do so. If you want something done, it is probably better to do it yourself; delegating the responsibility could end up being more trouble than it is worth. It is a good day to engage in some sport. Invigorating exercise is the ideal way to recharge your batteries. This is a great evening for getting together with a group of friends at a favorite restaurant.

11. SATURDAY. Variable. It is in the Leo nature to be open with others, but it may be wiser to hold back with a certain individual until you are sure that personal confidences will be treated with respect. Not everyone necessarily rates loyalty as highly as you do. Someone from your past might get in touch today. This could bring back a mixed bag of memories for you; it is unprofitable to dwell on the less happy ones. If you intend to renew your acquaintance, your best policy is to start with a clean slate. You might not be in a sociable mood this evening. Do not allow yourself to be talked into a night out if you would really prefer to spend some time alone at home.

12. SUNDAY. Deceptive. You may be suffering from a low energy level. Be kind to yourself; take it easy even if this means having to postpone plans to visit friends or family. Remind yourself that your health is your most valuable asset; look after it. Take extra care when preparing food. Do not use it if an expiration date has already passed. It is far better to throw something away than risk food poisoning. Avoid alcohol today; there is a greater danger of overindulging, which could leave you feeling depressed or aggressive. Conversely, do not allow a loved one to take out a bad mood on you; you could both end up saying things which will be difficult to retract.

13. MONDAY. Changeable. For Leos at home with young children, this is a time for varying your usual routine by visiting friends or going to a local park. By getting out you avoid the vicious circle of your stress rising in direct proportion to their boredom. Teenagers may be demanding at the moment; your best policy is patience and a willingness to discuss openly the facts of life. Remember that the more they are able to confide in you, the more secure they will feel. This is a good time for starting to keep a personal journal. You may discover the answer to a long-standing problem just by writing it down. Take extra care when addressing correspondence; it is more likely to go astray.

14. TUESDAY. Disquieting. Exert more self-discipline than usual, especially when it comes to furthering your own interests at work. Aggressive tactics could get someone's back up. Make a conscious effort to be diplomatic rather than going on the attack. If you are driving, be sure to observe the speed limit; there is a greater risk of being stopped or of not being able to make an emergency stop. Try not to take unnecessary risks just for the sake of cutting your journey by a few minutes. It is a good day for having your hair cut, but let the hairdresser know exactly what you want. A loved one may accuse you of being selfish; ask yourself if there is any truth in this before you rush to deny it.

15. WEDNESDAY. Uncertain. If you have been struggling with difficulties in a personal relationship, there is a chance that this could reach a crisis point today. The time has come to lay your cards on the table; this way you can both decide if it is worth making a fresh start. Be extra vigilant about your personal belongings. There is a greater risk of losing your wallet or having it stolen. A credit card may have expired without your realizing it; make sure that a replacement card has been sent to the correct address. Find out the balance in your account before writing a check. There may not be sufficient funds to cover a major purchase. Paying in cash allows you to escape finance charges.

16. THURSDAY. Sensitive. For Leos who are self-employed, this is a good time for seeking extra work. New customers may also come your way through referrals from exising customers. Try to secure payment up front wherever possible; delays in larger bills being paid could have a disastrous effect on your cash-flow situation. Refrain from extravagance; you could end up spending far more than you can really afford in an effort to impress someone. Cheer up your place of work with fresh flowers on your desk or a colorful calendar on the wall. This is a good evening for trying out a new recipe at home just for your family or to share with friends from work. Go easy on the spices.

17. FRIDAY. Positive. Think about ways to boost your income. Unattached Leos might consider part-time restaurant work, especially if it pays cash in hand as well as the added perk of tips. It is a favorable time for approaching your boss for a pay raise. Look for ways to save on tuition fees by learning from a self-help book or working without pay as an apprentice to an expert. Trade in an old vehicle against the cost of a new one, but make sure that the paperwork is up to date before you part with any money. This evening favors visiting a brother or sister who lives in your area. There is a lot of family news to catch up on, including an announcement that will please you.

18. SATURDAY. Mixed. Messages are likely to be flying fast and furiously this morning. There will probably be a mixed bag of personal calls and requests for payment of overdue bills. If you are looking for rental accommodations, buy as many newspapers as possible to see what is being offered in your price range. Be systematic; put together a list of places which sound suitable and make definite appointments to view them. Excellent references could swing a landlord's decision in your favor. It is a good day for getting to know new neighbors. If they have recently moved to the area they would probably appreciate some information about local public transportation, where to shop for fresh food, or the name and phone number of a reliable handyman.

19. SUNDAY. Misleading. If you are part of a large household there is a greater danger of arguments today when it comes to apportioning bills. It may be wise to have bills itemized in the future so that there can be no dispute over who owes what. If you are out with small children this afternoon, make an extra effort not to let them out of your sight; there is a greater risk that one of them could wander off. If you are nursing a broken heart over a recent breakup, now is the time to put painful memories behind you. Try to value the positive aspects of being single, especially your newfound freedom. Now you can live your life in the way that suits you best.

20. MONDAY. Variable. Leos who work from home may be slowed down by a series of interruptions. If you do not have an answering machine, this is a good time to invest in one so that you can return your calls during the most convenient period of the day. Meetings with other staff at work are unlikely to go as smoothly as you hoped; you might have to agree to disagree over certain issues. It is a good day for bringing insurance policies up to date, especially for house contents. Make sure that you are covered for accidental damage as well as theft. Take extra care when filling in forms; write first in pencil so that you can alter mistakes before inking the final form.

21. TUESDAY. Fair. Someone in your immediate family may receive an exciting proposition for a new job. This could mean a breakthrough in their career, but may involve moving away from the area. Guard against being quick-tempered today, especially with someone close to you. But if someone continues to irritate you, it would probably be better to say so. By expressing yourself you can avoid harboring resentment, which is bound to explode eventually. This is a good evening for entertaining at home, but make sure that you have all necessary ingredients before you start cooking. You may have to discourage offers of help from one of your guests; his or her well-meaning efforts could turn out to be more of a hindrance than a help.

22. WEDNESDAY. Changeable. Business associates could be enthused about new schemes. However, it may be up to you to point out the financial implications of what they propose. There is a chance that they have not really thought matters through on a practical level. If you have an advertising budget, this is not the best of days for taking risks with new publications; a trial run could be worthwhile if the cost is negligible. For Leos who are unattached but looking, this is a good day for taking the initiative. You are likely to get a positive response if you ask someone out or even strike up a conversation with a complete stranger. Remember, nothing ventured is nothing gained. Act confidently.

23. THURSDAY. Happy. Look for ways to develop a hobby into a money-maker in anticipation of making your living from the activity you enjoy doing most. If life seems to be all work and no play, now is the time to make changes. Do not fall into the trap of thinking that you cannot afford the adjustment time. If you resolve to take up an outside interest which really appeals to you, the time factor will probably cease to be a problem. Children can be entertaining company; entering into their world could be just what you need to take your mind off personal pressures. If you are divorced, this is a favorable evening for introducing your children to the new romantic interest in your life.

24. FRIDAY. Good. This should be a pleasant end to the workweek. You can afford to be more relaxed about your professional duties. Remind yourself that good health is often directly linked with an ability to handle or minimize stress. If you are applying for a new job, you may have to endure a medical checkup; take advantage of having a thorough examination at someone else's expense. This is a good time for taking up yoga or meditation, especially if you are not into physically demanding sports. Leo homeowners may not be actively looking for a lodger, but a workmate might need a spare room for a short while. Do not dismiss the idea too quickly; extra cash could come in handy.

25. SATURDAY. Changeable. Try to get through household chores quickly this morning. Resist a tendency to daydream that slows you down and leaves you short of time for more interesting tasks. This is a good day for practicing a musical instrument or learning a new song. If you have a roll of film to be developed, make sure that you use a reputable company; there is a greater danger of some beautiful shots being spoiled in the developing process. Now is a good time to handle repairs around the house, but leave plumbing work to an expert or you could end up with a flood. This evening favors relaxing at home with a good book. A rumor currently making the rounds is pure speculation.

26. SUNDAY. Deceptive. Remind yourself that this is traditionally a day of rest. Spend at least part of the day just relaxing or working on a project which has nothing to do with your job. Time spent with your mate or other loved one could not only be enjoyable but essential. You may realize that several weeks have slipped by since you last had a meaningful conversation. Do not hesitate to let family members know how much you value their company. Children are likely to be out for the day, involved in their own interests; make the most of the opportunity to enjoy some peace and quiet. This is a favorable evening for a first date. Choose a destination where you will not have to compete with loud music.

27. MONDAY. Uncertain. Combine tact and firmness in your business dealings. Refuse to rise to the bait if an associate appears to be deliberately antagonistic; arguments are likely to end in stalemate. Stick to the facts, especially if you are reporting to a superior. This is a good day for entertaining influential clients, perhaps by taking a hospitality box at a sporting event. It is a lucky day for placing a moderate bet, but guard against getting carried away or you could end up out of pocket. For Leos in managerial roles, this is a favorable day for conducting interviews for forthcoming vacancies. Be wary of someone who seems to be exaggerating their past achievements.

28. TUESDAY. Difficult. Try not to let financial anxieties escalate out of proportion. Panic moves, such as cashing in a bond or an endowment policy before the maturity date, could be regretted later. Take a careful look at your spending habits, and make some adjustments accordingly. If you share a joint account with your partner, be sure to discuss your ideas for economizing with them; this way you can avoid being accused of meanness or bossiness. Someone close to you may be suffering a bereavement. Although there is probably not much that you can do or say that will help, make an extra effort to be emotionally supportive until they are ready to talk and make new plans.

MARCH

1. WEDNESDAY. Changeable.   Interest payments on loans or an overdraft could be the root of current money problems. Resolve to dig yourself out of debt once and for all. Be methodical; start by reducing the most expensive debt first, such as a credit card. An offer of extra work may come out of the blue. This could be worth taking on even if it is only temporary because it might lead to other opportunities. An ongoing health problem could be resolved by a change of diet or by cutting out one particular food. Guard against harboring small resentments toward your partner over a recent disagreement; they would probably welcome some frankness rather than silence.

2. THURSDAY. Lucky.   A pay raise for either you or your partner could come into effect sooner than you had expected. It may be a wise move to open a savings account to start banking some of the extra before you get too used to having it. Remember that expenditure always rises to meet income. For Leo students, this should be a particularly productive day. The afternoon is good for work which will look good on a future resume. Marks on work returned to you today should be more than satisfactory. Begin now to plan how to finance further education for yourself or your children. This could include research on the choice of schools in your area that offer a reduced tuition for residents.

3. FRIDAY. Variable.   Today is good for long-distance traveling; there are unlikely to be delays. A fellow passenger could prove to be entertaining company. You may even decide to swap addresses or telephone numbers so that you can stay in touch. If you have a clear idea about how you want to spend your summer vacation, this is a favorable time for booking reservations. There is a greater possibility of a substantial discount for an early reservation. Avoid getting into arguments at work. If you stop and think before giving an unsolicited opinion, you will probably realize that it would make no difference anyway. A co-worker is set on a certain course of action; let them learn from their own mistakes.

4. SATURDAY. Deceptive.   You are likely to have itchy feet and be eager for some action. Partners may accuse you of being absentminded or of daydreaming too much. If you have no firm commitments, this could be a good time for taking off by yourself for the day. Take a trip to a local park, or enjoy more cultural pursuits such as visiting a museum or art gallery. Make sure that you have enough money in your wallet before setting off; you may need more cash than you had thought. Leo students might find it difficult to settle down to work. It could be quicker to change a plan rather than battle on with one which is proving too complicated or confusing.

5. SUNDAY. Sensitive. There seems little point in trying to put your foot down about a relationship matter. You are unlikely to get very far with ultimatums. Accept that you and your partner will not always want to do the same thing at the same time. Try not to impose rules or you could find yourself being accused of obsessive behavior. Socializing will probably revolve more around duty than pleasure. Make an extra effort not to let others bore or irritate you. This may mean taking the initiative in introducing more interesting or controversial topics of conversation. You could find that you have more in common with a certain individual than you thought.

6. MONDAY. Mixed. This is apt to be a taxing start to the workweek. Meetings are likely to run over schedule, leaving you pressed for time for other matters. A nonessential appointment may have to be postponed to a later date. It is a day when you cannot afford to make decisions without consulting colleagues; others need to know that their interests are being taken into consideration. Avoid a head-on confrontation with someone in authority; there is a greater risk that you will come off the loser. A new romance needs to be tended with care. Try not to force a commitment from someone; they may need more time to make up their minds about the future. Patience is your ally.

7. TUESDAY. Positive. This is a particularly favorable day for Leos who are starting a new job. Just guard against trying to run before you can walk; learning the ground rules first is essential. It is a good day for installing new technology in your place of work. This could be anything from a fax machine to computer terminals. You will be amazed at how these changes can make office work both quicker and more efficient. Conditions are ripe for approaching your boss about a promotion or pay raise. Leos who are new to parenthood may find the demands of a baby difficult to handle. Remind yourself that things will certainly improve once you can establish a routine. Do not hesitate to ask for help from those close to you.

8. WEDNESDAY. Strenuous. A disagreement with a friend could leave you feeling downhearted. Try not to let the problem grow out of all proportion. A difference of opinion does not have to mean the end of your relationship. Be cautious when it comes to lending money; someone may be only too quick to take your generosity for granted. It is up to you to make the terms clear in all financial transactions. Follow up a verbal agreement with written confirmation on both sides in order to avoid misunderstandings. Social arrangements for this evening need to be checked with all persons involved. It may be wiser to arrange your own transportation rather than relying on somebody else for a lift.

9. THURSDAY. Happy. The week may not have gone particularly well so far, but things should now take a turn for the better. A letter from someone you have been waiting to hear from could get the morning off to a cheerful start. A colleague who has been a thorn in your side in the past may now show themselves willing to meet you halfway. Do not stand on your dignity; grab the chance to be friendly with people who can make life easier for you. Spend some time catching up with administrative work either at home or at your place of work. Evening favors going out with a group of friends. Meeting new people could be in the cards; a new romance may blossom with someone you find easy to talk to.

10. FRIDAY. Quiet. Make the most of this quiet day when you should not be under pressure. Make or confirm a forthcoming appointment either for yourself or your partner. If a health worry has been nagging at you for a while, now is the time to do something about it. Ignoring the problem will not make it go away. You may find that your anxiety is unfounded. This is a good day for working alone. Let others know that you do not want to be disturbed, especially if you are trying to clear your desk for the weekend. This evening favors a relaxing night at home, either with a loved one or just to enjoy your own company. Get to bed early.

11. SATURDAY. Buoyant. You will probably feel like taking it easy; you need to recharge your batteries after the heavy week at work. Avoid stressful situations. Shopping for nonessential items should be delayed until a time when you are feeling more energetic. Begin now to plan a surprise party for a special person's anniversary. You may suspect that your partner is keeping worries to themselves for fear of alarming you. This is a good day for encouraging them to confide in you; be prepared to listen before offering your own opinions. Try to help them reach practical solutions while at the same time being sympathetic to their views.

12. SUNDAY. Uncertain. Plans for the day could be subject to upheaval. If you feel that someone is taking you for a ride, do not be afraid to say so; they may be taking advantage of your open nature. Guard against getting drawn into someone else's domestic problem. Trying to act as the peacemaker is likely to be a thankless task. For Leo parents, this afternoon is good for spending time with your children. Play a sport which you can all participate in, or join forces to complete a project all are anticipating finishing. No matter what your age, it is a good day for learning a new game such as bridge or backgammon. You could be surprised at how competition livens up an evening at home.

13. MONDAY. Variable. Take extra care when washing delicate clothes; there is a greater risk of a favorite item being damaged. It may be worth it to spend money on drycleaning. Finding an outfit for a special occasion could prove difficult. Look into the cost of having something specially made for you. This way you can guarantee getting a good fit and exactly what you want. In work matters there should be ample opportunity to further your own ambitions. However, guard against pushing someone else into the background in order to get your own way. Your victory is likely to be short-lived if you upset the wrong person. It is a good evening to get some physical exercise to combat built-up stress.

14. TUESDAY. Unsettling. It would probably be in your best interests to keep your opinions to yourself. A certain individual could be quick to misinterpret what you say and be only too willing to cross swords with you. Take extra care with written work, especially if you are preparing a report for a superior. Make sure that you have included all of the necessary backup information before you submit the final copy. Avoid carrying too much cash this afternoon; there is a greater chance of loss, which you may not discover until it is too late to backtrack your movements. Do not take the risk of wearing jewelry with a faulty catch. Take a favorite piece in for repair or to have a safety clasp put on.

15. WEDNESDAY. Fair. Collect money that is owed to you. Do not allow someone to put you off with lame excuses; they are probably just stalling for more time. For Leos who are becoming increasingly bored on the job, this is a favorable time for giving serious consideration to other offers. But guard against falling for a get-rich-quick scheme. Thorough investigation of any new company is a must. Look into alternative medicine, especially for a problem which more conventional remedies has failed to cure. Obtaining help could turn out to be more expensive than you had anticipated, but whatever it costs to obtain relief is money well spent. Positive thinking can have curative power also.

16. THURSDAY. Sensitive. For Leos who have been unemployed for some time, today could be a turning point. Recent efforts to secure work are likely to pay off, even if it means accepting a job quite different from what you had in mind. If you are involved in court proceedings, this is a favorable time for settling financial matters out of court. This may not be entirely straightforward, but with sensitivity on both sides you should be able to reach a mutually acceptable arrangement. It is a good time for taking in a lodger if you have a spare room. The financial help could make the essential difference between barely surviving and having a little money to spare; you may even make a new friend in the bargain.

17. FRIDAY. Routine. Letters you have been expecting could all arrive at once this morning. Take the trouble to reply at length to friends who have been out of touch for some months. This is a good day for Leo salespeople working on the telephone. You might be able to close some long-standing negotiations as well as set up appointments for next week. Call to purchase advance tickets for a show scheduled for the weekend; this way you can avoid disappointment or the tedium of having to wait in line. A brother or sister may need your company this evening, perhaps to discuss a family problem. Try to be gracious if this means having to cancel other social arrangements.

18. SATURDAY. Deceptive. Avoid driving if you are at all unsure about the safety of your vehicle. There is a greater risk of breaking down, which could prove especially expensive if you are not a member of an automobile association. If you plan to park at a meter, make sure that you have enough correct change beforehand; do not trust to luck that you will return before the meter maid does. It is a good day to shop for luxury items, although you should guard against being swayed by a hard sell before you have really made up your own mind. If you are a frequent letter writer, consider investing in some personalized stationery that looks especially impressive for professional correspondence.

19. SUNDAY. Fine. This is a good day for handling practical jobs around the house. There are many tasks, such as putting up shelves or stripping wallpaper, that you are able to do yourself rather than incurring extra costs from a professional. Simple instruction manuals can show you how to tackle the jobs you have never done before. If you have a garden, this is a favorable day for weeding or clearing away debris. Working with your hands gives you a sense of satisfaction and achievement. Devote some time to filling in forms related to your home, such as insurance or an application for a home improvement loan. This evening favors entertaining someone whose stimulating conversation you enjoy.

20. MONDAY. Useful. This is an especially productive day for Leos who work from home. If you are feeling overwhelmed by the amount you have to do, your best policy is to prioritize. Make a list of tasks in order of importance and check them off as you go. You could be surprised at how quickly you can produce order from chaos. Someone close to you may have been suffering from depression. By all means offer what support you can, but keep in mind that you are not their therapist. What they really need may be someone to encourage them to seek professional help. A partner could be irritable this evening; offers to cook or do other household tasks are sure to be appreciated.

21. TUESDAY. Harmonious. Leos who are urgently seeking new living accommodations may have to consider taking a day off from work to hunt around properly in the locales of your choice. Consider saving money by buying secondhand furniture or appliances. Items in thrift shops could be in surprisingly good condition and are also likely to be dramatically cheaper than the brand-new model. Be innovative at work this morning. Changes in routine which you suggest can be readily adopted by others who see the sense in what you say. Plans for a weekend away might have to be scrapped when a friend is forced to pull out. Visit your travel agent to investigate alternatives for a longer vacation.

22. WEDNESDAY. Fair. Most Leos are quick to show their enthusiasm for new projects, but today you have to contain your natural exuberance. Remind yourself that not everyone shares your sense of adventure. A colleague who lacks self-confidence might even feel a little intimidated by you. Make an extra effort to be objective when it comes to assessing how your behavior affects others. You cannot afford to waste time. Someone in authority could be piling on the pressure to ensure that a deadline is met; putting in some overtime may be unavoidable. This is a good evening for breathing new romance into your relationship. Having fun together is an essential ingredient to happiness.

23. THURSDAY. Disappointing. Leo business people may have to entertain clients today. If they are from overseas, be sensitive to cultural differences. Negotiations could be a struggle, but perseverance should win through in the end. If you are taking a client out to lunch, be sure to select a restaurant where you know the food and service are good. This is not a day for taking risks or for going on hearsay. Studying can be a source of frustration. Guard against battling on with work which makes no sense to you; you will gain far more by asking for help from a tutor or fellow student. An evening out may fall short of your expectations, but leaving too early could cause offense.

24. FRIDAY. Variable. This is a favorable day for attending interviews or mailing off job applications. Guard against a tendency to exaggerate your past accomplishments; stick to the facts, and let your references do the praising for you. You have the will-power to start a new health regime; an appraisal of your diet and exercise habits is long overdue. Try not to let your newfound enthusiasm lead you to set unrealistic targets. You are more likely to succeed if your initial goals are easily achievable. Leo parents may have to exert your authority this evening. Although you do not relish being seen as a disciplinarian, this is one of those times when you have no alternative. Be firm but fair.

25. SATURDAY. Deceptive. Household chores probably seem like a never-ending battle. If you and your partner work full time, consider some domestic help during the week so that you will have more free time to yourself on the weekends. It is a favorable afternoon for a family outing. Younger children would probably enjoy an amusement park or any place where they can make a lot of noise. Older children may opt for something more cultural, such as an exhibition or a museum. This is a good time for getting together with other parents to discuss mutual concerns. It is a favorable evening for a first date, but be prepared to work at drawing the other person out.

26. SUNDAY. Changeable. The day is likely to start off on a happy note. Time spent with your partner can give you a deep sense of contentment. For Leos who are unattached or who live alone, this is not a time for being by yourself. There is a greater risk of self-pity. Pick up the phone and arrange to meet a friend; once you are out and about you will probably be glad that you made the effort. Keep a careful eye on how much you spend later in the day. You need to guard against a tendency to be extravagant. It may be safer not to make any large bet this afternoon, although gambling with a small amount of money over a short period of time could make you a winner.

27. MONDAY. Positive. This morning should be excellent for conducting delicate business negotiations. Personal charm can work wonders when it comes to winning confidence, both in you and in the business you represent. This is a good day for starting a new job. Your new work colleagues are likely to go out of their way to put you at ease. Pay close attention to your sixth sense; an inkling that a certain individual could become a thorn in your side may be justified. This afternoon could be a trying time if you are stuck at home with children. There is a greater risk of suffering from feelings of isolation. Make an extra effort to contact other parents at home in your area.

28. TUESDAY. Unsettling. There are some days when you cannot seem to do or say the right thing. Unfortunately, this could be one of them. Try not to let other people's unfriendly behavior get you down. They may be caught up with personal problems that you know nothing about. On the other hand, do not let anyone use you as a scapegoat for their mistakes. It is possible to show compassion to others while still looking out for yourself. Outstanding bills need to be paid today if you want to avoid additional interest costs. If you cannot pay a debt in full, at least pay what you can; something is better than nothing. Avoid a social gathering where you know you will feel out of your depth with certain people or uncomfortable with one particular person.

29. WEDNESDAY. Lucky. Today is a favorable period for joint financial matters. Your partner may bring home welcome news of a pay raise or a healthy bonus. A gift of money from someone in the family could also be in the cards. It should be easier now to put personal anxieties into their true perspective; you may even be able to laugh at a problem which seemed overwhelming a short while ago. Use your intuition at work. Learning to read between the lines can put you in a powerful position. Keep plans for furthering your own ambitions firmly under your hat so that you will not have to rely on anyone's discretion but your own. Keep personal confidences for those whom you love and trust.

30. THURSDAY. Fortunate. This is a propitious day for Leos who are being interviewed or tested, especially if this is for the next stage in your career. All the hours put into study and planning are likely to pay off. Conditions favor all self-improvement endeavors. If you are unable to find the necessary time to attend college full time, look into the advantages of a correspondence course where you can choose the hours which suit you best. If you are in the process of claiming damages, this is a favorable day for meeting with your attorney. You may even be able to get a settlement without further hassle. This evening favors socializing with people from different cultures; you may be surprised at how much you have in common.

31. FRIDAY. Good. For Leo employees who have compensatory days off, this is a good time for leaving on a long weekend. A change of scenery and routine could lift your spirits and you may wonder why you do not go away more often. If your calendar is empty for the weekend, this is a good time to fill it; remind yourself of the importance of having something to look forward to, no matter how small. This is likely to be a productive day for Leos who work in the field of education. Students can be responsive and rewarding to teach. If you are unattached, romantic interest from a colleague will probably not be welcome, but decide if you really want the flirtation to go further.

APRIL

1. SATURDAY. Variable. If you have been going through a rough period with your partner, be prepared for a showdown today. There is a strong possibility that tensions could reach the breaking point. Some screaming and shouting may be unavoidable, but the positive side is that this could clear the air, leaving you both ready for more rational discussion. You might have to decide between making renewed efforts or facing a parting of the ways. Do not fall into the trap of staying for the wrong reasons. If you have brought work home from the office, try to get this out of the way as quickly as possible. This is a day to minimize stress and concentrate on activities you enjoy.

2. SUNDAY. Pleasant. Give active support to local community affairs, although fund-raising may not be as easy as you had hoped. Try not to be angered by what may appear to be meanness on the part of others; remember that not everyone has the wholehearted approach of generous Leos. Your interests favor cultural pursuits of all kinds, especially viewing an art exhibition or going to see a play. Check your local newspaper's entertainment guide; there could be a choice of new movies worth seeing. If you have young children, a matinee performance aimed at their age group could be great fun for all of you. Do not put off writing a letter to a loved one who now lives too far away for you to pay a visit.

3. MONDAY. Enjoyable. Leos usually have more than their fair share of energy, and today is no exception. You can probably achieve anything to which you put your mind. Make hay while the sun shines by taking on new challenges at work. For Leos who work in personnel, this is a favorable day for conducting interviews. Your judgment in selecting the right person is likely to be correct, even if others are not equally convinced. This afternoon is good for teamwork of all kinds. Pooling ideas and resources could result in finding a surprisingly easy solution to a problem. Meet up with a friend this evening who has been away, perhaps on a cruise. Be prepared for a late night.

4. TUESDAY. Changeable. Mail could be heavier than usual this morning. This might include letters or postcards from friends who are living or traveling in another country; an invitation to stay for a vacation later in the year may well appeal to you. Bills are likely to be hefty but probably no more than you expect. You may have to revise your budget for the month in order to pay your debts on time. For Leos working for a charity, this is a favorable day to launch a mail campaign aimed at raising public awareness and boosting donations. The initial outlay should pay for itself several times over. This evening is good for making long-distance telephone calls, but keep the cost in mind as the seconds tick away.

5. WEDNESDAY. Fair. Friends can be a mixed blessing. While one seems to be nothing but trouble, another could be the tower of strength you need in a moment of crisis. There is a lesson to be learned: see less of the people who leave you feeling drained and more of those who make you feel good about yourself. Discourage someone from entrusting you with money or anything valuable; there is a greater risk that you could lose the very thing that was handed to you for safekeeping. For unattached Leos, this could be a lucky evening for new romance. This may be with someone from a different culture, but you should share the same ideas about how to have fun.

6. THURSDAY. Quiet. You will probably feel the need for some uninterrupted time to yourself. If you are at home, try not to worry too much about catching up with housework. Put a few hours aside for relaxing with a good novel or listening to your favorite music. It is a favorable day for catching up with odds and ends at work, and also good for preparing reports or doing research of a confidential nature. Information can come your way through unofficial channels. If you are looking for work, remember that who you know is sometimes more useful than what you know. Someone in an influential position might be prepared to pull strings for you. Be generous in contributing to a charity close to your heart.

7. FRIDAY. Mixed. The less you disclose about your business tactics the better. There is a greater danger of information falling into the wrong hands. Correspondence relating to legal matters needs to be handled with extreme caution. Someone may be only too quick to misinterpret what you say. Guard against signing any binding document or statement which is unclear. Put any doubts to rest by seeking expert advice. In your personal life, you may be going to great lengths to avoid someone who has become a nuisance. Excuses or hints are unlikely to be effective with a person who is aware only of their own needs. Be forthright and direct if all attempts at subtlety fail.

8. SATURDAY. Deceptive. You could wake with the remnants of disturbing dreams this morning. Write down what you can remember; you may be able to make sense of it later in the day. This morning is good for offering your services to others. An elderly neighbor would appreciate a helping hand with shopping or gardening. It is also a good day for visiting grandparents, especially if their health has lately been giving you cause for concern. Partners can be temperamental this afternoon. You may have to walk on eggshells to avoid a distressing argument. Do not fall into the trap of rearranging your own plans for the evening in an effort to fit in with someone else's demands; it is unlikely to pay off.

9. SUNDAY. Variable. This is a good day for pursuing your own special interests. You may have to remind your partner that you need to lead separate lives from time to time; too much togetherness can be as negative as too little. Make a renewed effort to complete a complicated job or project which is beginning to weigh on your mind; a fresh start could be called for if you are not happy with results so far. Remind yourself of the sense of achievement you will feel when it is done. This is a favorable evening for cultural pursuits such as going to the theater or listening to live music. To avoid embarrassment, take extra cash or your checkbook with you; it could be an expensive evening.

10. MONDAY. Buoyant. The beginning of the workweek is likely to get off to a flying start. There is a greater possibility of your efforts being acknowledged or praised by those in authority. For Leos in managerial roles, this is a good time for working at motivating your staff; encouragement and affirmation can work wonders. Show someone that you have faith in their ability and their confidence will grow right before your eyes. Conditions favor job interviews, especially in the legal or educational professions. A letter from a friend residing at a distance can be entertaining; make an extra effort not to wait too long before writing back. This is a favorable evening for going out to eat with other members of your family.

11. TUESDAY. Disquieting. If you are paying bills by mail, it is very unwise to send cash; it may never reach the person for whom it was meant. Use a check or money order instead. You might need proof of payment at a later date, so be sure to hold on to the receipt. Final demands for household bills should be paid as quickly as possible; otherwise there is danger of your telephone being disconnected or your power being turned off. For Leos who are out of work at the moment, this is a good time to ask about benefits due you; a government bureaucrat may have overlooked your paperwork. If you are seeking a babysitter it should be worth trying a recommended agency for your own peace of mind.

12. WEDNESDAY. Routine. Scan the newspaper for secondhand sales, especially if you are looking for items for children. A new baby can be expensive; nearly new goods at vastly reduced prices should help ease the financial pressure. If you are at home with young children, make an extra effort to be enterprising. With your help they will invent their own games which cost nothing but a little of your time. Current investments may not be doing as well as they should. Make an appointment to meet with your financial adviser in order to investigate alternatives. A new romance is likely to be going strong, but guard against overwhelming someone with attention.

13. THURSDAY. Sensitive. If you are starting a new job you may find that you have inherited an administrative tangle. Your best policy is probably to concentrate first on establishing an effective filing system, which could transform the efficiency of your workplace. A new broom sweeps clean; changes you suggest are likely to be welcomed by others. Conditions favor trading in an old car for a new one, but an expert's opinion might be advisable before you part with any cash. Make sure that the service record is up to date on both vehicles. A surprise telephone call from an old flame might lead to your renewing the acquaintanceship strictly on a friendship basis without the stress of romance.

14. FRIDAY. Auspicious. Mail is likely to be more abundant than usual. Fortunately, this should consist mostly of personal correspondence rather than bills. A brother or sister has some exciting news about a new job opportunity that has come their way. Send out invitations to friends for a party; remember that you do not need a special occasion in order to bring your favorite people together. For Leo business men and women, entertaining clients from out of town can prove taxing. If there is an accent or language barrier, some minor misunderstandings could result. Make an extra effort to be clear. This evening is good for trying out a new restaurant recently opened in your area.

15. SATURDAY. Misleading. Leos who make a living creating can bring a piece of work to fruition this morning. If you work in journalism, be on the lookout for a good story right under your nose; do not let a rival beat you to the punch. Correspondence can be confusing, especially letters or reports related to legal matters. Make sure that you fully understand the implications before committing yourself to a course of action. Long-term aims and goals might seem further away than ever today. Be more realistic when it comes to setting targets for yourself. The here and now is just as important as the future. Some of the most positive events in the next few months will result from chance, not plotting and planning, but you must stay alert for the opportunity.

16. SUNDAY. Changeable. Other household members can be bad-tempered with one another today. You may find that the role of peacekeeper falls to you, but guard against interfering in the personal issues at stake. There is nothing to be gained from trying to fight other people's battles for them. Concentrate on practical jobs around the home such as mending broken furniture or repotting house plants. Be wary of taking the law into your own hands when it comes to family matters. Try not to make decisions on behalf of others; they would probably prefer to be consulted. This is a favorable evening for inviting close friends or relatives for a simple supper at home and some good conversation.

17. MONDAY. Mixed. This morning is good for working from home; this way you can start the workweek in a more relaxed manner. Make a start on spring cleaning. You may not realize how much there is to do until you actually begin. For Leo parents at home with small children, this could be a favorable time for initiating a child-minding trade-off with neighbors. The children would probably enjoy the variety as much as you would appreciate a few hours to yourself. At work this is a day when you need to treat superiors with extra respect. You might be curtly reminded of who is boss if you speak out of turn. Try to keep rebellious feelings under tight control.

18. TUESDAY. Good. This is a good day for a more experimental approach to your work, especially if your job involves creating new business. Boldness can pay off by bringing you into contact with the real decision-makers. Someone secretly admires your confidence. Working with children is likely to be entertaining. Their sense of fun should rub off on you, helping to put any personal problems back in their true perspective. Do not neglect joint financial matters. Leos in a committed relationship may decide to save an extra amount each payday in bonds or other securities designed to mature at retirement age. Keep your premiums to a realistic level.

19. WEDNESDAY. Sensitive. Restrain yourself from overspending, especially on clothes or accessories. By all means treat yourself to an item you have been eyeing, but try to be practical at the same time. You may hanker after something beautiful, but ask yourself how often you would wear it. If you are attending an exercise class such as aerobics, guard against pushing yourself too hard. Reaching a full fitness is a gradual process; forcing your body beyond its real ability could result in muscle strain or more serious damage. This is a good day for picking up vacation brochures from your travel agent. An early booking for your summer vacation might mean a substantial discount.

20. THURSDAY. Uneventful. If work has been going at a frantic pace recently you should get a breather today. With the pressure off for the time being, this would be a good day to catch up with odds and ends. Try not to put off till tomorrow what can be done today. Remind yourself that boring tasks need to be done sooner or later, so it might as well be now. A minor health worry can suddenly show signs of clearing up by itself; maybe it was related to stress. Place an advertisement if looking for a lodger or a handyman. Give yourself plenty of time to find the right person. Be sure to ask for local references and to check them carefully. Guard against being misled by appearances.

21. FRIDAY. Variable. This morning is a trying time at work. It may be impossible to make sense of a task because someone has not been clear in their instructions. Try not to waste too much time on routine matters, especially if there are other staff to whom you can delegate work. Afternoon is favorable for business negotiations of all sorts. You may have to stroke someone's ego if you want things to go your way. This evening can be good for socializing with old friends from your school days. Anecdotes from the past can be a source of great fun. A new love affair could be blossoming into a happy, secure relationship. Relax and enjoy it.

22. SATURDAY. Fair. This is a good day for spending time with your partner. Make an extra effort to enjoy the simple pleasure of each other's company. This is not a time for pushing your own plans; there is a greater risk that you will be accused of nagging. Because of the busy week there may be a backlog of personal telephone calls to return. Someone close to you might want to offload their problems. By all means hear them out, but do not allow them to tie up too much of your time. It is a good day for long-distance traveling. Do not hesitate to strike up a conversation with a fellow passenger; they could prove to be entertaining company. Someone at a distance is hoping you will apologize.

23. SUNDAY. Disquieting. Social arrangements can be subject to last-minute changes or might be canceled altogether. Try to take disappointments lightly; there is no point in raising your blood pressure about a problem over which you have no control. Money worries could be uppermost in your mind. Think of ways in which you can economize; consider giving up an expensive habit, at least for a short while. Children can be expensive when it comes to paying for their outside interests or for a school outing. A new romantic relationship is likely to cause Leo singles some anxiety. Suspicions that someone is not being entirely honest with you could be correct.

24. MONDAY. Good. Today is auspicious for new business ventures. Financial backing could be easier to secure than you had thought. For Leos involved with charity work, this is a favorable time for fund-raising efforts. Approaching a celebrity to lend their name to the cause can help boost public awareness. Your upbeat attitude makes this a fine day for interviews, especially if you are seeking a position in one of the caring professions such as counseling or social work. An individual who has been difficult to work with in the past may now start to unbend. This is the time to put your professional relationship on a more secure footing. You could find that you have mistaken their shyness for arrogance.

25. TUESDAY. Uncertain. You may not be able to avoid taking on extra responsibilities at work. This could include standing in for a colleague who is away on leave. Be sure to keep an up-to-date record of the work you are covering on their behalf. Presentations to superiors or new clients need to be carefully structured and researched in depth. People expect you to have all the answers at your fingertips, so try to be as well prepared as you can. Consider taking up a sport or activity aimed at reducing the stress in your life; swimming or yoga could work wonders. A bone of contention between you and a loved one needs to be resolved once and for all if harmony is to be restored.

26. WEDNESDAY. Variable. This is a good day for furthering your education, especially if additional qualifications are a necessary step to promotion. Employers are likely to support your request for time off to attend classes. It is a good day for business conferences out of town, but double-check arrangements before you set off. There is a greater risk of reservations for hotel accommodations going astray. Purchase train or plane tickets in advance in order to guarantee a seat. Legal matters need to be handled with caution. Guard against putting your signature to any statement or contract which is not entirely satisfactory in all details. This way nobody can accuse you of misrepresenting the facts.

27. THURSDAY. Lucky. For Leos who are unemployed at the moment, this is a good day for a renewed onslaught on the job market. A stroke of luck can put you in the right place at the right time. Employment agencies which you had written off could be worth contacting again. They are now likely to be offering more positions which sound suitable. If you are planning to go abroad soon, this is a favorable day for renewing your passport or applying for necessary visas. There is less risk of delay through administrative errors. Carefully fill out forms, especially if you are applying for a mortgage or a large loan. Insurance claims can be sorted out with a minimum of delay.

28. FRIDAY. Deceptive. If you are traveling a long distance this morning be prepared for delays which may keep you at a standstill for a while. Make sure that your luggage is clearly labeled; there is a danger that another traveler could mistake your bags for theirs. Keep valuable or important documents in your carry-on luggage; this way you are unlikely to lose them. Business meetings this afternoon can be tricky to handle. Do not rely on being able to predict someone's behavior. Your best policy is to keep an open mind and stay flexible. A farewell for a colleague who is moving on to new pastures could develop into quite a party. Be extra careful of your alcohol intake if you are driving.

29. SATURDAY. Buoyant. For Leo students and recent graduates, this is a prime time for seeking a weekend job. A few hours of work could give your bank account a welcome boost without interfering with your studies. You may be able to widen your social circle at the same time. Do not overlook entering competitions on the local or national levels. Someone has to win, and it might as well be you. For single Leos, a sentimental letter or phone call from a former lover could tempt you to try a reconciliation. If your general aims and goals in life are in keeping with theirs, it might be worth a second chance. But if you know you are each heading in different directions, it may be kinder to you both to stay away.

30. SUNDAY. Variable. Aim for a balance between duty and pleasure. You might feel like pulling out of a family get-together, but to do so risks hurting someone's feelings. Try to reach a compromise between what others want and what you would prefer to do. A colleague from work may call to see what you are doing today. An invitation for supper or to go to the movies will probably be greatly appreciated; this could be the beginning of a firm friendship when you discover how much you enjoy their company. Conditions favor participating in sporting activities of all kinds. But guard against playing solely to win rather than just enjoying the game for its own sake.

MAY

1. MONDAY. Lucky. The team spirit is what counts at work. Best results come from everyone being willing to pool their ideas and resources. Working alone can prove to be laborious; someone else's input could provide the inspiration you need to get a project finished. Concentrate on endeavors aimed at making the world a better place in which to live. This might include joining a political organization whose policies and views parallel your own. If a friend comes to you for comfort concerning a personal problem, an objective approach will probably be the most effective. This way you can help them to realize that an easy solution could be staring them in the face.

2. TUESDAY. Fair. You may need to remind yourself that mixing business with pleasure is not always good. Make an extra effort to divorce your personal feelings from your professional judgments. Leos in managerial roles must guard against promoting the wrong person out of a misguided sense of loyalty. Assess candidates on the strength of their individual merits or you could be accused of favoritism. Business dealings are favored with companies headquartered overseas. One in particular could prove to be a regular source of revenue. For Leos who are single at the moment, there is a greater chance of a friendship blossoming into a deeper attachment.

3. WEDNESDAY. Happy. The middle of the working week is likely to be unusually quiet. Make the most of the opportunity to catch up with minor but necessary tasks such as filing or letter writing. This is a favorable day for Leo salespeople to devote some time to research; you may be able to identify a new market for your product. Appointments for later in the week are likely to be more successful if you allow time for thorough preparation now. Professional ethics could be more important than you had realized; make sure that yours are above reproach. Studying can be fun as well as educational. Attending a seminar or lecture should help to broaden your own intellectual horizons and open up new options for you.

4. THURSDAY. Calm. Keep things to yourself when it comes to business plans and tactics. Associates do not always have to know what goes on behind the scenes. You can afford to trust your own judgment when deciding on a course of action. Partners may be keeping a problem to themselves for fear of worrying you. It is up to you to spot the symptoms of anxiety and encourage them to confide in you. As well as offering moral support, two heads can be better than one at finding a solution. This is a favorable day for arranging an appointment with a doctor or dentist either for yourself or another member of your family. Do not overlook the importance of regular checkups.

5. FRIDAY. Fine. For Leo business people, this is a good day for meetings of a confidential nature. Prepare a budget for the coming months, especially if you are approaching the end of your financial year. You may need to allow more money for administrative costs. Consider taking out private medical insurance if this is not provided for you by your employer. Take extra care to read the small print of a contract. Ask for more information if you are not entirely clear about what is included and what is not. This evening favors relaxing at home. Someone older than you may want to talk about the past and relive some old memories that you barely remember.

6. SATURDAY. Useful. This morning favors tackling housework and other domestic chores such as washing or ironing. If you have older children at home, insist that they make a fair contribution. You may need to remind yourself that they are not babies anymore. This afternoon is good for getting out of the house. Browsing around bookshops or markets can be fun; bargains should be easier to find. For recently separated Leos, this is a good time for picking up the pieces of your social life. Concentrate on rediscovering the advantages of being single, including having more personal freedom. Mix with those who are fun to be with and who make you feel good about yourself.

7. SUNDAY. Mixed. It would be worth getting up earlier than usual this morning, especially if you plan to go out for the day. This way you can get boring jobs out of the way and leave yourself free to enjoy your leisure time. You will enjoy playing sports such as tennis or basketball. Horseback riding can be fun even if you have never tried it before, but be sure to put yourself in the hands of a skilled instructor. If the weather is fine, this is a favorable afternoon for throwing an impromptu barbeque. You might be surprised at how many people turn up, so be generous when buying provisions. This is a good evening for attending an event in your community, such as an amateur dramatics production. Leo performers enjoy showing off in the spotlight.

8. MONDAY. Disquieting. A crisis at home, such as a burst pipe, could disrupt your usual morning schedule. Do not delay arranging for repairs, even if it means having to take the morning off work. House hunting can be a frustrating experience. It may seem as if you just cannot find what you really want. But do not give up hope too easily; you may regret settling for something second rate. If you find the ideal place, do not hesitate to make an offer right away. There is a greater risk of being beaten out by another buyer. A loved one may be suffering from depression over a broken relationship. Be prepared to sacrifice your own plans for this evening if they need your company.

9. TUESDAY. Demanding. Money matters demand your attention. You may have to do some careful juggling in order to make ends meet. It might be wiser not to write any checks unless you are sure that you have sufficient funds as deposit. This way you should be able to avoid extra bank charges. Try not to borrow money from a friend; they may secretly resent being asked even if they do not show it. For Leos who earn a living from creative pursuits, this is a day when you could suffer from the notorious artist's block. Try not to waste too much time struggling with something that will not come together. More research can get the ball rolling once again.

10. WEDNESDAY. Fair. Leos who are self-employed may have to deal with a cash flow crisis this morning. Certain customers might be delaying payment beyond an acceptable time limit. You may have been too trusting; try to secure a substantial deposit for new orders or contracts. This is a good day for small cash-in-hand jobs. Later in the day favors written work of all kinds, which might include letter writing to boost public awareness of a humanitarian cause. Confide your secret hopes and feelings in a diary; putting things down in black and white can be surprisingly insightful. Children are likely to demand your time and energy, but they will be great fun as well.

11. THURSDAY. Buoyant. This is an auspicious day for Leos who are taking a test. If you have never learned to drive, this is a good day for your first lesson. Both long journeys and short trips within your neighborhood are sure to be enjoyable. Traffic is unlikely to be heavy and parking spaces will probably be easier to find. You can afford to let intuition be your guide in work matters. Others will be impressed at your ability to sum up a situation at a glance. Shop for secondhand items through the classified ads in your local newspaper. Leo students might be able to pick up used books and other learning materials in very good condition. The day also favors hobbies and self-improvement activities.

12. FRIDAY. Strenuous. If you are planning to take your summer vacation with friends, this is a good day for finalizing details. There could be some dispute over the choice of a resort. Try to ensure that everyone is happy with the final decisions; this way you are less likely to hear complaints when you are away. For Leos who are unemployed, this is a favorable time for using your own initiative. You cannot afford to rely on luck alone. Write to the companies you would like to work for rather than waiting for them to advertise openings; your application might land just at the right time. This is a good evening for going out with a brother or sister; family updates can be full of pleasant surprises.

13. SATURDAY. Happy. If you are looking for rental accommodations, this is a favorable day for hunting. You may be tempted by a place slightly beyond your budget; decide if it is worth making other sacrifices to live there. Make sure that you are clear about the rules before you sign a tenant's agreement; for example, you might not be allowed to keep a pet. Auspices are good for working on your home, especially if you are restoring an old place to its original grandeur. You may discover some beautiful features which had been covered up by the previous owners. This evening can be good for dressing up and going out in style, perhaps to a recommended restaurant or nightclub.

14. SUNDAY. Changeable. For Leos who are enthusiastic gardeners, this is a good day for putting in new plants. Those with colorful blooms are likely to thrive the best as well as being beautiful to look at. But guard against overdoing physical work today; be aware of your own limitations or you could end up with aches and pains. Members of your household could be at each other's throats this afternoon, as their personalities clash. Your best policy is not to get involved. Let them fight it out between themselves and you will not risk being accused of interfering. You might end up doing more harm than good if you appear to be taking someone's side.

15. MONDAY. Fortunate. This should be a fun start to the workweek. You can afford to take a less serious approach to your work; colleagues warm to a sunny nature and your sense of humor. Remember that the enjoyable side of work can be the friendship and in-house jokes. You have every reason to feel confident about your own abilities; do not allow others to pour cold water on your new ideas. Have faith in your own beliefs. An unexpected gift from someone close to you can bring great pleasure. They may be remembering your generosity to them in the past. Take the lesson to heart that in the end you always reap what you sow. This evening can be lucky for a first date or any new beginning.

16. TUESDAY. Slow. There may be concern over a child's health. You might have to take a day off work to stay at home with a youngster. Even if the symptoms appear not to be serious, seeing the doctor can confirm this and put your mind at ease. An older child might be angling for a day off school. Be alert to the possibility that this might be a sign of a deeper problem; try to find out if they are getting along with the other children. Schedule a conference with the class teacher if you are worried. This is a good day to interview for a new job; there is a greater chance of striking up an immediate rapport with a potential employer. Evening favors entertaining an important client.

17. WEDNESDAY. Unsettling. Superiors can be in a difficult mood. It may be wise to wait until they are more approachable before bringing a work problem to their attention. At the moment you are unlikely to get either a sympathetic or a helpful hearing. Remind yourself that they may be suffering from personal worries which they are unable or unwilling to discuss. Leo salespeople need to guard against being too pushy. There is a greater danger of losing an important client if they feel that they are being hustled. Guard against making assumptions when it comes to dealing with other people's grievances; you might be barking up the wrong tree altogether. Listen more than you talk.

18. THURSDAY. Manageable. Take a long look at your general state of health. Now can be a good time for making changes in your diet such as eating less fat or cutting out a high-calorie food which you know is bad for you. Extra vitamins and minerals can boost your vitality. Cutting down on cigarettes or alcohol, or giving up altogether, might be easier than you think if you have the determination. If you work in an office where others smoke it would not be unreasonable to request a no-smoking area; let the democratic process rule and put it to a vote. Conditions favor closing a business deal which has been hanging in the balance for some time. This evening can be good for socializing with friends from your workplace.

19. FRIDAY. Variable. This is a good time for buying presents for someone close to you. Remember to keep the receipts if you are buying clothes so that they can exchange something if it turns out to be the wrong size. You may decide that your place of work needs cheering up. Ask your employer for permission to buy plants or pictures. At first, they may be reluctant to part with the money, but they are likely to change their tune when they see what a difference these little touches can make. It is a good evening for going out with your partner. Discussing current events can lead to some heated exchanges when your views differ; just remember how boring it would be if you always agreed on everything.

20. SATURDAY. Sensitive. Try to put work out of your mind this weekend, especially you married Leos with children. Partners may be complaining that you attach more importance to work than you do to them. If there is any truth in the accusation, try to find ways of dividing your time more equally. Your partner is likely to be more than willing to reach a compromise as long as their needs are being met. This is a good day for moving. Take extra care when packing valuable or breakable objects; there is a greater risk of something being ruined beyond repair. For Leos who are unattached, this evening can be a good time for joining a social club. Meeting new people could prove to be a great tonic.

21. SUNDAY. Fair. Leos are likely to be feeling out of sorts this morning. If there is no particular problem on your mind you may be short of sleep; sleep later, or take a nap this afternoon. Problems which seem insurmountable when you are run-down often fall into place once you recharge your batteries. If you usually play chef on weekends, this is a good time for handing over the cooking to someone else for a change. Alternatively, suggest that you go out for lunch; this way everybody gets a break, so it should be worth the expense. A surprise visit from a friend can turn a quiet evening at home into a party. They may have exciting news which they want to tell you in person.

22. MONDAY. Disquieting. Financial matters need your attention. A letter from your bank or credit card company can start the day off on an unhappy note. Do not delay in repaying; remember that they are more likely to cooperate with you if you keep them fully informed of your circumstances. Paperwork relating to joint finances can be laborious but necessary. Leos who are newly married may have to think about obtaining additional life insurance or making a will for the first time. The idea might not appeal to you, but there is no point in being superstitious. Make an extra effort to be realistic. You have a duty to those you love to make proper provisions for them for the future.

23. TUESDAY. Changeable. This morning favors efforts at making your home burglarproof. If you live in an area where break-ins seem to be on the increase, you may want to consider fitting locks on the windows as well as the doors. Installing an alarm system could be expensive but is one of the best deterrents of all. Learning basic self-defense could also be worthwhile, especially for Leo women who live alone. You should be able to get details of classes through your local police station or library. This afternoon is favorable for conducting legal business. If you need advice on your rights in a controversy, contact a lawyer who is recommended by a friend or the bar association.

24. WEDNESDAY. Good. Going on vacation for the first time with a new partner can make or break the relationship. This is a favorable time for discussing what you both look for in a holiday. If you have different expectations it is better to find out now so that you can work out a compromise. A new romance can make life rosy. Do not be afraid to let someone know how much they matter in your life. For Leos who work in the arts, this should be a productive day. Your natural creativity is at its most powerful. This is a good day for setting out to learn about a new academic or vocational subject. Picking up a new skill, such as keyboarding, can be quick and easy.

25. THURSDAY. Deceptive. If you are traveling a long distance you may be prone to a bout of travel sickness. Carry some medication with you just in case. Trips to other countries in the not too distant future necessitate bringing your inoculations up to date. Although these can leave you feeling under the weather for a few days, this is infinitely preferable to coming down with the real thing. You may also have to produce proof of your shots in order to be granted entry into certain countries. For Leo students, preparing for the end-of-year examinations can be demanding. Be methodical; do not forget to schedule some leisure time to keep yourself fresh and free from fatigue.

26. FRIDAY. Quiet. Your employer could leave you holding the fort while they take a long weekend. There are unlikely to be any major crises; just be sure to keep things ticking over as smoothly as possible. Have confidence in your own judgment if you are called upon to make decisions in someone's absence. If you have been out of work lately, today could bring new opportunity your way. You may hear of a suitable opening through word of mouth. Devote some time to revising long-term career goals. You might have to acquire extra skills to keep your plans on course. This evening favors a quiet dinner with your partner or a few close friends. Discuss home improvement plans in depth.

27. SATURDAY. Auspicious. This is a good day for lending support to a function in your local community. This could include visiting an exhibition of work by local painters or craftspeople. You may find an object of beauty for your home or office. A friend may ask you to sponsor them in a marathon walk or swim; try to give as generously as you can. If you are physically fit you might consider taking part yourself; testing your own powers of endurance may be an irresistible challenge. Deal with paperwork on behalf of someone who is suffering a loss. Take responsibility for the administrative side of home finances and there is less chance of overdrawing your joint bank account.

28. SUNDAY. Sensitive. A weekend job that you took when you needed to boost your income may no longer be essential. This is a good time for handing in your notice and reclaiming your weekends for yourself. Entertaining friends at home this afternoon can be fun, but you may have to restrain certain individuals from making too much noise. Loud music could be too much for an elderly neighbor to cope with. Try to avoid arguments with your partner later in the day, especially over money matters. You may have conflicting ideas about how to spend disposable income. Guard against losing your temper, even if you feel that you are being unfairly criticized.

29. MONDAY. Mixed. You may discover that not everyone has the same philosophy about life as you do. Someone you thought was a close ally at work could show their true colors by breaking a promise or withdrawing support at a time when you need it most. Try to learn from the experience; be more discerning when it comes to placing your trust in others in the future. Young children can be more of a handful than usual today. It may seem they never stop talking or asking questions which are tricky to answer simply. Your best policy is to be patient; try to let some of the chatter wash over you while you get on with other things. Accept a friend's offer this evening without any pangs of guilt.

30. TUESDAY. Disquieting. A recent disappointment at work may leave you feeling unable to cope with additional responsibility. Try to realize that you are suffering from a momentary lapse in confidence. There is no reason you should not push ahead with plans to better your career prospects. You may feel that someone who has been with your employer for a long time is deliberately trying to block your progress. Although this might be the case, it is probably due to jealousy over your undoubted ability. Try to take the competition in stride; let your achievements speak for themselves. This is a day when you should refrain from extravagance. You could easily spend far more money than you can really afford.

31. WEDNESDAY. Good. This is a good day for working in privacy. You are likely to get far more done if you can arrange to be undisturbed. For Leos thinking of becoming self-employed, this is a good time for doing some research. The financial factors need special attention; for example, find out how your tax situation would be affected and what your initial outlay is likely to be. There is no point in approaching the bank for a loan or a line of credit until you have worked out some basic sums. For single Leos, a new attraction can leave you intrigued but unsure. It may be better to keep your feelings to yourself until you are more certain that the interest is mutual.

JUNE

1. THURSDAY. Disconcerting. Deal discreetly with problems at work. This morning is good for off-the-record meetings with someone in an influential position; they are likely to have your best interests at heart. Teamwork can be unproductive unless someone is prepared to take the lead. Enthusiasm alone is not enough to bring a project to fruition. It could be a case of too many cooks spoiling the broth, so try to be clear about what it is that others expect of you. Married Leos may be struggling with feelings of guilt if you are attracted to someone new. Remind yourself that this is a totally natural reaction, but it is up to you to keep the situation in check.

2. FRIDAY. Mixed. If you are at home today, this morning is a good opportunity for an onslaught on the housework. This way you can leave the weekend free for pursuing more interesting activities. Introspection is not always healthy, but this is a time when reviewing recent mistakes in your personal life could be helpful. Knowing where you went wrong can help you to avoid repeating the same patterns in the future. Be aware of your own inner strength, and do not allow others to make you feel inadequate. Although partners may be in an argumentative frame of mind, do not swallow your own feelings just to keep the peace. Maybe they should be told just how alienated you feel when they go on the attack.

3. SATURDAY. Fine. You can afford to spend more time doing the things you enjoy, either alone or in the company of others. Let household chores take a backseat for once. Younger children are likely to be less demanding of your time. They may be engrossed in new games of their own which do not require adult supervision. Try to turn a blind eye to the inevitable mess. This evening can be good for socializing with a group of friends. One in particular may seek you out for a heart-to-heart talk about a personal problem. Some plain speaking is needed if you are going to be of any real help. Do not be afraid to give your friend a hearty dose of constructive criticism.

4. SUNDAY. Disquieting. Family get-togethers can be more hard work than fun. A certain individual may insist on dredging up past grievances in an attempt to win an argument. Try not to get hooked into exchanging recriminations; this is unlikely to be profitable and may even widen the rift between you. If you intend to start decorating at home, make sure that you have enough of the necessary materials. Running out of paper or paint halfway through can be frustrating. A social arrangement for this evening may be the last thing you feel like doing. It might be better to postpone it until a later date rather than going along under duress. What is favored tonight is any form of artistic self-expression.

5. MONDAY. Sensitive. Leos who work in the finance department of a company or as bill collectors may have to get tough with those who still owe money. If the friendly approach has failed, you might have no option but to resort to a threatening letter in order to get a response. If you are self-employed, try to avoid giving credit to new customers. Someone can be quick to take advantage of the chance to spend more than they should; your cash flow situation could suffer as a result. Single Leos may be attracted to someone in authority at work. This could be an infatuation. Be alert to the potential problems of mixing business with pleasure. Stay away from speculation or any kind of gambling.

6. TUESDAY. Fair. This can be a good day to apply for a promotion or a new job. While you may be offered the position, you are unlikely to secure the salary you had hoped for. It is up to you to decide if it is worth taking on extra responsibilities now in the hope of securing better prospects for the future. Going out for lunch with a friend can be expensive because they are short of money and you end up paying for them. Remind yourself that they would probably do the same for you if the situation were reversed. Minor health problems can be improved through relaxation techniques such as yoga or meditation. Try swimming to relieve general aches and pains.

7. WEDNESDAY. Happy.   A cheerful disposition can be your best ally. Someone at work who is difficult to get along with will probably thaw eventually if you show a willingness to be friends. Leo salespeople can afford to be more informal with clients. Try not to overlook the value of entertaining conversation as well as talking about your product. Bring written work of all kinds up to date. You are in a good position to explain a new procedure. If you are writing a report, concentrate on the essential details; you have a tendency to go off on a tangent. This evening can be good for an informal dinner with other members of your family.

8. THURSDAY. Lucky.   This is likely to be a productive day. Your local community can be buzzing with all sorts of human interest stories; it is up to you to ferret them out and also check the gossip to see if it is true. This could be an excellent day for canvassing on behalf of a political party; people can be easily drawn into conversation. Listening is often the first step toward shaping policies which will benefit society as a whole. Conditions favor market research or sales via the telephone. Promoting new products could prove easier than you had hoped. A dinner party at a friend's should make for a fun evening; other guests can be well informed and lively company.

9. FRIDAY. Demanding.   This can be a tiring end to the workweek. Meetings are unlikely to go as smoothly as you would like. It may seem as if someone is determined to put a crimp in your plans. Your best policy is to keep cool; try not to overreact to criticism. If you can stick to your guns in the face of fierce opposition, others may think twice about trying to push you around in the future. Leos in the process of buying property could run into some problems. Financial arrangements appear to be sound, but the difficulties could lie with a seller who wants to push the price up or even pull out altogether and cancel the deal. Patience pays off.

10. SATURDAY. Buoyant.   This morning is likely to be uneventful. Take the opportunity for a leisurely start to the day, perhaps by treating yourself and your partner to breakfast in bed. Spend some time on the garden, especially if the weather is fine; new plants can transform a plain border into a blaze of color. Surprise visits from friends in the afternoon can liven up the day. If you are at home alone, this is a good time for picking up the telephone and arranging a night out or inviting friends over for dinner. Single Leos could meet someone new through your existing social circle, just when you least expect it. Evening is good for group activities of all kinds.

11. SUNDAY. Uncertain. This morning is a good time for cleaning out closets and drawers at home. You may be amazed by the amount of junk that you have managed to accumulate over the years. Make an extra effort to be ruthless when it comes to throwing things away, especially if you need the extra storage space. Items which are still usable, such as books or old clothes, can be donated to the next charitable sale. Later in the day is good for sporting activities of all kinds, although you might receive some flak from your partner for not spending enough time at home. Introducing a new partner to long-standing friends can be tricky; they need time to get to know and like each other.

12. MONDAY. Unsettling. Guard against making rash promises. Someone is relying on you far more than you had realized. Try not to make arrangements unless you are certain that you can honor them. Applying for a new job is unlikely to be straightforward. You might feel that your age counts against you because you are perceived as either too young or too old. Concentrate on selling your abilities and proven track record; personal confidence could tip the balance in your favor. Leo parents may be under pressure from children to allow them more freedom. Try not to deny requests without thinking them over; remind yourself that you cannot keep them tied to the apron strings forever.

13. TUESDAY. Demanding. For Leo employees, the prospect of going to work this morning may be more difficult to cope with than usual. You might feel tempted to call in sick, but this is unlikely to go over well with those who have to cover for you. Once you are there it should not be as bad as you thought. If you work on commission, this may not be a productive day. Clients who have made promises to you could fail to come up with the goods for a variety of reasons. Take to heart the lesson that closing a sale means getting a check; verbal agreements count for little. Children can be exhausting work this evening; you all need to get to bed early.

14. WEDNESDAY. Difficult. A health problem could be nagging at you today. If you are delaying seeing a doctor for fear of what they will say, this is the time for taking your courage in both hands; make an appointment for the next available opening. The matter could be far less serious than you imagine. Shop for a birthday present for a special friend, but try not to get carried away when it comes to cost. It is the thought that goes into a gift that counts. If you work in a large office, guard against taking part in gossip. Someone may be looking for allies in what amounts to a private vendetta; refuse to get involved. The boss will notice your ability to remain neutral but on good terms.

15. THURSDAY. Changeable. If you are looking for rental accommodations, this is the day when something suitable is likely to turn up. This could happen quite unexpectedly; be prepared to view an apartment at a moment's notice. If you have a spare room, this is a favorable time for taking in a lodger. Begin with a trial period to avoid the risk of being stuck with someone you cannot get along with even though they seemed ideal to begin with. Do not forget to ask for receipts for anything you buy today. Later in the day is good for spending time alone with your partner. It may suddenly dawn on you that they are also your best friend; tell them so. Children, too, need an extra hug for reassurance.

16. FRIDAY. Calm. For Leos in managerial roles, this is a good day for meetings with individual members of your staff. Some of them may be more willing to confide to you in private rather than letting their problems be known in a general meeting. Your support and discretion at this time can help someone move forward in their career instead of falling by the wayside. The human touch can work wonders. It is a good day for holding out the olive branch to a loved one with whom you recently had a falling-out. They are probably feeling just as bad as you are. Try not to let pride stand in the way of a reconciliation. This evening can be good for going out to a club or restaurant with someone you are trying to impress.

17. SATURDAY. Disappointing. Leos who have been in a healthy relationship for some time may be thinking of making it permanent. This is a good time for beginning a trial period of living together, which is the real proof of how compatible you are. A new romance can set your head spinning, but try not to rush into making commitments too quickly. It is the Leo nature to be impulsive, but the novelty of anything new may wear off sooner than you had anticipated. This is a favorable day for making contact with your parents or other older members of the family. They probably appreciate an effort on your part to touch base more frequently, either with a phone call or a visit.

18. SUNDAY. Unpredictable. If money problems seem to be going from bad to worse, this is a good time to dig yourself out of debt. Write down all your income and expenses to see how they compare. Once you have done this, finding ways in which you can economize may be more obvious. Spending less on your social life might be unavoidable. Try to get into the habit of inviting friends over rather than always meeting them in a bar or restaurant. Someone may try to talk you into joining a health club with them. Make sure that it is the sort of place you would enjoy before you part with a membership fee. If you go along with suggestions just to keep the peace you could feel resentful.

19. MONDAY. Variable. If your job involves handling large amounts of money, this is a day when you need to take extra precautions. Try not to leave cash lying around; there could be a thief in your midst who would find the temptation impossible to resist. It is a good time for submitting an application for a mortgage or other loan well in advance; the process could be subject to more delays than usual. Consider opening a separate savings account earmarked specifically for emergencies such as structural repairs to your home. Investing money in home security is a good idea. Learning how to install new locks yourself could save you from having to rely on the services of a locksmith. A large dog is also a good safeguard.

20. TUESDAY. Good. Today is auspicious for Leos setting off on vacation. Your journey is likely to be pleasant as well as true to schedule. If you are going away on your own you do not have to worry about being short of company; you are likely to make new friends almost immediately. A holiday romance could be just the tonic you need to boost your self-esteem. Deal with legal matters of all kinds. If you are appearing in court today, decisions on the bench can go in your favor. It is a favorable time for taking examinations, especially a final test. The questions could be exactly what you had hoped for, and you should come out knowing that you have passed.

21. WEDNESDAY. Deceptive. Avoid getting involved in debates centering on controversial issues such as religion or politics. Even if you do not have particularly strong views yourself, there is a greater risk of upsetting someone else who does. A colleague may feel that they are being discriminated against at work on the grounds of their nationality. If this is evidently true, then you might question the ethics of staying in the job yourself. But this is not a time for rash decisions; secure another position before you leave your current one. Take extra care when buying clothes. Something may not be as well made as it first appears despite the cost. Keep all receipts just in case.

22. THURSDAY. Productive. For Leo business people, this is likely to be a productive day. Deals you have been nursing along behind the scenes could now come to fruition. Patience and discretion can pay off when it comes to beating competitors. An employee who has been with you for a long time could be hankering after a promotion; maybe this is the time to delegate more of your own responsibilities to let them prove their ability. If you are attending a final interview try not to feel intimidated by the big boss; remind yourself that most powerful people are really quite human behind their facade. This evening can be favorable for meeting future in-laws; just relax and be yourself.

23. FRIDAY. Lucky. This should be a satisfying end to the workweek. Leo salespeople could find it easier than usual to reach your targets or even go considerably over them. If all or part of your salary is based on commission, this is likely to be a bumper week. This can be a good time for Leo employers to introduce a bonus scheme; this could do wonders for staff motivation. It is a favorable day for taking a collection for a popular colleague who is about to leave; co-workers can be more than generous in their donations. Conditions favor fund-raising ventures of all kinds, especially those aimed at providing better services locally. The community spirit is alive and well, and Leos will be encouraged to take a leading role in special events.

24. SATURDAY. Fair. A new job may include the proviso that you be willing to travel. This can mean being away from home on a regular basis. Married Leos need to discuss the situation in depth with your partner; remember that the decision should be as much theirs as yours. If you are contemplating starting your own business, try to avoid signing over your house or other personal property as security. Investigate alternatives to putting your property at risk. You may be able to find a guarantor who has faith in your scheme. This is unlikely to be a good evening for entertaining at home, especially if you have had a tiring week. Eating out with friends or a loved one should be far more enjoyable. If children act up, do not be afraid to lecture them in public.

25. SUNDAY. Changeable. Today favors participating in sporting activities of all kinds. If you have always felt that you are not the sporty type, you may be surprised at how much you can enjoy a match just as a spectator. Leos who are unattached may be introduced to someone you find instantly attractive, but you need to guard against a tendency to impress. They might mistake your enthusiasm for showing off. Do just as much listening as talking. Someone cannot fail to like you if you show a genuine interest in getting to know them. Children can be bursting with excess energy. Ignoring them will only make them worse; concentrate on finding games which will capture their imagination.

26. MONDAY. Sensitive. Teamwork is important, especially if you are part of a large department. The left hand needs to know what the right hand is doing; otherwise overall efficiency can break down. A new colleague is looking to you for assistance when it comes to learning the ropes. This may be the beginning of a friendship which could last a long time. If you are unemployed at the moment, do not hesitate to claim benefits due you. Avoid relying on being told automatically what you are entitled to; it is up to you to insist on more information. You might be able to get a tax rebate on previous earnings, and you have nothing to lose by requesting the necessary forms and sending them in. A small gamble is apt to pay off.

27. TUESDAY. Happy. This is a good day for working from home. You need extra peace and quiet in order to get a new project up and running. The less you say about new business ventures at the moment the more successful they are likely to be. Well-meaning associates are full of advice, which will only serve to confuse you rather than help. This is a productive day for Leos who work in the health field, especially in a laboratory. There can be welcome news of extra financial backing for research which was in danger of being abandoned. A friend who is hospitalized is making a surprisingly swift recovery; a visit from you or others in their circle of acquaintances would probably be much appreciated. In matters of romance, let your heart rule your head tonight.

28. WEDNESDAY. Quiet. This is unlikely to be a busy day for Leo employees. You may be able to take a longer lunch break than usual, or use the extra time for personal shopping or meeting up with a friend. It is a favorable day for a visit to the dentist or the optician for a checkup. For Leos who are approaching retirement, this is a good day for making plans for the future. It may be wiser not to discuss these too much with the rest of the family just yet;

give yourself time to reach your own decisions first. A new relationship needs to be handled with extra care. Someone who has been badly hurt in the past might not want to make a commitment until you have won their trust.

29. THURSDAY. Inactive. You may not be feeling particularly energetic or inspired. It might take you longer than usual to get going with today's tasks. Try to let things proceed at their own pace; trying to impose discipline on yourself could end up having the reverse effect. An unexpected communication from someone in your past can leave you feeling unsettled; decide on the wisdom of renewing your acquaintance. There is a danger of stirring up jealousy from your current partner. It may be better to leave the past well alone; the here and now is what really matters. Rely on your own judgment rather than collecting varied opinions from other people.

30. FRIDAY. Disquieting. You can expect recognition today for recent efforts at work which you thought had gone unnoticed. The boss or others will take the trouble to let you know that you are not taken for granted, even if it may seem that way sometimes. An associate might display jealousy at your popularity; remind yourself that this probably stems from their own insecurity or fear of failure. Try to show compassion to those less able than you while at the same time taking justifiable pride in your own achievements. This evening is good for a family outing to the movies or to a concert in the park. Remember that everyone needs spoiling from time to time. Conditions also favor all forms of artistic self-expression, especially for Leo performers.

JULY

1. SATURDAY. Fine.   This is a good day for shopping with a friend. New summer clothes or swimwear will probably be at the top of your list, especially if your vacation is coming up. Be on the lookout for sale items; you may be able to pick up several bargains. This is also a good day for buying accessories such as a hat or jewelry. You may decide to spend some money getting your hair not just cut but styled. Looking good can do wonders for your confidence. A new hairstyle is likely to be successful if you are ready for a whole new look. Try not to let work matters prey on your mind; this is a day for doing what you enjoy. It is a favorable evening for a night out with special friends or with someone close to your heart.

2. SUNDAY. Disquieting.   Children are likely to be underfoot throughout the day. Boredom may be at the root of the problem. You will probably have to summon all your creative powers in order to keep them occupied. If you do not have a garden where they can play, this is a good day for taking them to the park or a sports center. Guard against frittering away money; stick to essential purchases only. Try to pay for anything you buy with cash rather than on credit; this way you are likely to be more realistic about how much you can afford to spend. This is a good time for revising your personal and household budget for the rest of the month. Also review your savings for the first half of 1995 and decide how to save more from now till December.

3. MONDAY. Variable.   You need to guard against a tendency to be short-tempered with those who are only trying to be helpful. Words spoken in anger may be difficult to retract. Leos are not usually prone to bearing a grudge; you can flare up but then just as quickly forget why you did. Remember that others might not find it so easy to let an argument drop. Be careful when it comes to confiding in anyone, especially a colleague who works in the same department. A certain individual can be only too quick to misquote you if it suits their own ends. Written work can be a laborious process; you will appreciate why you need to learn to type or to use a word processor.

4. TUESDAY. Good.   Now is a favorable time for collecting any money that is owed to you from an insurance claim or a tax rebate. You may need to make a fuss in order to speed up matters; otherwise you could end up waiting much longer than necessary. Red tape can be frustrating; it is up to you to find a way around it. For Leos who are house hunting, this is a favorable time for investing in older property. You may be able to get more financial assistance for renovation work than you had thought, but patience will be needed to see the project through. Agree to put in some overtime at work if offered the opportunity. Taking on extra work that can be done from home could also be a way of boosting your bank balance.

5. WEDNESDAY. Difficult. Events today could start on a worrisome note. Illness in the family or of a work colleague who is close to you is a possibility. While there is little you can do on a practical level, sending a card or flowers can let them know that your thoughts are with them. Try not to let other people's problems or bad news affect you too much. By all means be compassionate and offer help where you can. However, keep your anxiety in perspective by realizing that you have your own life in the meantime. An old car may prove more trouble than it is worth. You might have to decide on the wisdom of spending any more money to keep a clunker on the road; it might be better to sell it for scrap.

6. THURSDAY. Mixed. Today's mixed bag of mail is apt to include a letter from a friend who has not been in touch for a while. Their entertaining news may include an invitation to visit. On the other hand, there could be disappointment about a recent job application. A social arrangement lined up for the weekend might be canceled; scurry to plan something else that you can look forward to. This is a favorable day for taking the bull by the horns when it comes to problems with neighbors. If you are constantly being bothered by loud noise, now is the time to draw this to their attention since they may not realize how intrusive they are. A polite request from you is likely to be taken to heart.

7. FRIDAY. Routine. This is a good day for working from home, especially if other members of your household are out for the day. Lapses in concentration can be a problem. The fewer interruptions you have, the better for bringing a project to a satisfying conclusion. Someone you work closely with may not have been pulling their weight recently. It is up to you to point out that shirking their responsibilities means extra burdens for you. But tread carefully if you want to offload your grievances onto someone; there is a greater risk of giving offense where none was meant. This is likely to be a frustrating day if you are involved in research; information can be difficult to get.

8. SATURDAY. Fair. Luck goes hand in hand today with Leos who are moving. Transporting your goods is likely to be more straightforward than you had dared hope, although unpacking at the other end may seem like an impossible task. Try not to worry about items which appear to be missing; they should turn up again once the chaos is brought under control. Spend some of your savings on furniture, new lamps, or acoustical equipment such as a music center. If funds are low at the moment, you might be able to buy on interest-free credit; just make sure that the monthly repayments are within your means. Entertaining at home is starred, but be prepared for one guest failing to show up.

9. SUNDAY. Buoyant. This is a good day for going in pursuit of pleasure. This could include participating in a sport or enjoying the role of spectator. Devote as much time as possible to hobbies of all kinds. If the weather is fine you may opt for a day in the garden or the park. Be sensible when it comes to sunbathing; by the time you realize that you have overdone it, it may be too late. Be sure to use a sunblock both for yourself and for children in your care. This is a lucky day for a new romantic encounter. Someone will capture your interest with their refreshingly cheerful outlook on life. Do not let them slip away without at least exchanging telephone numbers.

10. MONDAY. Disappointing. In work matters, it would probably be wise to stick to tried-and-trusted methods. You may be strongly tempted to follow a hunch, but bear in mind that you might not have all the facts. A gamble could prove expensive in terms of both money and the cost to your professional reputation. You could find yourself arguing with those closest to you. What starts as a minor disagreement can all too easily blow up into a full-scale argument. Guard against a tendency to point the finger and cast blame without examining your own behavior first. This way you can know which accusations are justified and which to take with a grain of salt.

11. TUESDAY. Useful. Leos may be inclined to dwell on past mistakes. There is a lot to be said for learning where you went wrong, if only to avoid repeating the same errors in the future. But there is also a point when you need to break from the past and let yourself off the hook. Concentrate on the positive aspects of life. A dream for the future can become reality with enough determination. This is a good day for approaching higher-ups concerning a pay raise; they may even be more generous than you had expected. Conditions are also favorable for joining a health or sports club. When you have to pay dues you are more likely to stick to a regular exercise plan.

12. WEDNESDAY. Worrisome. A hectically busy day makes you wonder how you will do everything you are supposed to do. Your best policy is to first get organized; rushing into jobs will probably only result in chaos or high blood pressure. Deadlines can be met as long as you refuse to let others panic or confuse you. Set the example of being calm and systematic. Your loyalty could be put to the test. Someone may try every trick in the book to make you share confidential information, but they will probably give up the game if they see that you are not going to play. This evening favors closing the door on the outside world. Enjoy a peaceful dinner at home, then relax in the arms of your loved one.

13. THURSDAY. Good. For Leo business people, this can be a good day for face-to-face negotiations. The secret of success is often a combination of your own personality backed up with hard work and careful planning. Avoid delegating work which needs an experienced touch. This is a favorable time for Leo parents to encourage your children to make new friends; a social education can be just as important as an academic one. Partners can be a source of joy to you. If you have been together for a long time, this could be the perfect moment for planning a second honeymoon. It is a propitious evening for someone new coming into your life if you are unattached but actively looking.

14. FRIDAY. Unsettling. You are likely to be thrown back on your own resources. At work several colleagues could be absent for varying reasons, and those who are physically present may be preoccupied with their own tasks. Insist on advice if you really need it; making decisions without consulting other staff members or superiors could land you in a heap of trouble. If you are about to embark on major home improvements, this is a favorable time for obtaining estimates from a local contractor. Do not fall into the trap of employing the cheapest just to save money. Shoddy workmanship will probably prove more costly in the long run when it has to be put right.

15. SATURDAY. Unpredictable. Leos who live alone may suffer from feelings of isolation today. Although it might appear as if everyone else has a thriving social life except for you, remind yourself that appearances are very often deceptive. Make an effort to contact old friends; they will probably be delighted to hear from you. Find out about weekend events in your neighborhood from your local newspaper. Even if you go alone, you could find that entering into conversation with strangers is easier than you imagined. Leos with young children may be ready to hand over the reins to a babysitter this evening. Someone in your immediate family is just waiting to be asked.

16. SUNDAY. Deceptive. Family responsibilities are at the top of today's agenda. This may include visiting relatives with whom you do not really have a lot in common. Remind yourself that the more effort you make, the easier the day will be. Entering into the spirit of the occasion is probably the only way to stop yourself from clock watching. It may also be time to stop seeing someone you always end up arguing with; maybe they feel the same. Avoid overindulging in food; eat several small meals. If you are offered alcohol, sip just enough to put you in a genial mood. If you are out this evening, avoid squabbling over the bill, even if it means paying more than your fair share.

17. MONDAY. Excellent. Leos who are on vacation should be in for a thoroughly enjoyable time. If you are staying in a foreign country make the most of the opportunity to travel around the area; local culture and customs can be fascinating. This is an excellent day for broadening your intellectual horizons as well. Find out about degree or diploma courses for the next academic year. These do not have to be related to your career. You may get more enjoyment out of studying if it is purely for the personal challenge. Money invested in property can bring good returns. If you are selling you should get at least the asking price. Trust your intuition about the motives of prospective buyers.

18. TUESDAY. Sensitive. Leo students who are now on vacation can afford to revel in the freedom from studying. By all means enjoy a well-deserved break, but try not to fall into the trap of ignoring summer projects for too long. Remind yourself that the more you do now, the less arduous it will be to get everything finished in time for the new term. Correspondence related to legal matters needs to be treated with caution. There is a greater risk of unwittingly compromising yourself by putting down your views in black and white. Do not enter into any negotiations without first obtaining expert advice. Look for ways to boost your income through overtime or an evening job.

19. WEDNESDAY. Strenuous. You cannot afford to be complacent when it comes to business matters. A certain individual is more than capable of pulling the rug from under your feet just when you thought things were going your way. Nothing is definite until it is signed, sealed, and delivered. Buying shares in a foreign company could be more risky than you realize; some behind-the-scenes investigating could bring more information to light. A personal relationship may be causing you anxiety, probably because you both look at the world from opposite ends of the telescope. You might just have to accept the fact that your views on life are incompatible.

20. THURSDAY. Happy. This is a starred day for Leos interviewing for a new job. Even if you are sure that you will be offered the position, it may be wiser to keep these feelings to yourself for now. Wait to break the news until you have written confirmation. It is a favorable time for thinking through a personal problem in depth; the solution can be easier to find by yourself rather than sifting through conflicting advice from others. Let intuition guide you; it is unlikely to let you down. Write a long letter to a close friend who now lives far away from you. This evening a loved one may surprise and touch you by telling you how valued and special you really are to them.

21. FRIDAY. Uncertain. Leo employers should not delay contacting references before taking on a new member of the staff. Someone may not have told the whole truth about their reasons for leaving their current position. Avoid making a final decision until you are in full possession of the facts. This is a good time for installing new equipment in your place of work. Even if you are technology shy, you probably realize that you cannot put off becoming computer literate much longer. Buying or selling property can be risky at best. A deal you thought was watertight could fall through at the last moment. An independent surveyor's report is essential before a contract is finalized.

22. SATURDAY. Misleading. Try not to agree to any social arrangements unless you are sure you can honor them. If something does not appeal to you, it would probably be better to say so now; this way you can avoid letting someone down at the last minute. Broken promises can create a sinkhole of bad feelings. Guard against putting yourself in a position where you might be accused of insincerity. You may get the feeling that a loved one is keeping something from you, but avoid leaping to conclusions. There is a danger of letting wrong impressions lead you astray. If you are partying this evening, be sure not to accept a lift from someone who has obviously had too much to drink.

23. SUNDAY. Enjoyable. This is a good day for socializing with friends, either at your home or theirs. With old friends, conversation is likely to run along nostalgic lines. Reliving happy memories from the past can be fun. A new romantic relationship could be losing that first flush of excitement, but there is no cause for anxiety. You can find that the newness is being replaced by deeper feelings of comfort and security with each other. You may be able to enjoy a companionable silence for the first time. An evening with someone close to you can easily turn into a very late night; you may end up talking happily into the small hours.

24. MONDAY. Variable. This can be a difficult beginning to the working week, starting with your morning commute. Traffic is likely to be heavier than usual. Inexplicable delays can be irritating, especially if they make you late for an appointment. Stay calm; there is no point in getting uptight about events which are beyond your control. Your decisions at work could be questioned by someone who appears unwilling to trust you. Refuse to rise to the bait if they are spoiling for an argument. There is no need for you to do more than just state the bare facts without offering an opinion. This is a good evening for relaxing at home. Do not be afraid to say that you want to be left alone.

25. TUESDAY. Challenging. Seek advice regarding long-term financial investments. You may decide to make additional contributions to a pension plan. If your employer does not offer the benefits of a retirement or life insurance plan, look into setting up one of your own. Do not postpone making a will so that you have peace of mind that everything will be left exactly as you would wish. For single Leos, an old flame could reappear in your life. If the attraction is still there for both of you, this could be a case of second time lucky. Take it one step at a time; there is no need to rush into making a commitment until you are both sure that this is what you want this time around.

26. WEDNESDAY. Slow. If you are at home, this can be a good morning for an onslaught on the heavier household jobs such as washing windows, shampooing carpets, or taking curtains to the dry cleaners. If you are at work, there is a greater chance of feeling restless or plain bored. You may have outgrown your job, and now it is up to you to discover new challenges. Try not to fall into the trap of staying where you are out of a sense of loyalty; this is almost certainly misguided. You owe it to yourself to find employment which will maximize your abilities; make your plans accordingly. If someone close to you is sick at home or in the hospital, put this evening aside for a visit to cheer them up.

27. THURSDAY. Good. This can be a propitious day for new starts of all kinds. Do not let the grass grow under your feet when it comes to new schemes; this is a time for taking plans off the drawing board and putting them into action. Personal determination can work wonders. It is also a favorable day for speaking in public or giving a lecture; clarity and enthusiasm for your subject should capture the interest of your audience. For Leos who work with children, this is likely to be a rewarding day; a child who has made slow progress in the past could show signs of coming into their own. Check out a new book from the library and find out about borrowing music or artwork as well.

28. FRIDAY. Positive. You are likely to receive past due recognition for your efforts. Someone in an influential position at work secretly admires your positive attitude; you could be closer to a promotion than you realize. Your cheerful, upbeat approach to problems can rub off on your colleagues. A certain individual who has a tendency to panic could benefit from some direct advice. This is a favorable day for creating more storage space, perhaps by clearing out closets which have not been properly emptied for years. The day is good for advertising unwanted items for sale, especially children's toys and clothes that they have outgrown, but keep favorite items for their nostalgic value.

29. SATURDAY. Disquieting. For Leos who are moving, this is likely to be a rather sad day, especially if you have lived in the same place for years. There could be a sense that part of your life is coming to an end, but remind yourself that this inevitably means a new beginning too. Try to concentrate on what you will gain through change rather than dwelling on what you have lost. Decorating or home improvements can take longer than you thought; this may be compounded by someone withdrawing an offer of help at the last moment. If you are out shopping this afternoon, guard against a tendency to overspend. Buying on credit may seem like a good idea now but could be regretted later.

30. SUNDAY. Lucky. A brother, sister, or close friend may be celebrating some good fortune today; this may be news of a birth or of a baby on the way. This is a favorable time for investing some savings in a new hobby; money spent in this way can enrich the quality of your life, so there is no need to feel that you are being indulgent. By putting equal value on work and play you get the best out of life. It is also possible that a new interest could become a money-maker or even your full-time occupation once you become proficient at it. Arrange an evening of sport or games which the whole family can enjoy together. It may be more difficult for you to be a good winner than a good loser.

31. MONDAY. Fair.   If you are paid at the end of the month, be prepared for a delay in receiving your check. A computer glitch or an administrative error may not have been detected. This could tilt your finely balanced bank account into the red. You may have to ask a family member or a close friend for a loan to tide you over until you receive the pay you have earned. For busy Leo professionals, this is a favorable time for hiring a cleaning service to help out with the housework; they could be worth their weight in gold. Consider investing in labor-saving devices for the home such as a dishwasher, food processor, or microwave oven. The initial outlay may seem expensive, but more free time can be invaluable. The day also favors efforts to improve personal appearance.

AUGUST

1. TUESDAY. Useful.   For Leo salespeople this is likely to be a busy day, especially if you are on the road. Your appointments should run to schedule; make use of the extra time you allotted by dropping in on potential clients in the area. There is a greater chance of picking up some unexpected business by being in the right place at the right time. Self-employed Leos should find that more work is coming your way by referral from satisfied customers; do not neglect to thank them for recommending you. This is the time to get your car serviced, even if it seems to be running perfectly; regular maintenance is essential for road safety and can prolong the life of your vehicle.

2. WEDNESDAY. Manageable.   Paperwork could well reach alarming proportions this morning. Search for ways to improve your existing filing system. You may not realize how much time you can waste searching for a certain document or past correspondence. Aim for the sort of organization where you can put your hands on any paper at a moment's notice. A telephone call to a friend could turn into a marathon conversation; just remember that this will be reflected in the bill. Try to make calls at the cheapest time. Plan a special night out with your mate or current date. Spending time as well as money on your appearance can give you that extra bit of confidence that comes when you know you look great.

3. THURSDAY. Unsettling. Leos who are unemployed at the moment may begin to doubt your own abilities. Realize that this is a totally natural reaction to being turned down for a job that seemed perfect for you. Try not to become disheartened; have faith in yourself and refuse to be daunted. Your luck is bound to change, and sooner rather than later. If you are at home today, housework is probably the last thing you feel like doing. Put at least part of the day aside for creative work you enjoy. Feeling cooped up is likely to make you depressed or resentful. This evening favors abandoning your own kitchen in favor of a restaurant; this way you do not have to shop, cook, or clean up.

4. FRIDAY. Mixed. Take extra care when addressing letters or packages. Check the address rather than relying on your memory, or something may never reach its destination. Telling a white lie might seem a safe alternative to hurting someone's feelings, but honesty is usually the best policy in the long run. Looking for a place to rent can be a tedious procedure. Save yourself time and energy by reading between the lines in advertisements. You are more likely to find a place through word of mouth; for instance, a colleague may be looking for a tenant. A formal occasion this evening can be glitz and glamour, but it could be uphill work to put a polish on your conversations with strangers.

5. SATURDAY. Good. For Leo parents, this is a good day for taking your children shopping. A sale on summer clothes will probably be at the top of your list; try to buy garments with plenty of room for them to grow into. Having lunch out at their favorite place can be a noisy but fun occasion. Splurge on something new at a marked-down price for yourself as well, such as an item of jewelry or a bathing suit. Conditions favor participating in sporting events of all kinds. Learning a new game could be easier than you imagined; you may find that you have a natural aptitude. If you have always wanted to learn to play a musical instrument, this is a good time to start; you should be able to make swift progress if you are coached by a tutor.

6. SUNDAY. Useful. A relationship which is still in the early stages could present a few problems. There may be conflict over how to spend leisure time. Try not to be obstinate. Part of sharing your life with another person is knowing when and how to make compromises. There is no point in behaving as if you were still single with no one else's needs to consider. This is a good day for talking through worries or anxieties of all kinds. There is very little that cannot be sorted out as long as you are prepared to be honest. Do not let pride stop you from facing up to a situation as it really is. Others admire you for sticking up for what you believe in whether or not your views are in vogue.

7. MONDAY. Fine. This is a surprisingly easy start to the working week. Tasks which you thought would take hours can be dealt with in far less time than you had allowed. Catch up with the routine jobs which always tend to get pushed to the bottom of the list. For Leos who are newly qualified in a marketable skill, this is a propitious day for setting up your business. Working from home can save on rent until you can afford to expand. Be selective when it comes to advertising; a few choice publications should be all that is needed to reach your potential market. Find a way for getting to know work associates on a more informal basis, perhaps by entertaining them at home.

8. TUESDAY. Deceptive. This is a favorable time for Leo employees to join a trade union. Recent events at work indicate the need to be absolutely clear about your rights; a representative backing you in a dispute can be invaluable. Although it is usually wiser to ignore gossip, today you may have to take steps to stop someone from bad-mouthing you. Although you might not be able to find out what their real grievance is, you can protect your own reputation with those who matter. A health problem affecting someone in your immediate family could be causing anxiety. This may be because a diagnosis has not been properly explained; insist on a second opinion.

9. WEDNESDAY. Happy. Conditions are perfect for Leos entering into a new contract or business, especially if you are joining forces with a partner. You can afford to follow your hunches; taking a risk is likely to get far better results than sitting on the fence. Sign up to attend a business convention. Getting together with other people in your profession can expand your thinking and open up new possibilities. You should come away from any discussion with plenty of new ideas just waiting to be tried out in practice. Unattached Leos can suddenly be in demand; someone has set their sights on you. Leos are not usually slow on the uptake; do not hesitate to follow up an invitation if the interest is mutual.

10. THURSDAY. Disquieting. Guard against crossing swords with a superior, for they may not hesitate to use their influence against you. Look long and hard to find the happy medium between following a direct order and standing up for yourself; do not allow anyone to walk all over you. If you have been having more downs than ups in a long-term relationship, you may not be able to ignore the real problems any longer. The time has come for an honest confrontation; this way you can both decide if this is the parting of the ways or if you are willing to renew your commitment. A decision one way or the other is preferable to living with ongoing doubt and insecurity. You may be able to forgive, but forgetting is not as easy.

11. FRIDAY. Strenuous. Unforeseen expenses, such as repairs that cannot be delayed, could put a substantial strain on your finances. Making ends meet until next payday can be a struggle; some careful budgeting is necessary. This may mean having to cancel out of a social arrangement for this evening, or you might suggest something less expensive, such as cooking a simple supper at home. The fun you have is not necessarily in direct proportion to the amount you spend. Babysitting for a friend can be much harder work than you had anticipated; younger children can have you running around in circles. Guard against losing your temper when in charge.

12. SATURDAY. Misleading. You may feel unable to talk to anyone about a personal problem. Maybe you are not sure who to trust or fear that no one will really understand. The last thing you want is to be told to pull yourself together. Consulting a trained counselor could be the ideal answer; this way you can guarantee a good listener who should be able to help you reach your own conclusions. An objective perspective can be an eye-opener. If money problems are slipping out of your control, this is a good time to take decisive action; ignoring the situation will only make matters worse. Write to your bank or credit card company and propose a new payment plan; it is in their interests to help you pay off your debt.

13. SUNDAY. Lucky. Try to get all your chores finished early so that you can devote the rest of the day to doing what you enjoy most. Someone close to you who has been ill should now be making a remarkable recovery. An offer to help with housework or shopping would probably still be gratefully accepted. Sign up to do some volunteer work that will let you put the skills you have to use in helping less fortunate people. If you are going on vacation soon, make a list this afternoon of all that you will need to take with you. Be realistic about the amount of clothes you should pack; you will probably not wear half of them. Travel as lightly and economically as possible.

14. MONDAY. Demanding.   Leo students who are on vacation need to get back to your studies today. If all your good intentions to finish off a project in advance have gone out of the window, try not to let things slide any further. Getting motivated again can be difficult; just remind yourself of how virtuous you will feel when you start to make headway. If you are involved in litigation you may be reaching a crucial stage in negotiations, but final decisions are still far in the future. Be wary of engaging in any correspondence that is not okayed by your lawyer. Avoid taking the law into your own hands over any issue; you are likely to come away a very disappointed loser.

15. TUESDAY. Deceptive.   If your business interests are spread over a large geographical area, you may not be able to conduct affairs from your desk today. Some traveling is unavoidable in order to bring your personal influence to bear on current issues. Usual work routines can be disrupted. Deadlines may be moved forward with hardly any warning. Your best policy is to keep cool, especially if everyone around you is madly rushing around. You are far more likely to deal with pressing problems effectively if you refuse to be rushed. It is up to you to set an example for less experienced colleagues to follow. This is a good evening for trying out a new restaurant featuring ethnic cuisine.

16. WEDNESDAY. Happy.   Conditions favor applying for a new job. Even if you think you might be underqualified for a certain position, there is no harm in trying. You may have other qualities that can count for more than classroom learning. Leos who are interviewing today are likely to come across with confidence. Your intelligent questions can impress a potential employer and possibly swing the balance in your favor. If you work on commission, this can be a productive afternoon. The deals that you are able to close now could make up a large part of your next paycheck. Creative work intended originally for pleasure may be good enough to sell.

17. THURSDAY. Sensitive. Sort out a health concern by seeing a specialist. Even if you do not have health insurance to cover the cost, a consultation can be money well spent. In dealing with any professional you are paying for their time as well as their knowledge, so make the most of the session by asking as many direct questions as it takes to gain a full understanding. Consider long-term investments, especially the type that allows you to increase your contributions over the years. If you decide to get a haircut, it may not be wise to try somebody new. The style you want and what you actually end up with could be worlds apart.

18. FRIDAY. Difficult. You may be getting tired of a friend who seems to contact you only when they want to offload their problems. You might also suspect that they are exaggerating the latest crisis in order to win your sympathy. Maybe it is time to point out that this friendship has become too one-sided, if not tedious. Alternatively, start talking about your own problems and see how long they listen. Leos in charge of children today could find their constant demands tiring. Make an extra effort to think up new activities to keep them out of your hair. A night out with a loved one may end in a quarrel, probably over something which will seem petty tomorrow.

19. SATURDAY. Demanding. You may be jolted to find out just how unreliable other people can be. A friend could change their mind about a social arrangement which you had been looking forward to for some time. Even more annoying can be their lack of sincerity when it comes to apologizing for spoiling your day. Someone who owes you money may suddenly be keeping a low profile. It is up to you to hunt them down, especially if your own finances are not in the best shape. Take to heart the lesson that you should only lend money to those you know you can totally trust. Try not to rely too much on others for evening entertainment. Make your own plans and let others mesh their plans with yours.

20. SUNDAY. Fair. Talk through a career problem with someone older than you who has seen it all before. A dose of worldly wisdom could be just what you need to keep your ambitions on course. Advice about your personal life may be harder to accept, but rest assured that it is offered with your best interests at heart. Try not to mistake genuine concern for interference. If you are serious about starting a new diet, plan meals for the week ahead. It may be helpful to anticipate the times when your resolve is likely to waver, such as between meals or when you are out on a dinner date, and make allowances accordingly. Flexibility is the key to success. The evening is favorable for quiet get-togethers at home.

21. MONDAY. Unsettling. This can be a frustrating start to the week. In work matters, it may seem as if a certain individual is deliberately blocking your efforts to get ahead. You might be forced into the realization that you have made an enemy of someone who can make life difficult for you. Try to set the record straight; it is up to you to bring grievances out into the open. Only in this way can you hope to reclaim your own power and prestige. Current strains on your finances mean that you are unable to afford the little luxuries of life. Try not to get green-eyed with envy over a friend or co-worker's newest acquisition. Making small economies now should pay dividends later in the month.

22. TUESDAY. Deceptive. If your car has been acting up recently it may be wiser not to rely on it for a journey. There is a greater risk of breaking down in an inconvenient place. A problem you thought had been repaired could still be causing trouble. This is a good time for joining a road service; membership could pay for itself several times over. A brother or sister can be going through a crisis in their personal life but be concealing the true extent of the problem for fear of burdening you. The whole picture will probably emerge in the not too distant future. In the meantime, let them know that you are available when and if they need your support.

23. WEDNESDAY. Changeable. This can be a lucky day for new business ventures. Certain associates will probably urge caution; some may even try to dampen your enthusiasm by being downright pessimistic. Try not to let other people's negative attitudes deter you from following your chosen path; getting results may be the only way in which you can prove them wrong. Remind yourself that most brilliant ideas are usually ridiculed by someone to begin with. For Leos who have found a partner for life, this is a good day to pop that all-important question. But a dream wedding may have to wait until finances are a little healthier, especially if parents are unable or unwilling to help out.

24. THURSDAY. Quiet. This is a good time for taking a day's leave, especially if you have had very little time off lately. Everyone deserves time for themselves occasionally; there is no reason to feel guilty about putting your own needs first. If you have young children, try to make arrangements for them to be minded; this way you have the freedom either to go out for the day or to relax at home in peace and quiet. Family members are likely to cater to your desires, so make the most of getting your own way. Consider brightening your personal image with a hairstyle change or a colorful new outfit. Fill your calendar with events for the weekend ahead. Play the role of social director.

25. FRIDAY. Mixed. Leos who are job or house hunting may have to take a disappointment in stride this morning. A position or place you had set your heart on can be filled at the last moment. Someone close to you may also suffer a setback in their career plans. Try not to let bad news spoil the rest of the day for you; there is no point wasting energy on matters that are beyond your control. The day should get progressively better. This afternoon there could be some welcome news on the financial front; this may be a long awaited pay raise or perhaps a gift of money from someone in the family. It is a good evening for treating someone special to a fun night on the town.

26. SATURDAY. Sensitive. For Leo parents with children about to go back to school after the summer break, this is likely to be an expensive day. Shopping for clothes can cost more than you had budgeted; some nonessential items may have to wait until next month. A child preparing to enter a new school might be suffering from nerves that makes them act defiant or sulky. It is up to you to spot the signs so that you do not make matters worse by punishing them. Be tolerant and sympathetic and they are more likely to confide their fears in you. A friend may offer tickets to a play or concert this evening; do not hesitate to take up the offer.

27. SUNDAY. Tricky. Hunting for a lost object could take the greater part of the morning. Try to think back to when you definitely last had it in your possession; this might give you a useful clue. If you need to confront someone close to you on a personal issue, it would be a wise move to first write down what you want to say. This way you are less likely to be sidetracked onto issues which are irrelevant. Have the confidence to insist that your antagonist hears you out. Even if their initial reaction is one of anger, they will probably secretly respect your assertiveness. Entertaining at home should be pleasant if you steer the conversation away from controversial topics.

28. MONDAY. Worrisome. A letter or postcard from a loved one can get the day off to a cheerful start, but your heart may sink when you see the size of the bills which arrive at the same time. You may have been spending too freely with your credit card; resolve to stop using it until you can reduce the balance to a more

manageable sum. Conditions favor starting a new advertising or
marketing campaign, especially if you have the backing of a professional agency. Their fees may seem steep, but the creative ideas
they produce should justify the cost. Find time this evening to
catch up with personal telephone calls and correspondence that
you have been putting off.

29. TUESDAY. Deceptive. Distinguish between fact and fabri-
cation; an associate is not beneath abusing your trusting Leo
nature. You may realize too late that this was an attempt to win
you over to their side in a dispute which does not really concern
you. Disentangle yourself from those whose business tactics seem
dubious; your suspicions that you are being taken for a ride could
be justified. Listen to your intuition. Decisions or actions taken
against your better judgment will probably be regretted at a later
date. A running battle with a neighbor can come to a head this
evening. Make an extra effort to be diplomatic in order to defuse a
threatening situation.

30. WEDNESDAY. Upsetting. This is a favorable day for bargain hunting for household items. You may be able to find furniture or appliances at a fraction of the list price if you are prepared
to shop around. You may be tempted to browse around a local
antique shop; items such as lamps or mirrors can be an investment
as well as adding a classical touch to your living room. Do not
postpone buying a new set of everyday china or a food processor.
Try not to be too adventurous if you are buying a gift for someone
you have not known very long; they might be more fastidious in
their tastes than you had realized. Keep receipts so that you can
return or exchange merchandise.

31. THURSDAY. Good. This can be a good day for dealing
with paperwork related to your home. Renew or update insurance
policies. Make sure that your security provisions are adequate; if
you have young or elderly people living with you, it may be wise to
invest in a new smoke or burglar alarm. For Leos who are first-
time home buyers, this is a favorable day for shopping around for
the best mortgage offer. A seller may be wiling to drop an asking
price once they learn that you are on a tight budget. This evening
is good for attending a formal function. Leos rarely lack social
graces; a dinner party or other gathering is likely to provide a good
time for everyone.

SEPTEMBER

1. FRIDAY. Fair. If this is the end of your working week, make an extra effort to bring ongoing projects to a satisfying conclusion. A project which has been dragging on for too long needs to be finished once and for all; you may be surprised to find how quickly you are able to dispose of a job once you focus on it. Remind yourself of how pleasant it will be to start next week with a clear desk. If you are at home today, the morning is the best time for housework or grocery shopping. Leave the afternoon free for more pleasurable pursuits, such as calling on friends or working on a creative project. A date this evening can live up to and beyond your expectations.

2. SATURDAY. Disquieting. Efforts to keep your home clean and neat may seem like a waste of time this morning, especially if you have children. Try not to attach too much importance to domestic chores; there is more to life than waging a constant war against other people's mess. Think practically; consider designating one room where toys and games are not allowed. This way everyone can be happy and comfortable. Get out and about in your local area. You may find some intriguing out-of-the-way shops if you wander off your beaten track for a change. If you are selling a car or other major item you are likely to find a cash buyer more quickly than you had hoped.

3. SUNDAY. Fine. Plan a day out with all the family. Visiting an amusement park or the zoo can be just as much fun for the adults as the children. Older children may prefer something more educational or more stimulating, such as a battle of wits or a test of skill. Your local library can be a gold mine of useful information when it comes to finding out about new hobbies. Treat yourself to books related to your outside interests. For Leos who are involved in a new relationship, this can be a favorable day for introducing your partner to other family members. They are likely to be given a warm welcome; your only problem will probably be getting a word in edgewise.

4. MONDAY. Good. If you have been waiting to hear about the outcome of a recent application you are likely to get some good news today. What started as a part-time or temporary job may now be offered to you as a permanent position; the increase in

195

salary should make this a tempting proposition. Consider joining a health or sports club, perhaps with a friend or a colleague from work. Keeping fit can be more fun if you have the company and support of someone who is enthusiastic. Leos may decide to improve your public image. Start by giving away old clothes and shoes that you have had for years; replace them with a few classic, carefully chosen designer items or good copies of designer bests. New eyeglasses can also give you a new look.

5. TUESDAY. Deceptive.   Guard against taking part in gossip, especially if you work as part of a large company. Rumors may seem harmless at the time, but there is a greater danger of hurting someone's feelings in a way that you had never intended. Avoid making hasty decisions either at work or in your personal life. Acting on impulse is unlikely to achieve intended results. This may be because you are too closely involved in a situation to see things clearly. Forcing the issue over emotional problems might even blow up in your face; your best policy is to be patient and wait until you are feeling less vulnerable. Avoid alcohol altogether if driving this evening; try to be home before dark.

6. WEDNESDAY. Lucky.   This is likely to be a productive day for Leo business people. Contracts which you have been counting on for some time may now be finalized. But no matter how solid a deal might appear, it is still advisable to protect your interests by following up all verbal agreements in writing. If you are self-employed, some strategic advertising at this time could bring in enough work to keep you busy for the rest of the month. In your personal relationships this can be a good day for talking through any difficulties. If you are able to discuss things honestly you are unlikely to drift apart. Your partner should be only too willing to give you the affirmation you desire.

7. THURSDAY. Mixed.   Be wary of making key decisions without consulting others who are involved or will be affected. Someone is sure to resent the fact that you appear to have made up their minds for them. Disagreements over business tactics are likely; at least give everyone a chance to air their opinions. This way you should be able to find mutually satisfying solutions. Meetings can be poorly attended today; you might have to hold some issues over until a later date. If you are in charge you may have to face the unenviable task of disciplinary action against an unsatisfactory employee. There could be more to the matter than first meets the eye; be prepared to hear their side of the story before passing judgment.

8. FRIDAY. Discomforting. If you work with money belonging to others you could have a long day. Allocating funds or preparing financial reports may take much longer than usual. There are certain individuals who consistently overspend with no thought of the future. Leo parents may decide that the time has come for your children to learn how to handle their own money, perhaps by having their own bank account. Try not to keep household expenses a secret; it may be invaluable education for all family members to discover how much it costs to live. Avoid lending possessions which are valuable to you; there is a greater risk that you might never see them again. Stash away jewelry so that it is not out in plain sight.

9. SATURDAY. Disquieting. This is not a day for allowing boredom to get the better of you. Complaining that you have nothing to do will probably only make you feel worse as well as irritating those with whom you live. Try not to rely on others for entertainment or suggestions. A swim or a long walk could get the adrenalin racing again. Consider treating yourself to the luxury of a sauna or a massage; some pampering might be just what you need. This is a good time for adopting a pet such as a puppy or a kitten, especially if they have been abandoned by their previous owners. Be realistic about the responsibilities and time involved, particularly if you are often away overnight.

10. SUNDAY. Happy. Focus on self-improvement of all types. If you need an intellectual challenge, now can be a good time for finding out about evening classes or correspondence courses. Learning a new skill such as carpentry or flower arranging can fill a gap in your creative life. Attending classes with others who share your same interests is also almost guaranteed to widen your social circle. Do not hesitate entertaining visitors from abroad; an invitation to return your hospitality could be in the cards. Long-distance travel is likely to be trouble-free as well as fun. Consider taking a late summer vacation to a popular resort area.

11. MONDAY. Misleading. You may have to deal with one or two disappointments or setbacks in your career. Maybe you are having second thoughts about the type of work that you are doing or are training to do. Decide if this is just a transitory feeling or something more serious. While there is nothing wrong with admitting that you have made a mistake, this is not the time for quitting on impulse. Give the job and yourself a fair chance before you make any final decision. Studying can be uphill work today. Leo students who have just started classes might be worried that you have bitten off more than you can chew. This is a natural anxiety while you are getting adjusted to new teachers and classmates.

12. TUESDAY. Demanding. Working Leo parents may find that juggling home and career obligations is even more tricky than usual. Just when you undertake to be home at a reasonable time, something urgent is likely to crop up at the office. At the end of the day you have to accept that you cannot be in two places at the same time. Make sure that your family understands the pressures that you are under; this way it will be more realistic to expect their support. Someone in a position of authority can throw their weight around today; you may suspect that this is a display of egoism. Stay out of their way by getting on with your own tasks and not volunteering for anything.

13. WEDNESDAY. Good. Decisions which you made recently with your fingers crossed should now be bearing fruit. The fact that your judgment has proved to be correct will probably come as a relief. Be sure to give yourself a pat on the back as well. Success usually breeds success; have confidence in your ability to overcome obstacles that others may see as insurmountable. Identifying potential markets now can prove to be a lucrative source of revenue for the future. Look into claiming a tax rebate or collecting money which is owed to you. If you are waiting for a lawsuit to be sorted out, there is a good chance that matters will be resolved before too long.

14. THURSDAY. Sensitive. For Leo salespeople the pressure could be on to boost sales. If a deadline is looming, teamwork is essential in order to meet your target dates. You should find colleagues more than willing to pull their weight. There is unlikely to be much time for casual chat, but try not to ignore a new staff member who might be feeling like a fish out of water in the face of all this activity. If you recently received a new credit card, be sure you have signed it. If someone is paying you by check, be prepared for a delay in this reaching your own account. It could also be returned due to insufficient funds in their account.

15. FRIDAY. Disquieting. For Leos who work in managerial roles, this is a day when you need to concentrate on personal detachment. Try to put your own feelings aside when making decisions for the good of everyone. The law of averages indicates that there will probably be at least one individual in a team with whom you cannot see eye-to-eye, but do not let this blind you to their good qualities. A friend who appears plagued by a run of bad luck may be desperately in need of moral or financial support. Think of a way in which you can cheer them up; a surprise gift or an invitation to dinner could be a welcome respite for them. It may be wiser to keep your own problems to yourself for now; you are unlikely to get full attention.

16. SATURDAY. Variable. If you are involved in fund-raising activities for a charity, try not to expect too much generosity from other people. You may find it difficult to accept that certain individuals are unable to give to a cause that does not directly affect them. On the other hand, a small number of lavish donations can restore your faith in human nature. Do not hesitate buying raffle tickets or entering your name in a drawing; there is a greater possibility of winning something worth having. A social engagement this evening is likely to be canceled at the last moment, or a friend may fail to turn up. Have an alternative plan in mind so that you are not left stranded.

17. SUNDAY. Changeable. You have to put the needs of others first today. This may include giving someone a lift when their car breaks down. Helping out could take more time than you can really spare, but remind yourself that they would undoubtedly do the same for you. Begin now to do the groundwork for home decorating, such as stripping old paint or wallpaper. Make life easier for yourself by hiring or borrowing equipment designed to speed up the job. A recent disagreement with a loved one may be troubling your conscience. If you know in your heart that you are at least partially at fault, now could be the time to swallow your pride and make a sincere apology.

18. MONDAY. Frustrating. Money you have been salting away for a rainy day may have to be withdrawn for an emergency. This could be for repairs to equipment used for work, such as a word processor or your car. A member of your family may come to you for a loan. Because this is likely to be a case of genuine hardship, try to be as generous as you can. If your work requires long periods of concentration, this is a good day for investing in an answering machine so that you can return calls at more convenient times. Written work of all kinds can prove difficult to compose; get down the essential information first and worry about the style later. Double-check facts and figures with more than one source.

19. TUESDAY. Fair. Recently retired Leo people may find that you have too much free time on your hands. Working on your home or garden can be rewarding but might not be enough to keep you fully occupied. Look for a part-time job; there could be more opportunities than you realize. Remind yourself that it is never too late to learn about new subjects or acquire new skills. Varying your usual routine today can be productive. Seek ways of managing your time more effectively. Someone who is ill or recovering from an operation would probably appreciate a visit this evening. Although they should be making a good recovery, they are likely to be suffering from postoperative blues.

20. WEDNESDAY. Uncertain. Being at home with children can be tiring because you are trying to get on with other jobs at the same time. It might be easier to let nonessential tasks wait until later in the day. Take extra care not to leave sharp instruments such as work tools or kitchen knives lying around where children can reach them. There is a greater risk of an accident, which can happen in that split second when your back is turned. If work matters have been taking over your life recently, this is a good time for resolving to take up a sport or a hobby. Do not fall into the trap of thinking that you cannot spare the time; it is up to you to make the time available.

21. THURSDAY. Useful. Today's mail can be heavier than usual, but the one thing you have been expecting is unlikely to turn up. There is a greater possibility that it has been lost. This is a good day for shopping for birthday cards; stock up with a selection now so that you always have one on hand. Personalized stationery or glassware can make a beautiful present for a friend. Paying bills should be high on your list of priorities, especially if you have already received a first reminder. Put the telephone bill at the top of the list so that there is no chance of being disconnected. Consider taking on an assignment which can be done at home if finances need a shot in the arm.

22. FRIDAY. Variable. For Leos who are out of work, this can be a good day for claiming government benefits to which you are entitled. Try not to be turned off by the amount of forms that need to be filled out. It will all seem worth it when the first check arrives. Do not rely on a bureaucrat to volunteer information about other benefits that may be available; ask directly for relevant information, or speak to an officer whose job it is to help you. If you have older children living at home, this is a favorable time to ask them to make a contribution to household expenses. Even a small amount could teach them to place a value on comforts they may take for granted.

23. SATURDAY. Unsettling. Be more selective about whom you spend your free time with. There is no rule which says that you have to see people who depress you or who undermine your self-esteem. Nor is feeling sorry for somebody a sound basis for a healthy relationship. By all means acknowledge a certain responsibility to those who depend on you, but look out for number one as well. Spend more time with those people whose company you genuinely enjoy. If you are separated by circumstances from a loved one, this afternoon is good for writing a long letter to pass on the week's news. This evening favors socializing, which gives you a chance to meet new people.

24. SUNDAY. Good. Treat yourself to a lazy start to the day, especially if you have spent the whole week rushing around. Do household chores in your own time rather than trying to race against the clock. Do not forget to go through pockets before putting clothes into the washing machine; there is a greater chance of finding some money that you had forgotten was there. Consider selling household objects that you no longer have any use for, such as an item of furniture or a painting. Try to be more ecologically minded today by taking bottles or newspapers to designated collection areas. If you go grocery shopping, bring along your own bags and help to save a tree.

25. MONDAY. Buoyant. This is likely to be a fun start to the workweek. Colleagues can be full of entertaining stories about the weekend and know just how to appeal to your sense of humor. Leos are likely to be kept busier than usual, but tasks should be straightforward. Working on the telephone can produce excellent results, especially if you are canvassing or selling a new product. Do not put off making business appointments; someone who has refused to see you in the past may now be more approachable. This is a favorable time to sign up for a course aimed at quickly acquiring a new skill such as learning to drive, type, or use new computer software.

26. TUESDAY. Disquieting. If you have been waiting for a medical report you may get some news this morning, but you could be in for a long wait before getting another appointment. You might want to consider seeing a private specialist in the meantime if you are worried about the delay. Taking in a lodger could be the answer to current financial difficulties, but be discriminating about where you advertise. Someone who is recommended by an associate may not really be your sort of person; arrange a meeting before you make a commitment that you could live to regret. Business negotiations of all kinds need to be followed up immediately in writing. Take promises or verbal assurances with a grain of salt.

27. WEDNESDAY. Strenuous. Statistics reveal that a high percentage of accidents happen in the home, but there are many steps you can take in order to minimize the risks. Make sure that you have taken every possible precaution in your own home, especially if you care for children or an elderly relative. Gates at the top of stairs or a mat in the bathtub make a lot of sense. This is also a good day for increasing your insurance coverage. Friction with someone in the family can lead to a falling-out later in the day. This is one of those times when a good argument may be the only way to clear the air. Try not to let bad feelings linger on; holding a grudge benefits nobody.

28. THURSDAY. Mixed. Self-employed Leos who have been working from home may be running out of space. This is a favorable day for looking for property to rent. You might find that the cost is not quite as steep as you had imagined. Taking on an assistant could also make life easier. Freeing yourself of administrative work is likely to give you more time to spend with clients. Leos who are in the process of establishing a new living arrangement may still have many things to discuss, such as the division of household goods. Stressful negotiations would probably be less painful if you arrange to meet on neutral ground such as at a restaurant. Give a little and you will get most of what you want.

29. FRIDAY. Happy. Your workload is unlikely to be heavy; you should have more than enough time to tie up loose ends from work earlier in the week. Entertain influential clients either at lunch or at a sporting event. Someone you have always been slightly in awe of could turn out to be amusing company in an informal setting. Single Leos may be asked out on a date by someone you have known for a short time. Even if you do not feel wildly enthusiastic, you have nothing to lose by giving someone a fair chance. You could well be in for a pleasant surprise when you discover how easy they are to talk to and how much you have in common.

30. SATURDAY. Calm. Devoting time to your children can remind you of the most enjoyable side of parenthood. Their capacity for fun could be just what you need if you have had a grueling week at work. Looking at the world through their eyes is likely to help put your own problems in perspective. Consider taking part in a sponsored sporting event such as a marathon walk or swim;

you should be able to raise a substantial amount of money for a good cause. This evening can be good for an informal gathering with close friends, either at home or at a favorite restaurant. Put any worries firmly out of mind, at least until tomorrow; use all your energies for enjoying yourself.

OCTOBER

1. SUNDAY. Disquieting. Your services may be called upon by a brother or sister to help with work at home, or they may ask you to look after a niece or nephew. You will probably feel reluctant to give up your free time, especially if you have a full schedule of jobs to do yourself. Aim for a compromise by suggesting the morning or afternoon, but not both. Deadlines for written work, such as an essay or a company report, could be looming. This means having to curtail social activities later in the day. Working on your car can present difficulties. Even if you are mechanically minded you may not be able to isolate a particular problem; a garage bill seems inevitable.

2. MONDAY. Variable. Starting a new job or work assignment can be a daunting experience; you may wonder what on earth you have let yourself in for. Keep in mind that everything is bound to be confusing and unfamiliar at first. Try not to judge colleagues on first impressions; once you have found your feet you will probably realize that they are true professionals. Try not to be seduced by new health products; you could end up wasting a lot of money. But boosting your vitamin intake could be beneficial, especially if you drink or smoke. Seek advice from a health-foods specialty store if you are unsure about which vitamins or minerals you should be taking. Strive to improve your overall diet as well.

3. TUESDAY. Good. This promises to be a productive day. Others seem willing to hear you out, probably because they are responding to your enthusiasm. A positive attitude can open doors to even the most reluctant customers. If you are seeking new staff members, this is a good day for conducting interviews; recent advertising could have attracted just the caliber of applicants you are hoping for. Leos who are unattached may receive a telephone call from someone you met over the weekend. Their obvious interest can boost your self-esteem; do not hesitate to agree to a date. This is a favorable day for making or accepting social invitations of all kinds.

4. WEDNESDAY. Deceptive. This is not a good day for staying indoors; there is a greater tendency to feel lonely and housebound. If you have young children, make an extra effort to get in touch with other parents in your area; some variety should be beneficial to all of you. An argument with an associate can leave you feeling resentful, maybe even angry enough to think of quitting. But this is not a day for rash decisions. Remind yourself that it is unrealistic to expect total harmony all the time. Being in an intimate relationship can bring you face to face with your own faults and shortcomings. Try to acknowledge your part in the issues which seem to create friction.

5. THURSDAY. Changeable. If you are buying goods on behalf of another person today, at an auction for instance, guard against a tendency to be too open-handed. Try not to go over budget, even if you think that you have found a bargain. Your first responsibility must be to your client; abide by their guidelines. Investment plans may appear attractive on the surface, but do not allow yourself to be hustled into making long-term commitments. Take time to think carefully about the costs involved; there is no point in beginning monthly premiums unless you are sure that you can keep them up. Helping children with homework could keep you busy this evening.

6. FRIDAY. Fair. If you have a financial application in the pipeline, perhaps for a grant or a loan, this could be a favorable time for checking up on it. Refuse to accept delays beyond a reasonable amount of time; making a complaint may be the only way to cut through the excuses or red tape. Return faulty merchandise to the store where it was bought. Guard against being apologetic; knowing your rights and having confidence in your own authority can make others less inclined to argue with you. Working late might be in the cards. Concentrate on finishing a job which cannot be left over the weekend. Putting in overtime is preferable to taking work home with you.

7. SATURDAY. Disquieting. This is unlikely to be a good day for traveling. Long-distance journeys can be subject to delays or rerouting without advance warning. Be sure to keep travel documents such as your ticket and passport in a safe place; there is a greater danger of losing them or of having them stolen. Luggage labels need to be clearly legible and firmly attached. Avoid leaving your car in a risky parking place; you might return to find that you have been towed away. If you are throwing a party this evening, be sure to let your neighbors know. They are far less likely to complain about the noise if they have been forewarned, or even invited to drop by.

8. SUNDAY. Demanding. You may be disappointed in your attempt to secure tickets for a concert or theater production. It might be worth scanning newspaper advertisements to see if you could buy them elsewhere. Be prepared to pay extra if you buy from a ticket agency. Long-distance telephone calls may be unavoidable, but keep an eye on the clock in order to avoid a hefty bill. Write friends or relatives who now live overseas. For married Leos, a visit to your in-laws can be an ordeal rather than a pleasure. Avoid arguing over personal beliefs about politics or religion; if certain family members hold opposing views you could be accused of being antagonistic.

9. MONDAY. Unsettling. Legal matters can be particularly stressful. If you are involved in litigation you may be tempted to give up altogether; you probably are tired of fighting what appears to be a losing battle. Take advice from your lawyer; you are likely to be encouraged to hold out for what is rightfully yours. For Leos in school, work could be piling up at an alarming rate. Your best approach is to be systematic; put your assignments in order of priority. If written work is due soon, do not fall into the trap of leaving it all until the last minute. Try to impose your own deadlines so that pacing yourself becomes second nature.

10. TUESDAY. Good. This should be a satisfying day for Leo business people. Even if you are not earning as much as you would like, true job satisfaction is just as important. Chances for a promotion could be nearer than you realize. If you run your own business, this is a favorable time for improving public relations; widespread publicity can boost your image and consequently your revenue. Afternoon hours are good for viewing properties if you are looking for some place to rent; there is a greater possibility of finding exactly what you have in mind. Accept an invitation to go out after work with an associate. Developing a personal relationship can improve everyday cooperation.

11. WEDNESDAY. Uncertain. Work matters should be mostly straighforward. Routine jobs can be disposed of surprisingly quickly. If you are looking for a better position, your current employer will probably be sad to see you go, but they are likely to give you a glowing reference to help you up the ladder of success. At home, this could be a day of disruptions. Home repairs or redecorating may be creating more chaos than you had thought possible; it might seem as if the place will never get back to normal. Try to be patient and keep out of the way as much as you can. Take extra care when handling valuable or breakable objects; an accident could result in an item being damaged beyond repair.

12. THURSDAY. Lucky. This is a good day for a scoop, possibly related to the world of politics at the local or national government level. If you work in a creative field such as marketing or advertising, this can be a favorable time for pooling ideas with your colleagues. Teamwork should produce the best results; inspiration from general discussion can set off a whole new train of thought. Conditions favor joining clubs or societies with a view to widening your social circle, especially if you have recently moved into a new neighborhood. You could find that getting to know people is easier than you had anticipated. Do not hesitate to take the initiative in striking up a conversation with someone you would like to get to know better.

13. FRIDAY. Changeable. If you are a decision-maker when it comes to allocating funds, this is a day when you should exert extra caution. Certain investments are unlikely to yield the level of profits that they promise. Reducing budget allotments may produce a storm of protests, but if you are careful to explain the rationale behind your policies you should be able to win grudging acceptance. Strive to organize group activities of all kinds. This evening is favorable for a get-together with old friends or former colleagues. There is plenty of news to catch up with regarding events going on in their lives. Try to be a good listener for a loved one who needs a shoulder to cry on.

14. SATURDAY. Strenuous. Be careful when it comes to confiding in others. Personal anxieties may not get the sympathetic hearing that you were hoping for. It may be wise to follow your own counsel rather than looking to others to provide you with answers. Leos in relationships of long standing may be suffering from pangs of boredom, but becoming involved in another romantic entanglement is unlikely to be the answer. Secret meetings or telephone calls are bound to come to light sooner or later. Concentrate on breathing new life into the relationship you already have. This evening can be good for staying home; relax with a good movie or music that puts you in the mood for love.

15. SUNDAY. Happy. This is an ideal time for finishing off repair jobs around the house. A how-to magazine or do-it-yourself manual can provide useful tips which might save a lot of time. This is a good afternoon for inviting close friends or family for lunch or dinner. Be prepared for a welcome but uninvited guest as well; someone who has been out of touch for some time may decide to drop by out of the blue. If you have just had a breakup with your partner you could be troubled by feelings of regret. But all is not lost; this is a starred time for healing the rift and making a new beginning. You never appreciate what you have until you come close to losing it.

16. MONDAY. Variable. Acknowledge your own limitations when it comes to business matters. There is little to be gained by trying to pull the wool over someone's eyes. The best policy is to admit to mistakes you may have made rather than trying to cover them up. Try not to bluff your way through an interview or presentation; if you do not know the answer to a question, say so. Being honest is unlikely to make others think any less of you. Do some bargain hunting for household items. Your best chance of success is to stay away from department stores. Instead, try hunting around a discount store or thrift shop away from the main shopping malls. Traveling some distance can prove rewarding.

17. TUESDAY. Cautious. Make your own needs clear at work. This may include putting in a request for more modern equipment or a private telephone line. Employers are likely to agree to changes which can help you to be more efficient. Consider employing an assistant to help ease your administrative burdens. For Leo salespeople, this is a favorable time for attending a course aimed at improving your negotiating skills. Learning how to handle difficult customers on the telephone as well as face to face could prove invaluable. Partners may not have a particularly easy day; take the pressure off them this evening by offering to cook or take them out for dinner.

18. WEDNESDAY. Quiet. Contemplate ways of furthering personal aims and ambitions. If you work as part of a large organization, it is up to you to let superiors know where your real interests lie. Find out what experience or qualifications you need in order to reach a coveted position, then make your plans accordingly. It is a favorable time for brightening up your personal image by buying new clothes or shoes. You have the confidence to make a dramatic change in your appearance such as a new hair color or wig; this might take some getting used to, but others are likely to compliment you on your new look. Partners are making an extra effort to put you first; enjoy being spoiled this evening.

19. THURSDAY. Disturbing. You may not be feeling in the best of spirits, probably due to tiredness. If you have been burning the candle at both ends recently, resolve to catch up on your sleep. A couple of early nights could work wonders. If you suspect that the stress of work is more to blame, this can be a good time for finding ways to reduce your workload. Remind yourself that there is no point in sacrificing your health in an attempt to reach the summit in your career. Guard against a tendency to be overly demanding in personal relationships. You might have to make an extra effort to understand someone's point of view; they have a right to their own opinions.

20. FRIDAY. Changeable. Household bills could arrive all at once in today's mail, putting an unwelcome strain on your finances. This is the time to find out about alternative methods of payment, such as putting quarterly bills on a monthly basis. A separate bank account for regular expenses may make it easier for you to budget. Cheer up your home or place of work with fresh flowers or colorful plants. Blank walls can be transformed with some prints or a framed mirror. Do not delay getting an electrical appliance repaired, especially if the guarantee period is about to expire. Be flexible this evening; last-minute plans can lead to a memorable time.

21. SATURDAY. Good. Something valuable which you lost earlier in the month could be returned to you, just when you had given up hope. Other people's integrity can restore your faith in human nature. A small reward would probably be gratefully accepted. It is a good time for employing a local tradesperson to fix an electrical or plumbing problem at home. Not only are they likely to be efficient, they should be surprisingly cheap too. Bills for car servicing or repairs will probably also be more reasonable than you had expected. A night out with friends could prove to be the highlight of the week. Unattached Leos may find that a certain individual wants your undivided attention.

22. SUNDAY. Lucky. Expect a number of telephone calls to or from members of your family. Do not put off writing letters to friends you met on vacation earlier in the year; try to stay in touch even if you live some distance apart. You can afford to focus on activities you find relaxing; a new hobby can be absorbing. A crossword puzzle which usually takes all day to complete may be surprisingly easy this time. If there is a new contest being advertised, send in at least one entry; somebody has to win. For Leo parents, this afternoon should be a good time for taking your children to a local exhibition or other event related to their interests. If you are in the presence of a famous person, try to get an autograph.

23. MONDAY. Deceptive. Getting to work this morning can present problems. Allow more time than usual for commuting. Traffic is likely to be heavy for no immediately apparent reasons. An alarm clock which you have had for years may suddenly fail you; it would probably be cheaper to buy a new one rather than paying to have it repaired. If your work involves using computers or other technology, be prepared for some technical hitches today. Electrical faults can occur without warning and may prove impossible to trace. Get into the habit of copying your work onto a backup disk; this way you can avoid losing an essential document as well as work in progress.

24. TUESDAY. Buoyant. This promises to be a propitious day for Leos who are moving. The upheaval is likely to be far less traumatic than you had feared. If you have been in a happy relationship for some time, this should be a favorable day for discussing the prospect of living together or getting married. New beginnings of all kinds can bring you a renewed sense of purpose in life. If you are at home today, spend some time raking leaves and tidying up the yard. Family relationships can be put on a firmer footing. Bring a long-standing issue out into the open; remember that grievances which remain unspoken never really go away. A compromise solution can be hammered out.

25. WEDNESDAY. Fair. A transaction which has been dragging on for a long time needs to be brought to a close. Whether or not the outcome is positive may not be that important. But the matter may be holding you back because you are unlikely to throw yourself into new ventures until the way ahead is clear. Try not to waste time crying over spilt milk; resolve to learn from mistakes you might have made. Do not be afraid to state your point of view in business matters. Others will respect your opinions once they realize that you are talking from experience rather than just airing your theories. Offer to organize and host a birthday or anniversary party for someone close to you.

26. THURSDAY. Happy. This is a rewarding day for Leos who work in the field of education. Working directly with children can be especially enjoyable. Worries that you may have had about presenting certain material will probably be unfounded; this could give you the confidence to break with traditional teaching methods when the situation calls for it. Do not be afraid to be innovative as long as your aims are clear; results are what count. This is a favorable day for taking a written exam; you should find that you are able to answer questions in full without running out of time. If you are attracted to someone, this is a good time for taking the plunge and asking them out; you will be glad that you did.

27. FRIDAY. Disquieting. New business plans can be subject to a series of frustrating delays. Try not to lose heart too quickly; perseverance should win through at the end of the day. Certain individuals may try to influence you with their own pessimism or hard-luck story. It is up to you to separate the good advice from the bad in order to keep the courage of your convictions. An evening out which had promised to be fun could turn out to be deadly dull; you may find that you have nothing in common with the other people present. Teenage children are likely to rebel against coming home by a certain time, but Leo parents have to be firm in imposing a curfew.

28. SATURDAY. Lucky. This can be a good day for shopping for clothes. Leos looking for a special outfit for a forthcoming event, such as a wedding, are likely to find exactly what you are seeking. Finding accessories to match should be easier than usual too. Add to your music collection. Be adventurous in your choice of performers; you may discover someone new who is just your cup of tea. If you are entertaining at home this evening, take advantage of the opportunity to experiment with a new recipe. Guests will be impressed with your culinary expertise. Being in the audience at a live concert or musical production can be a magical experience.

29. SUNDAY. Uncertain. A friend may cancel a social arrangement with very short notice. You might have difficulty in believing their reasons for letting you down, but try to give them the benefit of the doubt for the time being. Certain facts could come to light later to prove if your suspicions were justified or not. If you are buying from a mail-order catalog, make sure that you are dealing with a reputable company. Sending cash through the mail is always risky, but especially so today. Make payments by check; this way you can always prove that they have been cashed and that you have paid. Avoid driving a long or even a short distance if you feel sleepy.

30. MONDAY. Deceptive. In business matters this is a day when you cannot afford to be too trusting. Verbal assurances, even from a client who is usually reliable, are likely to come to nothing. For Leos who are self-employed, suspicions of someone's inability to pay in full could be well founded. Ask for a substantial deposit for larger commissions so that you have some financial protection. A disagreement with someone close to you may blow up out of all proportion unless one of you is prepared to back down. Try to accept defeat gracefully if you are clearly on the losing end. Dealing with paperwork of all kinds can be laborious; do not hesitate to ask for clarification if a certain document is confusing.

31. TUESDAY. Fine. Request information about vacations or weekend getaways. Newspaper advertisments offering flights or accommodations at discounted prices are well worth investigating. Your creative powers are likely to be at full strength today. Leos who earn a living from creative work should be able to make great strides with your latest project; get new ideas down on paper as soon as possible while they are fresh in your mind. Sharing work with someone whose critical ability you respect can be surprisingly helpful. A sudden rush of social invitations could leave you with very little free time; be careful not to overcommit yourself and then have to invent an excuse to back out of the engagement.

NOVEMBER

1. WEDNESDAY. Variable. You cannot afford to depend too much on the help of others, especially this morning. Offers of practical assistance which you thought you could rely on may simply not be there when you need them. Leo business people are well advised to take extra care of important customers; there is a greater danger of losing vital contracts to a competitor. You may have to give certain clients substantial incentives if you want to guarantee future business. The afternoon may not go quite according to plan. Sorting out other people's blunders could use up a lot of precious time. An evening at home with a loved one can restore your sense of security.

2. THURSDAY. Demanding. This is apt to be a tiring day. Demands on your time could reach such unmanageable proportions that you have to keep certain individuals at bay. Do not hesitate to say no, especially to associates who always seem to take a yes for granted. This could stop them in their tracks, but they are unlikely to take advantage of your generous nature so quickly in the future. You should be systematic in order to achieve both short-term and long-term objectives; try to plan ahead. Thinking on your feet can rescue you from a difficult situation. But guard against giving glib answers to serious questions; someone's respect may be hard to win back once it is lost.

3. FRIDAY. Good. A kindness shown to you can be a heartwarming experience. Be sure to show your appreciation even though it seems clear that your benefactor may not be acting purely from altruistic motives. This is a rewarding day for Leos involved in counseling. There is a greater chance of getting to the real roots of a client's problem or a friend's dilemma. Money that is owed to you, such as a tax rebate or an insurance claim, can finally materialize. If this is a substantial amount it could be wise to invest part of it in a high-interest savings account. Seek alternative methods of treatment for a health problem; a remedy could be easier to find than you have been led to believe.

4. SATURDAY. Enjoyable. This can be a good time for a weekend trip to friends who live some distance away. Traveling is likely to be hassle-free. If you make your journey by car, choose a picturesque route even if it does take a little longer. A change of scenery can have beneficial effects on your health and general well-being. If you are unable to get away, spend at least part of the day on a hobby or special interest. This is a favorable time for entertaining visitors from other countries; you may learn historical facts about your own neighborhood through showing people around. Exchanging information about your different cultures could lead to lively informative debate. Accepting cultural diversity can give you a new perspective.

5. SUNDAY. Deceptive. Leos may be under pressure today to finish a project. Do not rely on being granted an extension to the deadline; this is unlikely to be given unless you can prove that unusual circumstances caused your delay. You might not be totally satisfied with the end product, but remind yourself that finishing is of paramount importance now. Be circumspect when airing your political beliefs in front of strangers. A certain individual may accuse you of prejudices and refuse to be persuaded otherwise. In-laws or other older relatives may be hard to convince when it comes to seeking a loan from them or their signature on a certain document. You need to use charm along with hard facts.

6. MONDAY. Disquieting. Leos whose work involves dealing directly with the general public could be in for a taxing day. You will probably have to call upon all your powers of tact and diplomacy in order to handle a difficult customer. Do not allow yourself to be subjected to unreasonable verbal abuse. A business associate may try to pass the buck for a mistake for which they are responsible. It may be a case of your word against theirs at the moment, but this is not an occasion when you can afford to take the rap just to keep the peace. The implications of such an act could be more far reaching than you realize. Put agreements of any sort into writing for future reference.

7. TUESDAY. Changeable. Patience in furthering your career prospects is likely to pay off. Although it might have seemed that there was no chance of promotion in your current job, the sudden departure of a colleague could leave a gap for you to fill. If you have been unemployed for a while, there could be an offer of work today. Even if the position is not exactly what you wanted, getting a foot in the door is what counts; prove yourself and you could soon be in line for better things. If you have recently moved from your neighborhood, you may have to contend with feelings of homesickness. But these should pass as soon as you become more familiar with your new surroundings.

8. WEDNESDAY. Demanding. For Leos who live in rented property, this could be a good time for putting your security on a firmer footing. If your landlord is pushing for an unreasonable rent increase you may need to take legal action. Household bills need to be paid promptly; there is a greater risk of having your gas, electricity, or telephone disconnected if you ignore an overdue reminder. Power outages either at home or at your place of work are a possibility in the morning. Later in the day is good for teamwork of all kinds, although minor disputes can delay progress. Delegate easy jobs so that you can concentrate on your particular area of expertise.

9. THURSDAY. Unsettling. If you are thinking of joining a club or association in order to expand your social circle, this could be a good time for doing some homework. Focus on a group that comes with a recommendation from someone you already know and whose judgment you can trust. Otherwise you run the risk of wasting a lot of precious time and money. At work you may get ahead faster if you map out a detailed plan of action. Advice or suggestions from colleagues can only serve to complicate what are basically simple issues. A friend could be going on and on about a personal problem, but remind yourself that what seems trivial to you is obviously very important to him or her. The evening favors study and writing projects.

10. FRIDAY. Uncertain. No matter how much you trust a friend or associate, this is not a good time for lending money. By all means offer what is safely within your means and could be written off as a gift. But larger amounts are unlikely to be repaid on time or in full. Try to guard against setting too high standards or being overly critical of other people's behavior. Unrealistic expectations can only lead to disappointments sooner or later. Also bear in mind that others will probably be less inclined to tolerate your own shortcomings if you cannot make allowances for theirs. Although children can show you up in public if they do not get their own way, giving in is likely to make the next battle of wills even worse.

11. SATURDAY. Rewarding. This is a good day for shopping for antiques. Old books or art can be an investment as well as a joy to own, especially if they relate to a particular interest of yours. You may also want to find an expert to restore an old painting or piece of furniture which has been handed down through the generations. Tracing your family ancestry can be a fascinating project; given the right assistance, this could be easier to do than you imagine. Someone close to you may disclose certain secrets about their past; knowing that you have their confidence to this extent can do much to strengthen the bond between you. This evening favors contacting an old friend by letter or in person.

12. SUNDAY. Variable. This can be a good day for volunteer work, perhaps in support of a charity whose causes are close to your heart. Raising money is never an easy task, but you are likely to get a generous donation from an unusual or even anonymous source. An exhibition related to mystical matters may be worth a visit. Try to keep an open mind when finding out about beliefs which are totally new to you. You might find some spiritual theories confusing, but others could challenge your own views in a way that makes sense to you. Later in the day can be good for catching up with domestic chores such as washing and ironing so that you can avoid starting the new workweek in a disorganized state.

13. MONDAY. Strenuous. Plans to improve your career prospects need to be discussed carefully with your mate or partner.
Remember that changes in your life are bound to affect them at
the same time. Consider going back to school to acquire extra
qualifications even though this could mean giving up your salary
for a while. Your heartfelt desires are likely to be greeted with
support if you show consideration for the feelings of others. For
Leo parents who work, child-minding arrangements could be hard
to organize. You may have to sacrifice a substantial part of your
salary in order to employ someone who is both experienced and
trustworthy. Working from your home base is an option worth
pursuing.

14. TUESDAY. Fair. A member of your household is likely to
get out of bed on the wrong side this morning. There is little point
trying to find out what is bothering them; stay out of their way and
do not let their irritability rub off on you. A cheerful approach to
problems could be the most effective way of finding solutions. A
positive attitude can stop others from overdramatizing what is
probably a straightforward matter. Your qualities of leadership
are beginning to be recognized, but be prepared for jealous remarks from someone who feels that they have been passed over. A
person you are attracted to can make you tongue-tied at first but
will soon put you at ease.

15. WEDNESDAY. Mixed. Necessary household repairs may
require that you stay home this morning. Leaving a key with a
neighbor could be an alternative, but it is probably wiser to be on
hand yourself to ensure that the work is done the way you want.
Be extra watchful of your personal belongings later in the day. A
tendency to be absentminded could result in your leaving a bag or
important papers in a public place such as on the bus or in a store.
Documents are likely to find their way back to you, but money
may be gone for good. Conditions favor sending off written applications for a mortgage or a loan for home improvements; you
should get a speedy and positive response.

16. THURSDAY. Lucky. There should be ample opportunities
for finding ways in which you can boost your income. This may
include using the skills you already have to take in extra work at
home. Doing jobs in other people's homes, such as carpentry or
decorating, could also prove to be good earning opportunities. Be
sure to put in a claim for benefits if you are out of work. If you are
disabled or have been ill for some time, there may be other
payments to which you are entitled. Ask a friend or relative to find

out more information for you if you do not feel equal to the task
yourself. This is a promising evening for romance; a new relationship can start to blossom.

17. FRIDAY. Difficult. You have to decide if a social arrangement is really worth the expense. Put your desires in priority. It
seems clear that something will have to be sacrificed or be put on
the back burner for the foreseeable future. Partners are likely to
be extravagant today, but try not to be too critical even if you feel
that they have gone over the top. There is no point in making
someone feel guilty about something which cannot be changed.
This is not the right time to push for a pay raise. Wait until you are
in a stronger position before you deliver what might be interpreted
as an ultimatum; be prepared to bide your time and prove your
abilities.

18. SATURDAY. Good. Financial pressures should ease today. Bills which arrive in the mail could be lower than you had
anticipated. Letters from friends or family can be entertaining and
get the day off to a cheerful start. A thank-you card from someone
you have helped out recently may be an unexpected but touching
surprise. For Leo students, this is a good day for getting down to
some serious written work, especially on projects which require
imaginative input. Working in the library may be a wise move
unless you can ensure that you will not be disturbed at home. This
evening favors a trip to the movies or to a musical recital performed by a local group.

19. SUNDAY. Easygoing. For Leos who live alone, this is a
day to seek the company of longtime friends who know you well.
No matter how self-sufficient you are, there comes a point when
social interaction can be essential to your sense of well-being.
Remind yourself that intellectual growth can only really take place
if you are prepared to enter into debate and share your opinions.
Someone special can bring more fun into your life if you give them
the chance to get close to you. If you have been badly hurt in the
past, you can now try to trust again. Guard against drowning your
sorrows by misusing drugs or alcohol; the problems will still be
there when the hangover wears off.

20. MONDAY. Satisfactory. Leos who have been contemplating going into business should proceed with basic fact-finding and
research. Talking to others who have already taken that path could
provide some invaluable information and guidelines. It is also a
favorable time for house hunting. Contact a local real estate agent

to explain what you are seeking in the way of property. This way they can keep you fully informed of the properties available in your price range. A recurring health problem may be failing to respond to treatment because of your life-style. A prolonged rest or some radical changes in your daily routine could achieve surprisingly quick results.

21. TUESDAY. Encouraging. Bringing business negotiations to a satisfactory conclusion should be possible. This means having to be firm in presenting a client with a final offer. Once they realize that you are not going to back down they will probably be only too willing to go along with your proposals. This could be an auspicious day for Leo salespeople to meet or even surpass your monthly target. A sale you thought you had lost to a competitor could suddenly turn around in your favor. An impromptu invitation from an associate to go out this evening should be well worth accepting. You are likely to meet all sorts of interesting and unusual people.

22. WEDNESDAY. Happy. A new creative project started at this time is likely to succeed. Acquiring new skills, such as learning a musical instrument, can be fun. If you are so far self-taught, this could be a good time for starting some professional lessons; this way you could make swifter progress. For Leos who are unattached, this is a favorable day for seeking out the company of someone to whom you are attracted. Building a firm foundation of friendship could lead naturally to romance, so try not to rush the relationship. Give the other person a chance to get to know you. Consider advertising unwanted household items for sale; the extra money could come in handy. If you are traveling for tomorrow's holiday, get an early start.

23. THURSDAY. Disquieting. For Leos going through the process of a lawsuit, this is a day to guard against being drawn into old arguments. There comes a time when going over old ground becomes unprofitable, not to mention painful. Try to accept that there are certain issues which you will never see eye-to-eye on, no matter how hard you try. Looking after children may feel like a thankless task today. But if you are celebrating this holiday, you will give thanks anyway. Put your energies into thinking up activities to keep them occupied. Losing your temper in any situation is likely to get you nowhere fast. Money worries may be uppermost in your mind. Avoid entering into credit arrangements unless you are sure that the repayments are within your means.

24. FRIDAY. Tranquil. This is likely to be a pleasant end to the working week. There is less chance of last-minute crises. Deadlines should be easier to reach than usual; putting in overtime can be optional rather than compulsory. For Leo business people, this could be a favorable day for entertaining influential clients. Securing their personal friendship as well as professional respect can count for a lot. Consider attending a convention; mixing with others who share your same interests could be educational. A recent argument with a loved one appears to have been forgotten; perhaps it was not as serious as you at first thought.

25. SATURDAY. Mixed. If you have a spare room at home, this could be a good time for advertising for a lodger. But guard against taking people at face value. No matter how charming someone appears to be, do not fall into the trap of disregarding the usual formalities. Make sure that you check references before handing over the keys. Asking for a deposit against breakage or unpaid bills is essential in order to protect your own interests. Health anxieties need to be addressed rather than ignored; a condition may get worse if you do not seek treatment. A personal problem might not have a clear-cut solution, probably because you are not in full possession of the facts.

26. SUNDAY. Fair. A missing pet can cause a great deal of worry this morning, especially for children. Abandon scheduled plans so that you can organize a search. There is a good chance that it will be found safe and well. If you are buying an animal today, make sure that their vaccination papers are up to date; do not take the previous owner's word for it. Later in the day can be ideal for a family get-together at home. A sit-down meal is likely to develop into a lively but noisy affair. Make sure that you get enough help when it comes to cleaning up, even if you have to break up a conversation. A newcomer is likely to receive an enthusiastic welcome and fit in well.

27. MONDAY. Enjoyable. This is a good day for face-to-face negotiations of all kinds. Meetings may go on for longer than you had anticipated, but time invested with a client or supplier now is likely to pay dividends several times over. Winning other people's confidence does not often happen overnight; concentrate on earning the respect and trust which is crucial to every working relationship. For Leos parents, this could be a good day for employing a nanny or a part-time babysitter. References can be glowing, making it hard to decide on the best candidate. You can afford to let intuition be your guide. The evening is favorable for romance with someone new, as you will be at your charming best.

28. TUESDAY. Easygoing. This morning is the best time of day for teamwork. If you need a superior's endorsement for certain plans or decisions, try to pin them down before lunchtime. There is a greater risk that they will be suddenly unavailable later in the day. Offer to help out a colleague with a difficult job, but try not to let your own work suffer by letting this take up too much of your time. Important paperwork can seem lost this afternoon. This should turn up eventually, but take the lesson to heart that your routine organization needs to be improved upon. Guard against a tendency to be unsympathetic about someone else's problem; a bit of encouragement can go a long way.

29. WEDNESDAY. Disquieting. If you are attending an interview, leave as much time free beforehand as possible. You will benefit greatly from going over the ground you need to cover in your own mind first. Even better would be to ask someone to role-play with you so that you can anticipate which questions are likely to trip you up or lead you into contradictions. This is not a day when you can afford to take unnecessary risks, especially with money. Make an extra effort to budget in advance and stick to it. Use discretion when it comes to confiding personal information to others. There is a greater likelihood that someone will draw conclusions which are incorrect.

30. THURSDAY. Sensitive. An increase in your income is likely, but try not to see this as a license to spend too freely. Money can run through your fingers at an alarming rate. Concentrate on finding ways to economize more effectively. Colleagues can be helpful with a work matter that has you baffled. A certain individual can come up with solutions that had never occurred to you even though they were staring you in the face. Accompanying your partner to a social function later in the day can be more of a duty than a pleasure. You might not be in the mood for small talk, but try to circulate rather than monopolize the company of those people you already know.

DECEMBER

1. FRIDAY. Good. For Leo students, this can be a day of real progress with your studies. Work submitted today is likely to earn you excellent grades; encouragement from a teacher could spur you on to greater efforts. You can afford to have confidence in your own abilities, but remember also that knowing your own failings is a sign of strength, not weakness. Honesty can endear you to others. At work, your willingness to learn is probably the best way to win popularity. Do not hesitate to ask for further explanation if you do not understand something the first time around. This is an auspicious evening for lighthearted romance, possibly with someone from a different country or culture.

2. SATURDAY. Deceptive. Try to put work matters out of mind. Worrying over a project that awaits your attention next week can put a damper on what promises to be an enjoyable weekend. If you have not yet started your Christmas shopping, this is a good day for buying gifts for those closest to you. You may end up spending more than you had intended, but loved ones are undoubtedly worth it. If you are planning to spend the festive season away from home, this is a favorable time for booking a flight or making hotel reservations. Do not neglect to ask for confirmation in writing to be forwarded to you if you make arrangements over the telephone. This is a good evening for a party, but take it easy with alcohol and fatty foods.

3. SUNDAY. Happy. This is unlikely to be a day when you are satisfied to stay at home. Explore a part of your neighborhood which is unknown to you. Volunteer work aimed at helping others in the community can be physically hard, but a sense of achievement from knowing that you are making a practical contribution should be rewarding. Go out of your way to support local events. This is a favorable time for joining a health club, especially if you are conscious of not doing enough exercise. If you plan to use the facilities on a regular basis, it would probably be cost effective to opt for a fully paid membership. You may be able to get a two-for-one deal and bring along your mate or steady date.

4. MONDAY. Disquieting. If December is your busiest time of year for business, this could be a good day for getting an advertising campaign under way. Make an extra effort to stick strictly to your budget; additional expenditure may not prove worthwhile. For Leos who are self-employed, this can be a good time for revising marketing strategies. Try to identify where the greater part of your business really comes from; the results could be different from what you had imagined. Meetings can start off well, then gradually reach a stalemate due to someone who refuses to compromise. Try not to give into demands which you know will make life more difficult in the long run.

5. TUESDAY. Variable. This morning favors introducing a new bonus scheme for your staff or learning more about an incentive plan available for you. The added incentive should boost your income for the month as well as keeping everyone happy. Morning is the best part of the day for attending or conducting interviews. If you have belonged to a club or association for some time, you may be invited to take up an official position on the governing committee. Although this is obviously flattering, think carefully before you accept such responsibility. The position could be open due to a resignation; it may be enlightening to find out why. Later hours favor short trips or visits with neighbors.

6. WEDNESDAY. Demanding. You may have to make a critical decision with regard to career matters. You can no longer afford to keep sitting on the fence. If you have children, part of your dilemma may be a concern that you do not spend enough time with them. Taking a promotion could reduce that time even more. Talk things through with your partner; let their wishes have equal weight in your final decision. A business venture which you have been nursing along may have to be dropped because the risk factor has proved to be unreasonably high. Make a donation to a charity of your choice, but do not allow yourself to be pressured into lending support to a cause whose policies you do not uphold.

7. THURSDAY. Difficult. A personal relationship may be giving you cause for concern. While it is unrealistic to expect that you should agree on everything, there should be a basic sympathy between you when it comes to sharing aims and ideals. You might have to face up to the fact that you are incompatible. Do not fall into the trap of believing that you can change someone to suit your needs. Younger children can be more demanding than usual; it may seem as if you never get a moment to yourself. This is a good time for finding a reliable babysitter to take over in moments of stress. An evening out with friends can end in debate over current affairs; try to be open to opposing viewpoints.

8. FRIDAY. Fair. You might wake up feeling at odds with the world, but try not to take out your irritability on others. There is a greater danger of alienating someone who has your best interests at heart. A medical appointment may involve a long period of waiting around. Anticipate the boredom by taking along a book or crossword puzzle to keep you occupied. In business matters, this is a time when you need to stay one step ahead of the competition. This may mean having to rely on a secret source of information; take care not to compromise somebody or run the risk of being accused of unethical behavior. Later in the day is good for visiting a friend or relative recovering from surgery.

9. SATURDAY. Uncertain. You need to guard against being secretive with a loved one. While you quite justly feel that you have a right to thoughts of your own, remember that evasive answers to innocent questions can stir up feelings of jealousy or of insecurity. If you conceal information, you are indirectly inviting someone to make interpretations which may be wide of the mark. Leos shopping for holiday presents may have difficulty in finding exactly what you had in mind. Do not postpone placing orders for gifts if delivery can be guaranteed to suit your needs. This evening is good for eating out at a reasonably priced restaurant.

10. SUNDAY. Unsettling. Take extra care if you are working out or jogging this morning. There is a greater risk of a minor injury such as a pulled muscle or sprained ankle. If you know you are out of condition, exercise of all kinds should be approached sensibly; remind yourself that fitness is not something you can acquire overnight. Start slowly and increase the level of activity gradually. If you are short of money, later in the day can be good for revamping old clothes; for instance, dyeing something a more modern color could give it a new lease on life. Making over a jacket or coat might be easier than you think. A night out with a group of friends or even someone special can be fun but expensive if you have to pay for two.

11. MONDAY. Good. This is a day when other people are kindly disposed toward you. A certain individual who has recently been a thorn in your side may go out of their way to be friendly; maybe they realize that they have been unfair in their judgment of you. Have the courage of your convictions in business matters. A bold scheme can work out even better than you had hoped. If you are presenting a new proposal to a client, your enthusiasm is likely to be the main factor in winning their support. It is also an auspicious day for romance. Do not be afraid to show someone that you are interested in them. They might just be waiting for the green light from you to give them the courage to ask you out.

12. TUESDAY. Quiet.   Spend some time attending to your personal appearance. If you cannot afford a new outfit for the upcoming holidays, you may be able to borrow from a friend. Or check a thrift shop stocked with once-worn castoffs. This can be a good day for treating yourself to a new hair style or for buying a kit to dye your own hair. For Leos who are self-employed, this is a favorable time for taking on extra help. Delegating routine work gives you more time to spend with customers who demand your personal attention. Superiors are willing to give you a freer hand in areas where you have proved your ability to cope and succeed.

13. WEDNESDAY. Fair.   Try to avoid carrying a large amount of cash. There is a greater chance of losing your wallet, and it is unlikely to be returned. This is a good day for putting your personal finances in order. Do not throw away receipts or old checkbooks just yet; you may need proof of purchase at a later date. Informal discussions at work should be productive. Do not beat around the bush when putting over your point of view; being direct and concise can be the most effective way to cutting through what is unimportant and getting to the facts. Leo salespeople stand a better chance of success if you resist using jargon. It might sound impressive to you but is probably a turnoff to others.

14. THURSDAY. Variable.   Money being paid directly into your bank account could be subject to delays. Save additional charges by checking your balance on hand before writing a check. Statements may not show transactions which should have cleared by now; this is likely to be an administrative hiccup which has gone unnoticed rather than an error on your part. If your work involves serving the general public, there is a good chance of earning extra tips. Part-time or temporary work for the festive season can be easier to come by, although the wages may not be particularly generous. Remind yourself that something is better than nothing in the short term.

15. FRIDAY. Stressful.   Buying Christmas presents this morning can be even more costly than you had feared. But with imagination you can make a small budget stretch a long way. For example, secondhand toys may look as good as new but cost a fraction of the original price. Catch up on routine work matters; you might be able to get away earlier than usual this evening. Later in the day is favorable for writing Christmas cards. Do not neglect to check the final mailing dates for cards or packages; you may have to pay extra to ensure holiday delivery. This evening is good for heart-to-heart discussions with a loved one; you should be able to clear up a misunderstanding once and for all.

16. SATURDAY. Deceptive.   Guard against acting in the heat of the moment. If you give vent to your anger you may end up saying things which you will regret later. Remind yourself that confrontations are usually better saved for a time when you are in a more rational frame of mind and are more likely to stick to the real issues. If you are planning to shop at a mall, it may be easier to use public transportation. Sitting in a traffic jam can waste a lot of time, and a parking space could be virtually impossible to find. Do not fall into the trap of staying home to wait for a telephone call from someone special; let your fingers do the dialing.

17. SUNDAY. Changeable.   If you still have not sent off your Christmas cards, this is a good day for disciplining yourself to do so. Friends you have been out of touch with for most of the year will appreciate an update on your life, although it might prove difficult to condense all that has been happening in a way which makes sense. Stick to the main events if you want to avoid being long-winded. Looking after other people's children is a possibility this afternoon. If you have your own as well, this is a favorable time for taking them all out to a local event such as a play or puppet show. Be generous in taking part in a sponsored event aimed at raising money for a charitable purpose.

18. MONDAY. Calm.   Send out invitations to a party you are planning. If you want to include colleagues on the guest list it may be easier to issue an open invitation; this way you avoid excluding someone by mistake or oversight. Someone who recently moved to the neighborhood would probably welcome the chance to make new contacts through you. Putting up Christmas decorations, either at home or at the office, can get everyone in a party mood. Go out for lunch with your own workmates and people from other departments. Taking part in a sporting event this evening can bring out your competitive side; do not overlook the value of just playing for the fun of it as well.

19. TUESDAY. Fair.   A deadline to meet at work this morning is likely to require all your resources. If you work as a manager you may have to exert your authority in subtle ways; knowing how to get the best out of each individual can be the key to success. If you are at home, the early part of the day is good for racing through the usual domestic chores. Do not allow older children to shirk their duties when it comes to giving you a hand. A social arrangement for later in the day may be canceled on short notice; have an alternative plan up your sleeve. A night out with a loved one may start promisingly, but an argument which has been brewing for a while is likely to erupt.

20. WEDNESDAY. Variable. You are unlikely to be snowed under with work, but guard against a tendency to let time slip through your fingers. Leo business people could benefit greatly from thinking ahead and making plans for the new Year. This can be a good time for interviewing to fill a position which will open up once the vacation period is over. If you store information on computer disks, be wary of deleting documents you now think you will no longer need. Such decisions could be premature. Avoid mixing business with pleasure beyond a sensible limit. A casual affair with a colleague could damage your working relationship as well as do harm to your reputation.

21. THURSDAY. Happy. Wind up business affairs in readiness for the Christmas break. Legal matters can be easier to resolve than at first appeared. A settlement made at this time is likely to be more than generous. With only three more shopping days to go, this can be a good day for buying last-minute presents in order to avoid the weekend rush. There is also a greater chance of finding the ideal gifts at reasonable prices, especially for the children in your family. For Leos who are single, this evening is auspicious for meeting someone new, probably at a party where everyone is set on having a good time. Serious conversation can always wait for another occasion.

22. FRIDAY. Demanding. If this is your last working day before the Christmas break you may not have the quiet day that you had expected. This may be a result of having to cover for other staff members who have already started their vacation. Thinking on your feet can get you through some tricky moments; snap decisions will probably prove to be the right ones. Try not to let workmates burden you with problems which could clearly be kept for another time. Once you get trapped into a conversation it might not be easy to get away. Leo parents should not delay making babysitting arrangements for Christmas or New Year's Eve.

23. SATURDAY. Misleading. You cannot afford to overindulge in rich food or too much alcohol; your system is likely to rebel unless you know your own limits. Last-minute shopping for gifts or groceries will be easier if you go alone. This way you can plan exactly where you want to go and not have to wait for someone else to keep up. Figure out menus for the next few days and stock up on what you need. If you are entertaining guests, make sure that you are aware of their likes and dislikes; also bear in mind any special dietary requirements. If you are planning to eat out this evening, make a reservation in advance rather than trust to luck. Candlelight will bring romance into clear focus.

24. SUNDAY. Good. This should be an enjoyable day as long as household members are prepared to cooperate with domestic chores. A fair division of labor can keep tempers in check and prevent someone from feeling put upon. Spend some time wrapping presents, but be sure that larger objects are hidden away in a place where nobody can stumble across them by chance. It is a favorable time for accepting an invitation to a formal affair such as a dinner dance. If you are socializing with people you have met through your professional interests, make sure that your partner does not feel excluded; try to avoid talking shop. Evening also favors attending a concert or theatrical production.

25. MONDAY. MERRY CHRISTMAS! This is likely to be one of those Christmas days when everything goes smoothly and according to plan. Your choice of gifts for loved ones could be met with even more delight than you had expected. In return, you could be overwhelmed at the generosity of a certain individual. Not surprisingly, children have a tendency to get overly excited. But their high spirits should calm down naturally once they become engrossed with new toys and games. Later in the day is good for taking a walk, although athletically minded Leos may prefer something more energetic such as jogging. Calm down this evening with improvised games which include the whole family.

26. TUESDAY. Calm. This day favors pure relaxation. Others seem content to be left to their own devices, so take the opportunity to enjoy some time to yourself. You may not feel inclined to keep a social arrangement later in the day, but you will probably be glad that you made the effort once you are on the scene. A friend who has not had a successful Christmas so far may need to unburden certain troubles to you. Make an extra effort to be a sympathetic listener; having someone understand his or her side of the story is probably all that is required. It is a good evening to include someone you suspect has been alone. Looking in on an elderly neighbor would probably be much appreciated.

27. WEDNESDAY. Variable. For Leos who are back at work, the morning is likely to drag because it is difficult to switch back into a work mode when there is not much to do. Try to keep busy with the routine tasks you do not normally have time for; this way you should forget to clock watch. The additional expenses of Christmas could mean that you are now feeling the pinch financially. It may be better to avoid a social get-together which is not that important to you but bound to be expensive. Be prepared for a certain individual to put pressure on you to change your mind; you may have to work hard to get this stubborn person to take no as a final answer.

28. THURSDAY. Deceptive. Make long-distance telephone calls to those you were unable to visit over the holiday period. Cards or packages which have been delayed could arrive in today's mail. Being separated from a loved one at this time can become more difficult to cope with, but the bond between you can be strengthened by their absence. Writing thank-you letters for gifts can be a tiresome process, but it has to be done sooner or later so you might as well make a start. This evening is favorable for a trip to the movies, or you may want to pick up several videos to watch. Keep entertainment on the light side.

29. FRIDAY. Tricky. If you are leaving for a New Year's vacation be prepared for delays in your journey. Flights can be rescheduled with very little prior warning. Try not to take out your frustration on those who are not to blame and probably no wiser than you are. Traffic jams may occur for no obvious reason; an alternative route is unlikely to be any better. Unless you know the roads intimately, there is a greater risk of getting lost if you veer onto side streets. Leo students may feel reluctant to get back to the books, but remind yourself that the more you do now, the less you will have to cram in just before returning to class.

30. SATURDAY. Uncertain. Entertaining visitors from abroad can be fun but unexpectedly demanding. It may be easier to abandon your usual routine for the duration of their stay. For Leo parents, this can be a good day for taking bored children on an outing; you may have to cope with disruptive behavior if you stay at home. Leos who have been unemployed for a while should give some serious thought to the path you want to pursue. You might find that you are ready for a new direction, which may include returning to school in order to get the necessary qualifications. Do not hesitate to take on a new challenge; change can be scary, but productive in the long run.

31. SUNDAY. Demanding. Guard against picking a quarrel with your mate or partner. You might find that plans for this evening are in conflict; make an extra effort to reach a compromise that is acceptable to you both. There is no point in spoiling the occasion over a disagreement which will probably seem petty tomorrow. If you have no plans to go out, consider throwing an impromptu New Year's Eve party. You may discover that there are a surprising number of people at loose ends who would welcome an invitation. If you are going out, it may be best to leave the car at home. This way you can relax and enjoy yourself without having to worry about going over the limit or having to give lifts.

October–December 1994

OCTOBER

1. SATURDAY. Sensitive. If you are harboring a grudge it is probably upsetting you more than the object of your anger. Find a way to relieve yourself of the burden, either by apologizing, accepting an apology, or putting the matter out of mind once and for all. Be aware of how other people view what you say and do. With your natural Leo enthusiasm you may be coming on too strong, causing people to back away from you instinctively. Your ideas are good, but if they are to become reality, you have to win supporters. Scale back a plan that is not working out. Test it in a small way to decide if it is feasible to continue. A lot can be learned by being observant of all that is going on around you.

2. SUNDAY. Mixed. Be alert for potential hazards at home and when visiting in another person's home. An accident is possible due to carelessness with flame or cutting tools. Also be wary of heights; let someone else climb the ladder to change a light bulb, hang a plant or rescue a kitten from a tree. Getting ready for a trip demands more than just packing a suitcase for yourself. You must arrange for care of your home and pets, if any. Figure out also what to do with mail and newspaper deliveries. It might be wise to give a neighbor a key in case of an emergency, as well as a phone number where you can be reached.

3. MONDAY. Manageable. Other people consider you better off than you think you are. Do nothing to dissuade them. You can look sharp without spending a lot on clothes or fancy props. Being well groomed is a key. Keep all of your possessions in good shape. Iron out wrinkles in what you plan on wearing even if they are not too obvious. Guard against being seen in anything with spots or stains. Practice courtesy with everyone you meet. You never know when an unobtrusive person could be a potential supporter or employer. Aim to break through a barrier that you have built around yourself for protection. You are probably holding yourself in rather than keeping danger out.

4. TUESDAY. Harmonious. An announcement being made late in the day should be a pleasant surprise. Your Leo intuition may let you down in this case, giving you a bigger jolt than if you had suspected something all along. There could be good reason for a get-together after work in celebration. Begin thinking about a present to honor the special occasion. Something you make, rather than an item anyone could buy, would be especially appreciated. Your ingenuity helps you come up with the unusual and save money in the bargain. Getting along harmoniously requires that Leos stand independently and not cling. Make up your own mind about a matter that has been up in the air for long enough.

5. WEDNESDAY. Rewarding. Unexpected income is foreseen, perhaps as a result of work done earlier in the year or a contest entered some time ago. You may want to bank part of it, but plan also on spending a portion for pure pleasure and entertainment. You deserve to reward yourself for hard work and creative risk taking. It is becoming clear that the way to get ahead is to be a little less conservative than expected. A subject you have been studying on your own, or a hobby you have worked on for a while, can be melded into your everyday job with most favorable results. Being well-rounded puts you a step ahead of competitors. Ability to speak a second language is also a considerable asset.

6. THURSDAY. Disquieting. What you believed would be a quick and easy job could turn into a marathon effort. Nothing comes easily today. Cooperation can be withdrawn, or active opposition could spring up. Circumstances put you to the test, but you can rise to any challenge if you stay calm, cool and collected. Do not allow any person or situation to goad you into acting recklessly. Choose words and actions deliberately. Unusual opportunity is foreseen involving someone at or from a distance. Together you can overcome obstacles that might trip up less determined people. Travel is not favored.

7. FRIDAY. Profitable. Coincidence may give you a break that others have been maneuvering to get for themselves. Be ready to take advantage of a chance encounter with an important official, especially an elected representative. There are ways to apply pressure even though you are not operating from a tower of strength. Let your views be known loud and clear. Speak up with valid reasons and some prime examples of why you believe changes are called for. Sign a petition, or consider joining a demonstration to publicize views that you share with a group. There is no reason to feel guilty for taking what is rightfully yours. Steer clear of anything underhanded or illegal, however.

8. SATURDAY. Happy. Ideas are flowing fast and furiously. Jot down those that you want to save for a rainy day. When your mind is fully occupied with one project you may find insight into another. A problem that has been hounding you can be resolved while you are sleeping or daydreaming. Twisting the scenario shows you the opening that you have been seeking. You are likely to receive a sincere compliment from a family member. They are behind you all the way. Be especially attentive to the old and the young. Go out of your way to please them without making it obvious what you are doing. Steer clear of strenuous socializing; relax and be your natural self even in a group situation.

9. SUNDAY. Stimulating. Today focuses on pleasure and entertainment, but the Leo with a mission can make it even more. Talk up your ideas and views among friends and neighbors. Together you can find a way to make an impact on those decision makers who could help you achieve your aims. A joint letter to a newspaper editor or initiating a petition drive is a good starting point. Look for ways to improve your local community through volunteer effort, perhaps at a hospital or teen center. Do not shy away from additional responsibility; the more you have to do, the more you will be able to accomplish. This is also a good day for reaffirming a personal relationship.

10. MONDAY. Positive. Go out of your way to boost the career prospects of a co-worker or friend who is just starting in a new job. Check to see how they are doing and if they need any suggestions or advice. Emphasize all that is positive while downplaying anything negative. With your backing they can become the success that you have envisioned all along. Hard work often produces extraordinary results for Leos, but today there is also a strong element of luck as well. Avoid anything secretive or underhanded. Be open and aboveboard in all remarks and all dealings. If you have something to say, come right out with it. People admire your forthrightness even if they do not agree with you.

11. TUESDAY. Buoyant. There is excellent opportunity today to advance your career through a job reassignment or new working conditions. Be quick to say yes to an offer that is almost too good to be true. Branch out in a new direction that incorporates a hobby with your paying work. Your Leo drive and outgoing personality impress higher-ups and give them confidence in you. Friends also figure prominently in your affairs. Pairing up with someone you have known since school days can be rewarding. A former colleague may supply necessary information or indicate a shortcut to save you time and money. A bureaucrat will bend a rule on your behalf. Sleep should be very peaceful tonight.

12. WEDNESDAY. Good.   Important work should be handled during the early hours. Later you want to get together on a more social basis with co-workers or friends to talk about a multitude of matters. Plans are forming slowly but surely. What starts out as casual conversation can take wing, becoming a brand-new intention. Your circus of friends and acquaintances is ever expanding. Joining a group of people interested in your line of work or a hobby can be useful in all areas of life. Romance, too, benefits from getting to know more people. Someone you have viewed as a work colleague could be seen in a different light. Taking a trip together for business could be the start of something grand.

13. THURSDAY. Demanding.   A bill collector may demand payment in full if you have fallen behind on your monthly payments. Or a friend may ask in no uncertain terms for return of money or an item loaned to you some time ago. Leos have to scramble today to accommodate all of these demands. Juggle available funds so that everyone gets enough to satisfy them, at least for a while. Look into alternative sources of financing. If a bank has turned down a loan request, you may be able to get money to tide you over till next payday from an older relative. A teenager can have money stashed away and be willing to help.

14. FRIDAY. Confusing.   Your mate or steady date can teach you something new. This is a good day to form a partnership or to formalize one with a contract or a vow. Confusion is present, however, when more than one person becomes involved. You will not operate well as part of a group. Shy away from anything that is so organized there is no room for spontaneity. Surprises are not going to be welcomed. If you feel you have not been getting a fair deal, appeal to the person at the top. Anxiety is likely regarding a work matter that you thought had been resolved. A deal could be falling through right before your eyes.

15. SATURDAY. Enjoyable.   Imagination is in top gear today. Let your creativity take you where it will. Do not set any constraints on yourself. You have a unique opportunity to display what you make and possibly get a commission from an individual or a business. Taking part in an exhibit or a crafts fair can also be worthwhile as well as enjoyable. Keep a camera handy to record special happenings. A get-together of friends is sure to be fun, with people moving in and out of the picture and Leos at the center. There could also be a formal celebration, possibly a welcoming home party. Keeping in touch with cousins, nieces and nephews can enhance your sense of family heritage.

16. SUNDAY. Lucky. Leos tend to be well positioned to receive or grant favors today. A special break is coming your way; take full advantage of it. Someone you meet while attending a sports event or other organized function may tip you off to new opportunity. A lottery ticket or raffle chance can also pay off, but in a small way. Be alert for rumors circulating through your neighborhood; they contain a kernel of truth wrapped in a layer of exaggeration. Good luck accompanies all of your efforts. Even when you are not particularly trying, you can benefit from the day's good fortune. You are at your persuasive best later in the day. Requests for favors should be made then.

17. MONDAY. Outstanding. A calculated risk can reward you with handsome dividends. Weigh the odds, then make your move. Leo instincts are not steering you wrong. Put humor into any presentation that you make. Do not allow fear of possible rejection to keep you from trying. Go after the big prize, although you may wind up settling for a very respectable second place. You cannot always come out on top, but you can aim to do so. You have the willpower to get your mate or partner to adjust to your way rather than compromising so that no one is satisfied. Keep a secret dream locked in your heart. If you reveal plans prematurely you will be besieged with people asking how you are doing. The timetable for action should remain your secret for a while.

18. TUESDAY. Variable. Put your organizing talents to good use. Come up with guidelines for everyone to follow in a group effort so that no one is confused or wondering. Without rules and regulations one person could be left holding the bag for the entire group. Look into ways to save more money. You might be able to arrange a carpool or buy food in bulk at a considerable discount. Analyze how other people have built up their nest egg, and learn from them. Any advice that you offer is apt to fall on deaf ears. If you have something to say, be direct. The blunt approach gets your point across, although it may not win any points for you. Possessiveness can doom a budding relationship.

19. WEDNESDAY. Successful. Interacting with other people who share your interests can enhance your creative and mental powers. Find out what has been going on at a distance. Consider attending a conference or taking some classes. Keep your eyes peeled and your ears open for news that may not be earth-shattering right now, but can develop into a major breakthrough. Visiting with an expert gives you added insight. Push yourself to do more than you think you are capable of at this point. Aim high and you will not fall short. It is also a fine time to volunteer for a job that no one else seems to want. When you make it a success your power base will expand and your reputation grow.

20. THURSDAY. Pleasant. You can afford to sit back and be more relaxed today. Allow ideas to jell in your mind while you concentrate on minor matters that require little thought. Working with your hands is favored. Do not burden yourself with too full a calendar. Keep some days open so that you can take advantage of unusual offerings. Someone with whom you recently argued is ready to make a full apology; accept it gracefully. Be sure to wear comfortable clothing and sturdy shoes for outdoor activities. Protect your health by keeping dry and warm. If you feel a cold coming on, get extra rest. Center stage belongs to other people today. Focus the spotlight on them if it moves in your direction.

21. FRIDAY. Unsettling. Although you would like to work as part of a team, your ideas and the group's may not coincide. Rather than putting restraints on yourself, act independently. Later you may be able to team up with one or two people who have become disenchanted with what is going on and want to give your ideas a try. Do not sit behind closed doors waiting for the phone to ring. Make some calls on your own behalf to stir up activity. Guard against allowing a minor upset to escalate into a full-fledged quarrel. You can give in without giving up. Keep an open mind to what your mate or partner is thinking.

22. SATURDAY. Excellent. Focus on family life rather than outside activity. Plan a special outing everyone will enjoy, including you. It is not wise to be too self-sacrificing. You can please yourself while making others happy. Chores around the house should be evenly divided so that no one person carries most of the burden. All personal relationships are happy and tension-free. Someone who has been on your mind due to a health or other problem has good news to share with you. It is a starred day for adopting a pet. Decide beforehand the amount of care you are willing to provide for an animal, and choose accordingly.

23. SUNDAY. Challenging. Rise to a challenge presented by a loved one. Do not shirk a duty unless you have a very good excuse. Family members are watching what you do more than they are listening to what you say. A calm discussion during breakfast could resolve a problem before it has a chance to escalate further. Nagging can destroy your credibility. Expect other people to fulfill their obligations; they are not likely to let you down often. It would be unwise to charge any purchases today. Pay cash or put off buying. A major item that you are saving for will be all the more treasured because you will own it free and clear.

24. MONDAY. Variable. The workweek starts for most Leos with the possibility of an awkward meeting. Someone you have been trying to avoid, and with good reason, may suddenly show up on your doorstep or make a telephone call that you answer unwittingly. Try to hash out differences before they become permanently ingrained. Be cool and aloof even if your heart is pounding. It is up to you to begin a thawing-out period that can lead to restored good feelings. Restlessness may set in later in the day. Visit a customer or contact at a distance to chat about what has been happening.

25. TUESDAY. Fair. Do everything in moderation. Avoid jumping to any conclusions, as your intuition is not as good as usual. Past experience is not a reliable guide to current action. You may react defensively when no criticism had been intended. Leos waiting for news about a job or other important matter will not receive word now. Get on with your life as though nothing was on hold. Put your agile mind to work thinking of ways to improve home life and your surroundings. Small changes that do not cost much can be worthwhile.

26. WEDNESDAY. Changeable. A relationship that has been smooth sailing for the past few months is undergoing change now. Be prepared to take on a different role in response to the other person's actions. You are on the taking side, not the giving. In a group you are apt to feel underappreciated and perhaps ignored. Speak softly and your words are more likely to be heard. It is necessary to control your own urges for the good of the team effort. A flirtation could create a jealous scene, so be careful. Discretion is needed in all affairs of the heart. Becoming involved in a secret romance can damage your reputation and hurt other people as well. Be as straight as an arrow where love is involved.

27. THURSDAY. Happy. The person closest to your heart may be farthest from your thoughts today. Togetherness is not a vital ingredient for happiness. Concentrate on a work project that has raised your level of excitement. Recent effort should begin to reward you with some surprising dividends. The positive interest that you have received so far may turn into an avalanche. You are especially successful dealing with a large corporation, particularly one based far from your locale. An overseas business offers special opportunity. Look for signs of a trend, then latch on to it. Be more aware of what the teenage generation is finding appealing.

28. FRIDAY. Enjoyable. Personal relationships remain excellent on all levels. You can communicate without having to say anything. This is one of those starred days when whatever you want is apt to be granted without questions being asked. You are ready to make a commitment with your eyes wide open. Leo singles interested in marriage can begin shopping for a ring; those of you who are married may want to look into larger living accommodations. Strive to keep your love life separate from work in every way. Catch up with half-finished projects so that you have a clear slate when new opportunity arises.

29. SATURDAY. Excellent. The outlook is for blue skies and sunshine even if the weatherman claims otherwise. All activities are positive and on track. Teamwork is favored. Leos who must be on the job today can look forward to special compensation. You should be particularly persuasive, making this a time when commissions increase and rewards come your way. Your reputation precedes you. People are turning to you for ideas; a group would welcome suggestions to raise money for a worthwhile cause. A goal you have been working toward since last year is coming closer to fruition. Do not let up now as success approaches.

30. SUNDAY. Rewarding. Go out of your way for a family member. Be extra considerate of their feelings, and they will respond in the same way. Children, in particular, can learn common courtesy simply by witnessing it at home. Cooperate with the plans of a loved one even if there is no thrill of excitement roused in you by the proposal. Once you are taking part you will discover that you are having fun. Travel can be enjoyable, although you should not be away from home overnight. Leo singles can successfully juggle more than one relationship.

31. MONDAY. Stressful. There is no escaping the pressure of work. Get an early start so that you have some uninterrupted time early in the day. A meeting is likely to last longer than expected, with everyone expressing views and no one listening to what others have to say. Do not count on any decisions being made unless you are the one to make them. Assign priorities so that you can figure out what must be done first and what can be put off. Take time for a nutritious lunch even though you are swamped with work. Getting away for a half hour or so can soothe your nerves and clear your mind. This is a day for stepping up salesmanship.

NOVEMBER

1. TUESDAY. Positive. Look sharp and stay alert throughout the day. You are apt to run into a person who can become your guide or mentor as you begin to branch out in a new direction. Although Leos do not need many close associates, a chain of contacts helps you stay informed and up to date. First impressions are especially important. Look the part for the role you want to play. You can find a way to turn what has been only a home-based hobby into a money-making proposition. Streamlining production methods and buying supplies in bulk are the first steps. There is also opportunity today to add to a collection through a private sale or a thrift shop find. Shake away the cobwebs and blow off the dust and you may discover a diamond in the rough.

2. WEDNESDAY. Outstanding. Do a favor even before you are asked. You are tuned in to the needs of family members, friends and co-workers. Come to their aid just as you know they would come to yours were the situation reversed. The help you offer will come back to you many times over. This is a starred day to talk with the boss or another higher-up about your future job possibilities. Knowing what they have in mind for you helps steer you in the right direction. Leo writers, artists and performers will shine as their talents are put on display. Do not be shy about having your work judged; you can learn a lot as well as get the recognition you deserve. A blue ribbon is very valuable.

3. THURSDAY. Mixed. Hopes and wishes sustain you while daily work goes on and on. Your mind is sharp and clear, open to all possibilities. Listen to what at first seems to be a far-out proposition. Dilute it with your down-to-earth approach and you may have a winner. Stay on top of income and outgo. Keep spending to necessities only today. You cannot afford to leave financial affairs to chance. Tally what you actually dole out in cash and also any credit card purchases. You may surprise yourself over how quickly small purchases add up. It is not wise to loan money to a friend or family member unless you consider it a gift.

4. FRIDAY. Difficult. A remark that makes you angry when it is told to you has a ring of truth. You can think about the message alone, then decide what changes, if any, should be made. Be wary of becoming too self-satisfied; there is always room for improvement. Someone you have been trying to avoid is likely to corner you and speak their mind. Be careful not to say or do something you immediately regret. Emotions that spring up suddenly have a way of overriding your better judgment on occasion. You have plenty to handle in dealing with the present. Do not lapse into regrets about what is over and done. Find a way to breathe new life into a relationship that seems to be backsliding.

5. SATURDAY. Variable. Prove to yourself that you are able to take a project from start to finish without outside assistance. A good how-to manual should help. Purchase the best supplies you can afford. If you do not have necessary tools and equipment, try to borrow them from a neighbor. Or rent them instead of spending money on what you may use only once. Give a definite maybe to an offer made by phone; later in the day you will know if you can accept. Friends are in a partying mood while you are determined to wait for results of your project. If you give in to them before you are ready there is bound to be tension. You get along well, but on your own terms. Write a love letter to that special person.

6. SUNDAY. Misleading. The Leo drive for individual freedom is strong. If people try to hold you back, you are likely to resist with equal force. Guard against allowing guilt to be the prime motivator for any activity today. Do what seems right, not what you feel you must do. Children are wizards when it comes to using subtle blackmail on their parents in order to get their own way. But you have some tricks of your own to counter these efforts. A united front is a good way to start. A rumor that is spreading like wildfire is likely to be false. Get to the bottom of it before telling another soul what you have heard. You do not want to be responsible for damaging someone's reputation.

7. MONDAY. Tricky. Leo's sensitivity to the feelings of others is strong now, and you should relate well to any group. Working in tandem is favored in all areas. Do not raise your expectations too high, however. You are more likely to plod along than to make significant progress. Committee decisions may be long and arduous, reminding you of time spent in a dentist's chair. The trick today is to remain neutral, but in a positive way. There are few guarantees being offered. If you begin to feel you are being backed into a corner, start pushing in the opposite direction. It may amaze you how people back down if you exert some force of your own.

8. TUESDAY. Unsettling. Someone at or from a distance has good news for you and your family. This could necessitate a trip or at least an overnight stay. Travel is not a high priority, but it may be unavoidable. Plans for the day go haywire as new demands are made; try to remain flexible. If your mind-set is locked in, you cannot take advantage of unexpected developments. Do your best to ignore small inconveniences instead of turning them into major problems. Your imagination is strong and your goals are well established. This can make you overly critical of those who do not share your intensity. Make sure that you express any aggressive feelings against the person involved, not whoever is around.

9. WEDNESDAY. Cautious. Put one foot in front of the other gingerly as you proceed with a project. Caution is the watchword today. If you try to hurry along by skipping steps you may only have to go back and start from scratch. There is rhyme and reason behind a plan that seems tedious because of all the checks that have been built in. Be extra thorough in filling out forms or other paperwork. Leave nothing to chance when it comes to explaining what you want and why. Keep notes of a meeting as a backup in case you have to justify actions at a later date.

10. THURSDAY. Successful. After the past few days of conservative action, Leos should be ready for this dynamic twenty-four hours. The Moon in Aquarius promises special success as you make your mark in a group. People are more than willing to listen to your ideas and plans; they are eagerly awaiting them. Your excellent reputation precedes you, giving you added leverage. There is no one to stand in your way once you make up your mind. Let higher-ups know that you are intent on moving ahead and cannot be satisfied remaining in your current job much longer. You deserve a pay raise and should pursue it actively.

11. FRIDAY. Variable. This is not a time to engage in any lengthy discussions about personal or work-related matters. Your logical thinking is not too sharp. You can easily settle today for less than you should get. Set your sights higher than what you imagine you deserve. Find a way to turn what could be termed a weakness into a source of surprising strength. Just being willing to ask for help sets you apart as someone who cares and is aware. Maneuver around an obstacle rather than charging at it headfirst. Tact and flexibility help you get what you want. Be more than ready to forgive and forget any wrongs that have been done. You will be the one who will be hurt the most by bearing a grudge.

12. SATURDAY. Easygoing. Quietly redo work that has not been completed to your satisfaction. Do not draw attention to your efforts. Leos have ample help available, but may not want to take advantage of it. Your sense of perfection bodes well for individual effort on your part. You cannot expect other people to meet your high standards on a regular basis. Personal relationships are easygoing, especially at home. Family members have their own agenda today, leaving you in peace. Consider inviting neighbors or friends for a potluck dinner or a game of cards. Shopping can also highlight the day if you read the ads before starting out.

13. SUNDAY. Disconcerting. A family member's announcement is apt to take you by surprise, but avoid either criticizing it or praising it until you have time to think. Your reaction is important to them and must be carefully worded. Shy away from an argument by refusing to be baited into revealing your opinions. Tempers may flare, then simmer down later in the day. That is the best time for a family consultation. What once seemed almost unthinkable could be seen in a new light. Traditions that have guided you are not as strong a force for the younger generation. Leo parents can guide, but not insist, once children reach the age of reason.

14. MONDAY. Mixed. Turn all your attention to a project that means a lot to you. Do not be distracted by other activity going on all around you. You may want to skip lunch or have a quick sandwich so that you do not lose your train of thought. Do not aim for perfection on the first go-round; later you can refine and improve your initial efforts. There is a strong indication of travel today, although probably it is someone coming to see you. A trip to the airport or train station is likely. Before starting out, check estimated time of arrival so that you are not kept waiting interminably. The winds of change are reaching gale force. New management wants, and will insist, that things be done their way.

15. TUESDAY. Excellent. Give a lot and you will get a lot in return. Go out of your way to help a co-worker or friend who has been struggling with a problem but getting nowhere fast. Your view as an interested outsider can be a big help. Share what you know and have experienced without holding anything back. You can also be effective acting as a mediator or go-between to bring together opposing factions. An important new relationship is in the bud stage; nurture it with attention and affection. For Leos looking for love, this is a starred day. A casual acquaintance is becoming more important to you every day.

16. WEDNESDAY. Disconcerting. A project may have to be put aside when other work demands priority treatment. Make some notes for yourself so that you can pick up at a later date where you leave off today. Handling more than one thing at once does not come easily for Leos oriented to getting results. Now, however, you can only go so far in one direction before having to turn your attention elsewhere. It could be necessary to wait for the green light from a higher-up before proceeding. Or a pending rule change may be keeping you from progressing. Negotiations are apt to slow down as positions harden. Come up with a new offer that is still less than you might be ultimately willing to accept.

17. THURSDAY. Demanding. Work has to be afforded top priority even though your family also needs attention. Try to arrange for a friend or relative to help out at home while you concentrate on a project with a fast-approaching deadline. Make things as easy for yourself as possible; hire a professional to do necessary work around the house because you do not now have the time even if you have the skill. You know a project has to be completed to your satisfaction before you can relax and let down your guard. Firsthand experience is the best indicator of what is going on. Schedule a trip to talk with people who have very definite ideas concerning changes you will be instituting.

18. FRIDAY. Good. Unexpected income is foreseen, based on work or service performed some time ago. You may also be awarded a prize, probably offering more recognition than money. This is a fine time to enter a competition based on your individual skills and talents. Do not be fearful of matching your talent with the best. New starts are favored after considering how you can fit them into your schedule. Avoid new investment unless you personally know about the management or product involved. Advice from a banker or broker may be too general to be of much use. See either your doctor or dentist to ease your pain that is bothering, though not restricting you now; it might worsen.

19. SATURDAY. Harmonious. Being at the center of things pleases you and gives other people an added measure of confidence. Take a leadership role in a neighborhood or community effort. A worthwhile cause would welcome your advice and active support. Strive to get family members interested in what interests you. A gift or talent you have been developing in your spare time can be put to excellent use. What is a serious matter should be presented in a lighthearted way so that you do not scare away anyone. Humor can also be a great teaching aid. Stand firm where spending is involved. You do not have to pay a lot for entertainment and enjoyment. Being with friends and family is enough.

20. SUNDAY. Easygoing. Pass up strenuous activity in favor of quiet pastimes. You may enjoy being a spectator at a sports match, though you do not have the energy to participate. Avoid making any demands on family members. Fetch and carry for yourself rather than expecting anyone to be your gofer. Material possessions are almost insignificant in importance compared with friendship and love. Be wary of a twinge of jealousy when someone wants to show off their new car or other recent acquisition. You have your own priorities and do not have to keep up with them in order to feel satisfied.

21. MONDAY. Mixed. Keep the various aspects of your life in separate and distinct compartments. Avoid mentioning home concerns to workmates, or on-the-job problems to family members. Friendship and love are also a volatile mix right now. Be wary of leading on an acquaintance with a hint that you might be interested in a romantic way. Make your intentions obvious enough so that no one gets a mixed message. Look for innovative ways to handle routine work that is becoming more of a chore than a pleasure. You may want to challenge yourself to beat your best time. A new technique is not automatically better than what you have been doing. Test it in a small way.

22. TUESDAY. Sensitive. Figure out the questions that have to be answered before looking for solutions. A problem that refuses to go away should be approached from an entirely new direction. What has worked in the past is a clue to the future. Study famous people and their methods of operation. You can learn a lot from a person who has achieved a well-deserved reputation. Guard against letting down a person who is counting on you. Come through with promised help or assistance even though doing so may be inconvenient for you. Be careful not to overlook a birthday or anniversary.

23. WEDNESDAY. Excellent. You are on the same wavelength as those you care about most. Any problem that has been interfering with your relationship, however slightly, can be sorted out now with frank, open discussion. The Leo in charge has the benefit of full cooperation. Self-confidence propels you toward long-term goals and the success you envision. Results of a test should be reassuring and satisfactory. Leo creativity is also excellent today. Put more of yourself into everything that you do. Leave a mark that makes it obvious you have been involved. There is no lack of mental and emotional energy. Your positive attitude inspires others to rise to their potential.

24. THURSDAY. Good. Friends and family members make the best companions for most of today, though you may want to get out to do some private exercising as well. Turn on the charm with a person who often gets on your nerves. Listen to the same story you have heard many times before without trying to hurry it along. Be especially gentle with an older person who wants attention. Avoid boasting or bragging; your accomplishments are recognized and appreciated with no extra publicity necessary. A serious discussion about politics or politicians can erupt into arguments, though it will not become divisive. Challenge yourself to consider other people's views as possibly the right ones.

25. FRIDAY. Quiet. Many Leos have the day off and can start their holiday shopping while merchandise is plentiful and sale prices are in effect. The more you do now, the less hectic will be your life at this time next month. It is also a good day to buy something special for your home. Curtains, rugs or furniture can make you more comfortable within your own four walls. Be good to yourself, just as you are generous toward others. A hobby should be a source of relaxation and pleasure. If it seems to be turning into work, put it aside for a while. A community project calls for your wholehearted support.

26. SATURDAY. Useful. Avoid dissipating your energy by trying to do too much. Focus on one or two projects that seem most vital. Repair work should not be put off; delay could force you to hire a highly paid professional later on. Give some attention to plans for an upcoming get-together which you will be hosting. Come up with a careful menu to take into account various tastes and diet restrictions. It is not too soon to get out holiday decorations in order to spruce them up. You may want to purchase some new lights or a few big red shiny bows. Offer help to a neighbor completing a major project.

27. SUNDAY. Happy. A family announcement puts a smile on your face that will not evaporate all day long. Now that the news is out, deciding what to do next could be a challenge. Other people have to be consulted and their views at least taken into consideration. This is a dynamic day for coming up with a list of possibilities, but do not initiate any action yet. All the help you need is close at hand. A loved one may surprise you with a small gift to commemorate the day. Do not try to contain your happiness with friends and neighbors; let them in on the news as soon as possible. You are not bound to follow tradition if you think you have a better way. Leo creativity is far ahead of the crowd.

28. MONDAY. Frustrating. An option that seems best to you may not be as acceptable to a family member or a co-worker. Arguments are foreseen, but the impasse may continue for a while. Frustration mounts as someone who usually takes your side now rejects your view. Keep a calm, cool bearing. Discretion is vital to a successful outcome. A shared bank account can cause some trouble, especially if you forgot to enter a deposit or record a check that you wrote. It will take a while to sort through past transactions and figure out your current balance. Reviewing the family budget can help come up with ways to cut expenses.

29. TUESDAY. Positive. People are now more adaptable and ready to go along with your plans. Lead them gently. Avoid even a hint of an I-told-you-so attitude. Your Leo optimism is a natural draw, putting you at the center of the action. Knowing what you want is a vital first step. Your vision is far-reaching. Have confidence in your own abilities as well as the cooperation you expect to receive. Obstacles that have been blocking your way can at least be sidestepped. An unfinished project could start nagging at your conscience. Try to finish it up in a rush. People help you find answers to questions that have a timeless quality.

30. WEDNESDAY. Confusing. Just when you thought you knew where you were going you may come to a crossroads and have to make a major decision. Do not rush into anything. Check out the possibilities with those who have been there before. Advice is likely to be contrary, but you can have confidence in majority opinion. Your Leo insight helps sort out truth from fiction and, even more important, the practical from the wishful thinking. An influential person is exerting considerable pressure. Giving in is the easiest choice, but it may not be the right one. You cannot rest easy unless you are true to yourself. Cultivate a closer relationship with a neighbor and you will both benefit.

DECEMBER

1. THURSDAY. Good. The struggle to keep your finances straight may mean you have to borrow. Try to arrange the most favorable terms. A friend or relative could provide a loan to tide you over. If you must borrow from a bank, shop around for a special rate. Doing without can be the best financial medicine, although the hardest to swallow. Put away credit cards until you have brought their balance down to zero. Indications point to a bonus or extra pay for overtime before the end of December. Romance is on the upswing. It does not take any money at all to keep that special person happy and satisfied.

2. FRIDAY. Fortunate. Work at developing a hidden talent that could become a cash-producer for you. Trust the judgment of a friend or co-worker who has been telling you for a while that a hobby is worth taking a step further. There is a strong element of good fortune today giving all of your plans a boost. A quiet person may come through with quite a surprise. Look beyond current horizons to the wider world. This is an excellent time to consider a merger with a foreign company or a minority-owned business. Diversity makes you stand out in both business and personal affairs. Do not limit yourself or your choices in any way. The strong Leo interest in travel makes you long to get away.

3. SATURDAY. Positive. Your careful planning ahead puts you in just the right position today. Some call it luck, but you know how hard you have worked and what you have done without. Take full advantage of a chance meeting. Do not allow yourself to become tongue-tied when filled with emotion. Someone you have had your eye on for a long time is likely to make you feel very special. Romance is starred throughout the day, although this evening you prefer being in a group rather than going off as a twosome. A romance that has snagged due to misunderstanding can be straightened out if you are willing to be the first to apologize. Do not hesitate to trust that special person with a secret.

4. SUNDAY. Mixed. Straighten up around the house so that you do not spend wasted moments searching for something you carefully put away, but cannot find now. Settle on one place for everything, and be sure everything is in its place. Do some rearranging and sorting out. Gather together clothes that you no longer wear and plan on donating them to a thrift store. Organization is the key to less stress at home. Check the refrigerator, too, for leftovers past their prime. A relationship that has been gaining momentum could begin to slow down. Do not think less of a person because their outside interests cannot always include you.

5. MONDAY. Variable. Look into plans for the upcoming holidays, especially if you intend to do any traveling. Confirm travel arrangements, or be quick to make them if you have not done so. A travel agent can help you locate the best deal. Do not count on a promise being fulfilled despite the best of intentions. Leos may have to do some scrambling to come up with alternatives today. Work should be anything but routine. The boss is expecting more of you than of other workers. Live up to these expectations and you can expect a pay raise or promotion. Trust a hunch.

6. TUESDAY. Difficult. Be wary of making any new commitments. You have more than enough of your schedule now, even though some good offers may be received. Give an excuse when you say no so that it is obvious you would like to be asked again. Making money is not enough for many Leos. You also want the respect and prestige that accompanies certain jobs. But you must earn this by starting at the bottom of the ladder and climbing up one rung at a time. Focus on current work by doing the best you can with it. Budget objectives are apt to cause disputes with your mate or partner as you tend to attract the opposite type.

7. WEDNESDAY. Changeable. Leo creativity is reaching a peak. Ideas are flowing so frequently that you cannot possibly put them all to use now. Jot down notes of what you would like to do in the New Year. Concentrate today on a project that has useful applications as well as showing off your artistic flair. What has been a low-key hobby can be taken a step beyond and become a money-maker. Relationships on the job are sensitive. Someone who has authority over you is worried that you are taking too much control. There may also be some jealousy about the attention you are receiving. Be sure to share praise with all who have contributed, no matter how little they may have done.

8. THURSDAY. Positive. After the past difficult days you deserve to have your plans begin to bear fruit. Self-confidence is soaring. Changes can be made now with little or no resistance. Do not pussyfoot around; take a bold step and do not back down. You can finalize a deal that has been on the negotiating table so long it seems to be growing moss. Your take-it-or-leave-it attitude forces action. A past experience could be influencing current actions. Look for clues in the way people speak about their family and their education. If you can fill their needs, they will respond to you positively. Travel is favorable later in the day.

9. FRIDAY. Outstanding. Jump right into the middle of an ongoing project without waiting to be asked more than once. Your help is needed, and you appreciate being in demand. A skill you have developed off the job could come in especially handy today. Once you have made a commitment, keep going until you have fulfilled it. It will not require much stimulation to inspire Leos so they slip into high gear. Do not be shy about publicizing your efforts and accomplishments. The more people who know about your work, the better. There is no holding you back once you begin; it is all or nothing. Other people have to join in or get out of your way. There is no room in your plans for negative thinkers.

10. SATURDAY. Quiet. Hang a sprig of mistletoe, sit back, and see what happens. Leos are particular about their home environment and want everything just so. It is up to you to do most of the arranging and planning; you cannot expect much help from family members, at least not without some arm twisting. You would rather do it yourself than cause a commotion among loved ones. Shopping can lead to bargains, especially for a special present that you want to buy. Check quality as well as price; in your hurry you could overlook a flaw. Enjoy a get-together tonight.

11. SUNDAY. Inactive. Keep more to yourself today so that you can rest and relax without interruption. Wish family members well as they go about their own plans, but do not accept an invitation to join them. Leo parents may offer to give some money to younger family members so they can go to the movies or ice skating, leaving the house to you. Be polite but noncommittal. You are under no obligation to provide entertainment for family or friends. A creative project could be an enjoyable way to pass the afternoon, provided you do not feel pressured to finish it.

12. MONDAY. Rewarding. Go on a safety search around your home or the office. Be sure that smoke alarms are in good working condition. Guard against plugging too much into one outlet or operating equipment with frayed electrical cords. Driving also demands extra caution, particularly on wet or slippery roads. Be alert for others behind the wheel who may not be paying close attention. Stay on the defensive in all areas. There is money to be made in a new offer or venture that is short-term. Put aside all but the most vital work so that you can concentrate on a quick project promising good financial rewards. Teamwork can be effective.

13. TUESDAY. Mixed. Focus today on current work rather than accepting anything new. Try to finish whatever you have before the deadline so that you are not under a lot of pressure. Worrying can rob you of energy needed to fulfill a commitment. Lack of support or cooperation may dismay you, especially if promises were made earlier in the month. You have to make do with whatever help is available. A younger person can be quickly trained to handle a repetitive job, freeing you for more detailed work. What is important to you is not a priority for co-workers or family members. They may even wonder why you care. Trying to explain your reasons is a waste of time. Romance is in a lull now.

14. WEDNESDAY. Changeable. Stick close to your usual base of operations. It can be difficult today getting along with people you hardly know. Someone from a different country or culture can force you to take a long, hard look at what you have come to accept as normal operating procedure. A meeting or other arrangement scheduled for later in the day may be canceled, giving you unexpected free time. Make good use of it. Strike a balance between what is expected of you and what you want to do. All work and no play can make you boring to yourself. A problem that has defied solution may have to be put out of mind. Refusing to rush to the aid of a person in a predicament forces them to find their own way out.

15. THURSDAY. Quiet. Sit back and relax. Let others do as much of the work as possible while you supervise and make plans for the future. Everything seems to be going your way now. Do not tempt the fates by making changes just for the sake of doing something different. Obtain promises that other people will fulfill their obligations just as you work to fulfill yours. You can trust people until they prove otherwise. A mystery that has been whispered about at home or work is beginning to become clear. There is a clue in conversation at mealtime. Do not pry and probe or you could spoil a surprise intended for you. Health will benefit from extra rest and a conservative diet so resist all the temptations.

16. FRIDAY. Variable. Concentrate on what you know inside and out and can practically do in your sleep. You do not need any new challenges today. Finish up what you do not want to have left over during the weekend. Joining forces with a neighbor or friend can lead to a satisfying partnership, especially for social purposes. Overhearing a conversation can give you something to worry about. You cannot ask questions, however, because no one knows you have a clue as to what is going on. An idea that is beginning to form could turn into a money-maker in the year ahead. Work on it independently for a while. Trying to rustle up a date for the weekend may be impossible.

17. SATURDAY. Enjoyable. A chance encounter can lead to a most welcome invitation. If you are the one hosting a party, be sure to include a new neighbor or to invite a friend of a friend.

Have ample food and drink on hand for drop-in visitors. You may also need a few general gifts in case someone with whom you have never exchanged them surprises you with a present. Advance planning is important so that you are not caught flat-footed. Children are a highlight of the day. Take part in a special activity just for them. Scale down your expectations to their level. There are also good opportunities to participate in a charitable project for the benefit of less fortunate community members. Giving time is more important than money.

18. SUNDAY. Harmonious.   Keep the lines of communication open with family members as well as friends. Be willing to listen when they decide they want to talk. Shared feelings help cement the bonds of love. Family ties can be stretched and twisted only so far or they will break. Do all that you can to preserve harmony by refusing to take sides in a dispute that seems silly from the start. An argument can mask the basic disagreement. Focus on the positive and be willing to overlook the negative. Avoid personal boasting or bragging. Let your actions speak for themselves without drawing extra attention to them. That special person in your life is in a serious mood and will not appreciate practical jokes.

19. MONDAY. Ambitious.   Carefully consider an offer that comes in today's mail. It is a good day to plot moves that you intend to make in the New Year. A chance to relocate should be given serious thought. Discuss it with your mate and partner, but do not make any hard-and-fast decisions yet. You may be one of a select few being considered for a promotion or a new job. Weigh the pros and cons of having to move and establish yourself and your family all over again. What you can do on your own with some degree of difficulty can be accomplished quicker and more easily with team effort. Reach out for help. You do not know what is available until you go looking for it.

20. TUESDAY. Excellent.   This is an excellent day to put your special Leo talents on display for all to see and admire. Romance can profit as well. People are turning to you for ideas and leadership. Acting naturally is the surest way to avoid letting them down. Keep personal emotions out of business transactions. Avoid showing impatience even though you may feel it. Some people take time to adjust to change, while you are ready and willing to reach out to whatever is new and different. Someone old enough to be your parent or young enough to be your child can open your eyes to even more opportunity. Select the best from all that is being offered, then mold it to your own liking.

21. WEDNESDAY. Promising. The present time is better than anything you may be able to conjure up in your imagination. An incident today proves that truth can be stranger than fiction. Keep your feet planted firmly on the ground; avoid a flight of fantasy. There are promising undertones from the boss or a government official that should give you good cause for optimism. Look for ways to expand your knowledge through formal classroom learning or on-the-job training. With the Moon in your sign, all indications point to financial luck through a relative. You can afford to take a chance now as well. The odds are in your favor because of the skills you have been developing.

22. THURSDAY. Outstanding. You may have some extra help available today to give you breathing room. Take advantage of their offers even if you might prefer to do it all yourself. What you would like to do and what you can fit into a mere twenty-four hours may not coincide. You will not be satisfied with a slipshod job just to get a project completed. Be wary of signing any document that has legal implications without first consulting an attorney. A financial planner could also be helpful in finding a way to cut taxes due. Your special Leo interest in home and family makes it easy to select a gift everyone would enjoy. A new TV or sound system will please young and old alike.

23. FRIDAY. Happy. Do not count on getting much work done today. Socializing can actually be good for business and job relations. Enjoy reminiscing about a joint project or mutual friends. The germ of an idea may develop from casual conversation. Nostalgia is sure to put a smile on your face even while you are making mental notes for the future. Leos going out of town today should get an early start. You have to expect delays, but should avoid becoming stressed or jittery while waiting. Take a book along to make the time fly. Romance is also on your mind. This is a starred day for a reunion with that special person, even if it has been only a short while since you parted. Love has a special glow tonight.

24. SATURDAY. Demanding. Many demands are being made today by friends and family alike. You cannot satisfy everyone and should not even try. Resist the temptation to ask for help, then turn around and do the work yourself, anyway. Last-minute shopping may keep you out for a while. It is too late to seek the perfect gift; anything appropriate will have to do now. Getting together with friends can be enjoyable providing you do not stay out too late. Your mate or date wants some undivided attention as well.

For the Leo with an important question in mind, this is the night to ask. You do not have to get down on bended knee; the sincere approach will get you the reply you are hoping to receive.

25. SUNDAY. MERRY CHRISTMAS! While others sit back and relax today you will be kept hopping in order to serve them. You are unlikely to be resentful, however, and will relish the compliments you receive. Show special appreciation for any hand-made gifts that you are given, even if you wonder what you are going to do with the item. Your mechanical ability may be put to the test with a toy that has to be assembled. Try to interpret the directions as you go along as they may not make much sense to you. Do not put on any airs, especially with a newcomer in the family circle. You have a lot of questions you would like them to answer, but do not pepper them for information.

26. MONDAY. Relaxed. Stay in bed late, or plan on taking a nap this afternoon. Conditions are slow and quiet. Another family member may be off looking for bargains, but you would rather stay home and avoid crowds. A particular present that was just what you wanted can keep you fascinated for the whole day. Instead of trying to do too much too fast with it, learn how it works step-by-step. Make allowances for younger family members who are still celebrating, perhaps too loudly. They have to act their age instead of the age you might like them to be. Unexpected visitors may bring along a special treat that is so delicious you cannot refuse it. Humanitarian instincts are strong; make a donation to a worthwhile cause.

27. TUESDAY. Easygoing. Ease back into the swing of your normal routine. Make no major plans for today. A morning meeting could start you thinking along different lines, but do not make a commitment of any sort. The news may not all be good today, but on the whole you should be pleased with the direction people seem to be taking. There is something for you in a pilot project about to be launched. Clear the decks so that you can say yes without any hesitation. Let your Leo talents be clear for one and all to see. Your special traits make you stand out both in public and in private. Your appearance and care about how you look identify you as someone who does not neglect details.

28. WEDNESDAY. Inactive. Another quiet day is on tap, which may make you wonder when the action will get under way. You are ready for a challenge, but have not found one to tempt you just yet. Keep all of your options open. A low profile makes

you invisible to someone who has busywork in mind. Appear to be
occupied even if you are whiling away the time on the job or at
home. A show of boredom is like a vacuum waiting to be filled.
Reach a decision with your mate or work colleague about rearranging furniture to accommodate a new piece of equipment. Try
to arrange storage so that it is more accessible. A headache or
other health concern is probably a sign of nervous anticipation.

29. THURSDAY. Mixed. Imagination and intuition are your
best guides now. Do what seems right at the moment. You cannot
even begin to imagine how whatever decision you make will affect
other people all down the line. Your high principles assure you of
excellent company. Others may second-guess you, but they will
have the benefit of total hindsight. You cannot be faulted for
taking action on the basis of information currently available. Once
you have made up your mind, do not allow anyone or anything to
dissuade you. Advice is apt to pepper you from all directions. Leo
creativity helps you pick and choose. Shun anything illegal or even
mildly underhanded or your conscience will not rest easy.

30. FRIDAY. Lackadaisical. Despite your desire to move forward there is insufficient energy today for anything but routine
work. Make some mental notes to help in planning for the New
Year. Decide where you want to be a year from now, and how you
are going to get there. A direct line is not always the quickest
route. If a friend or relative at a distance is on your mind, write a
letter with all your latest news. You may also want to consider
organizing a reunion with people you have not seen in a long time.
A wrong move in romance could force you to apologize, although
your intentions were good. Do not pressure your sweetheart into a
decision you could both come to regret.

31. SATURDAY. Exciting. A proposition involving your time
and someone else's money gives you added promise for the year
ahead. Do not make any decision just yet. Showing too much
enthusiasm cannot help your cause and could actually hurt it. But
you know excitement is in the air, with changes almost guaranteed
to be in your favor. Be leery, however, of anything that involves
an element of gambling and risk. You cannot afford to lose what
you have worked all year to achieve. Play it safe where your own
financial welfare is concerned. Look ahead, not behind. What has
been done is over; it is the future that beckons. So join a group of
friends tonight and celebrate 1994, then welcome 1995 at midnight!